# FREEING the CAPTIVES

Louise Ireland-Frey

To Hazel Miller, who got
me started at a Psychic
Fair!

With love,
Louise

# FREEING *the* CAPTIVES

*The Emerging Therapy of Treating Spirit Attachment*

## Louise Ireland-Frey, M.D.

HAMPTON ROADS
PUBLISHING COMPANY, INC.

for the evolving human spirit

Cover design by Marjoram Productions
Photos by Allen Russell and NOVASTOCK

For information write:
Hampton Roads Publishing Company, Inc.
134 Burgess Lane
Charlottesville, VA 22902

Or call: 804-296-2772
FAX: 804-296-5096

e-mail: hrpc@hrpub.com
Web site: http://www.hrpub.com

If you are unable to order this book from your local
bookseller, you may order directly from the publisher.
Quantity discounts for organizations are available.
Call 1-800-766-8009, toll-free.

Library of Congress Catalog Card Number: 99-71616

ISBN 1-57174-136-4

10 9 8 7 6 5 4 3 2 1

Printed on acid-free paper in the United States

# DEDICATION

*To the people who have been released*

*from oppressing or obsessing entities,*

*and also to the entities who have been released*

*from their imprisonment in living bodies*

*or their own negative desires,*

*this book is reverently dedicated.*

# TABLE OF CONTENTS

# FOREWORD

With the publishing of this volume on the subject of
Spirit Releasement Therapy, the author has taken an
irrevocable step for a woman, and has undeniably moved
humanity one giant step closer to a genuinely holistic
model of mental, emotional, physical, and spiritual
health and healing. Historically, the subjects of possession and exorcism were considered to be exclusively and
securely confined within the obscure, secretive, and
mysterious corridors of the Vatican underground. But
that is not the beginning.

Demons and devils were thought of as commonplace
in Babylonia and Assyria. The first written accounts of
the treatment of illness were deciphered from the cunei-
form texts of Assyrian tablets dating from about 2500
B.C. Eloquent incantations and prayers to the tribal gods
were interspersed with direct challenges to the demons
that imposed disease of every description. Through the
long annals of human experience, many people have
believed that there was a nonphysical existence parallel
and coexistent with the physical universe. People considered this world to be filled with spirits. The ancients
believed that most sickness was caused by evil spirits. In
ancient Egypt, the exorcism was performed by a team; a
physician to cure the ailment and a priest to drive out the
demon of disease.

The early writings of the Chinese, Egyptians, Hebrews,
and Greeks show that they generally attributed mental

disorders to demons that had taken possession of an individual. In ancient Persia of the sixth century B.C., the religious leader Zoroaster founded the religion that became known as Zoroastrianism. The God of Light was named Ahura-Mazda; the master of darkness was called Ahriman. Zoroaster, who was considered the first magician, was also an exorcist who used prayer, ritual, and the sprinkling of water to drive out the evil spirits. In India, the mother of Buddha was considered a great exorcist. King Solomon was perhaps the most noted of the Jewish exorcists.

In the New Testament, fully one-fourth of the healings attributed to Jesus consisted of casting out unclean spirits. He specified more than one type of spirit. Developed over a long period of time, the Roman Ritual continues as the model of exorcism in the Catholic Church. This concept of deliverance is based on the explicit command and example of Jesus to "cast out devils," though the Church to this day fails to differentiate between demons, the minions of Lucifer, and the earthbound spirits of deceased humans.

Hippocrates (460–377 B.C.), the great Greek physician, has been called the "father of modern medicine." He denied the possibility of intervention of deities and demons as the cause of disease. Further, he insisted that mental disorders stemmed from natural causes and, like other diseases, required more rational treatment. The physician Galen (130–200 A.D.) studied and described the anatomy of the nervous system. Among the causes of mental disorders he listed the following: injuries to the head, alcoholic excess, adolescence, fear, shock, menstrual changes, economic reverses, and disappointment in love.

With Galen's death, the contributions of Hippocrates and later Greek and Roman physicians were lost in a resurgence of popular superstition. There was a return of the belief in demonology as the source of illness. Not until the sixteenth century did another prominent physician, Paracelsus (1490–1541), reject demonology as the cause of abnormal behavior. He defied the medical and theological traditions of his time, for which he was hounded and persecuted until his death.

In the face of this ongoing dissent, demonology lost ground. Reason and the scientific method gradually led to the development of modern clinical approaches to mental illness. Even so, the belief in demonology was still widespread. Mental illness and demonology—the study of spirit possession—have been inseparably linked through the tortuous course of history.

Modern spiritualism began in America in 1837 in Mount Lebanon, with communications received from spirits. Spiritualism is concerned with two basic premises: the continuity of personality after death and the powers of communication with the spirits of the deceased. The early work on spiritualism was conducted with trance mediums, people who apparently have the ability to make contact with the "spirit world" in an attempt to communicate with the spirits of deceased persons.

Mediumship is defined as the phenomenon in which a nonphysical intelligence, usually a discarnate human, assumes some degree of temporary control or "possession" of a physical body in order to communicate something useful and meaningful. Mediumship is distinguished from the phenomenon of spirit possession in that it occurs only with the deliberate cooperation of the medium and produces a constructive result. The difference is in purpose, duration, and effect.

James Hyslop (1854–1920) was professor of logic and ethics at Columbia University, New York, from 1889 to 1902. He authored a book on psychology in 1895, and taught the subject at Smith College when the science was in its infancy. Dr. Hyslop was an experimentalist and empiricist. After he admitted the credibility of the existence of spirits, it required ten years of investigation to convince himself of the possibility of obsession by discarnate beings as a cause of mental illness. In the years that followed, he accumulated the facts that make it scientifically probable. He is the true pioneer in the systematic investigation of spirit obsession and possession as a cause of mental disorder.

Dr. Carl Wickland was an avowed spiritualist. He was also an exorcist. Wickland graduated from Durham Medical College in 1900 and nine years later became chief psychiatrist at the National Psychopathic Institute in Chicago. In 1918 he moved to Los Angeles and established the National Psychological Institute where he continued the work of healing spirit obsession. His seminal work in the treatment of spirit obsession and possession is chronicled in his two books, *Thirty Years Among The Dead* (1924) and *Gateway to Understanding* (1934).

Dr. Wickland first became interested in spirit possession after observing the frequency with which people suffered character changes after engaging in such practices as using the ouija board or automatic writing. Many such people required hospitalization for apparent mental illness. Wickland consulted discarnate intelligences through his wife, Anna, who was an excellent and gifted medium. He was told that possession of the living by the "earthbound" spirits of deceased humans was the cause, and that he could alleviate the symptoms of the victims if he followed their instructions. The work was conducted with the help of a "concentration circle," a small group of people assembled to support this Rescue Work. It is such Rescue Work that is described in later chapters in this book.

Into this centuries-old unresolved (and I suspect unresolvable) dispute between the intellectual forces that eventually fostered the mechanistic, reductionist Newtonian-Cartesian model of material reality and those individuals who perceive and believe in the higher, broader dimensions of a vaster spiritual universe of universes, stepped Louise Ireland-Frey, M.D. Working as a hypnotherapist in the later years of her medical career, she was, by wonderful synchronicity, called into the field of Spirit Releasement rather by surprise. More people heard of her successful work, and more cases came her way, as often happens in the nonlocal reality where Spirit Releasement is not only possible, but constitutes the triage procedures of spiritual healing. This is the first step before other healing treatment can be intelligently applied. Otherwise, it cannot be known just whose ailment is being treated.

It was my privilege to meet Louise in 1985 at the Spring Conference of the Association for Past-Life Research and Therapy, during a brief introductory workshop on "Clinical Depossession," which is the term I still used at the time. Did she volunteer or did I call on her as my demonstration subject? I don't recall, but it was another timely synchronicity for us both. It boosted her along her path of learning, and I was gifted with a new colleague, a medical doctor at that, in this arena, which, as many of my associates were quick to point out, was very "weird."

Courage is not the only requirement for a person to follow the path Louise has accepted and welcomed as her own. It requires perseverance with the work, precision in collecting data and case histories, documenting the near-miraculous results with the unbiased observation that marks the scientific investigator. In this unproven therapeutic modality, the therapist is operating in the unseen realms, square in the face of ridicule and rejection by family, friends, and professional associates.

"By their fruits shall they be known." The fragrant blossoms have emerged, the fruit has ripened, and it is good.

This is a book about Dr. Louise Ireland-Frey's adventure into an unknown land. She has returned and has chronicled an exciting journey. And now the pleasure of reading it is yours.

William J. Baldwin, Ph.D.
Author of *Spirit Releasement Therapy*

# ACKNOWLEDGMENTS

There are many to whom I am grateful for their help on this book: Lanetta ("Johnnie") Carson, R.N., first drew me into the work of Releasement; Nan Taylor gave me the first instruction in Releasement work; Bill Baldwin, Ph.D., taught the first workshop that I attended on "Clinical Depossession" besides demonstrating that I, too, could harbor an "entity" unknowingly and be released from it. Several friends gave generously of their time and channeling talents: Charlene Smith, R.N.; Mary L. Farmer; Kathleen Hawkins; Ann Jacobs, R.N., Cynthia Sharp, A.B.D.; Harry Rosenberg, A.B.D.; and "Lili," who prefers anonymity. As an active, not passive, channeler, Harry also provided thoughtful analyses of some puzzling aspects. Susan McGinness, Ed.D., edited each page of the manuscript and offered many valuable suggestions; and Kristy Soder typed the entire book and did the formatting.

I thank the authors of the books, lectures, and tapes who gave me further knowledge, especially F. Scott Peck, M.D.; Edith Fiore, Ph.D.; Annabel Chaplin, L.C.S.W.; William Baldwin, Ph.D.; Winafred Lucas, Ph.D.; Hazel Denning, Ph.D.; Irene Hickman, D.O.; and others listed in the Bibliography. To me they are more than names; a good many I consider friends.

My patients and clients, too, receive my thanks for their trust in me when they agreed to let me check them for the possible presence of entities. I am grateful for their cooperation and have rejoiced with them after a successful releasement.

In addition, I thank the invading entities themselves, especially the many who, sometimes with fear and yet with courage, allowed themselves to be persuaded to leave the living person and be escorted into the Light. But most of all I thank my Spiritual Advisor and the Bright Beings who gave protection, wisdom, and power in these sessions. Each time I sent out a mental call for assistance, an answer came from some higher realm.

Now I thank in advance all you who, reading this or other books about this work, begin to learn as much as you can and begin to release prisoners, too. The need is great. With humility and dedication, learn as much as you can and then just begin!

*chapter 1*

# INTRODUCING INVISIBLES

## How We Got Started

On an otherwise uneventful, pleasant day in September 1980, I received a phone call from my good friend Lanetta "Johnnie" Carson, a retired Army nurse with wide experience in nearly all nursing fields except psychiatric conditions.

"Louise, a neighbor of mine called, saying that for the past month she has become more and more convinced that her deceased mother is trying to push her out of her body and take over. She can't talk to anyone about it because people would think she's crazy. But she has become more terrified than ever, since even her husband comments on how much like her mother she is looking. I referred her to you."

To me! Why to me? But to whom else could she refer such a patient? Johnnie knew as much as I did about such things, for we were both taking courses in extrasensory perception from a young woman, Nan Taylor, who had studied these subjects for twenty years.

With considerable hesitation I agreed to see the neighbor. After hanging up the phone I called Nan Taylor to relay all I had heard and to ask her advice and assistance. Nan meditated silently a few moments and then said that she felt the situation was exactly as the woman had described it, and that the matter of getting the deceased mother to leave would be simple.

"Will it be all right if I have Johnnie sit in as backup?" I inquired.

"Oh, by all means. Her energy will be a help."

With less apprehension, then, I set up the appointment. For years I had been working with hypnosis and had discovered the immense power of the altered state. Moreover, since my teens I had known about "earthbound entities," the psyches of deceased persons that did not "go on to the astral level" as they normally should. To be suddenly forced to confront such an earthbound entity myself, however—especially one trying to possess a living person—well, that was different from sitting and quietly reading about such things.

When the lady, "Amy," came the first time, she came alone just to get acquainted with me. She looked like any well-balanced American woman in the mid-forties, slightly overweight. She told me that her body fat had been becoming redistributed to resemble her mother's pattern of fat deposition, and even the quality of her voice had changed so that when she spoke, she heard her mother's voice. In the mirror instead of seeing her face, she saw her mother's.

If she was frightened, I was at least somewhat nervous, too. I was glad that Johnnie was with us for the next meeting.

After leading Amy into a light state of hypnosis, I called the mother: "Maggie, we are calling you. Please come. . . . Amy, tell us when you see her."

In hypnosis, with her conscious mind still present, Amy responded, "I see her face. Her eyes are closed, but her lips are parted."

"Is she alive or is it her dead face you see?"

"Oh, she's alive."

"Speak to her," I directed.

"Mama, it's Amy. Open your eyes, Mama. Look at me. Look at me, Mama!"

"Reach out and touch her cheek."

"There's no response. But she's alive, not dead."

Johnnie reached for my notebook, took it and wrote, "Shake her." I relayed the message: "Shake her! Tell her to talk to you."

Weeping, Amy complied, "Mama, Mama, talk to me! You can help us both." She added, "Her lips are parted but her eyes are still closed; she has no desire to speak. I can *see myself* there: my mouth is her mouth, but she's not paying any attention to me. She can't hear me or see me."

"Does she look peaceful?"

"Oh, yes, not withdrawn—not hurt or angry or anything. My mouth is moving just like hers; it looks just like hers."

For a few minutes more we continued in this vein. I wrote for Johnnie, "Shall we send her away?" Johnnie was undecided. Then she signed that she wanted to speak.

I spoke to the mother: "Maggie, Johnnie is going to talk to you. We know that you need to understand how you have been hindering Amy and making her unhappy. The next voice you hear will be Johnnie's. Let your mind accept her suggestions."

Johnnie leaned forward. "Maggie, are you being sullen now? Are you pouting? Are you trying to punish Amy?" (Amy was in tears.) "You can't sit and pout and keep your eyes shut! Tell Amy what she ought to do. Let your thoughts flow into Amy and *tell her what you want!*"

"Johnnie, you're right; she is pouting. . . . Mama, I know you're here." Amy was still weeping.

"Maggie, we aren't going to let you get away with this. Now come on," ordered Johnnie, "and talk to Amy as a lady should."

"She's still there, but she's as far away as a doorpost."

"What did you do when she pouted in the years you were together?"

"I never manipulated her. No one could—she was strong!"

I put in again, "Maggie, put the *thought* into Amy's mind of *what you want!*" There was a long pause. "Amy, what do you see or feel?"

"I was thinking . . . I'm surrounded by her *things*: her furniture, her jewelry, her china and silverware—it's all here. All her *things* keep reminding me of her."

"Maggie, these *things* are not yours any more. They belong to your daughter now. Amy, say 'These things are mine.'" She repeated it weakly. "Say it again." (Still more feebly.) "Say it *again!*"

Amy burst into tears. "Mama, leave me alone! It's *her* mouth—it's *her* mouth saying, 'These things are mine.' *She's* saying it!"

"Maggie," snapped Johnnie, "you just leave Amy alone. Go away! She's grown up and these are not yours; they are *hers*. You must leave her!"

"I just saw her," said Amy. "She had on the robe she had on when she died."

"A good sign," remarked Johnnie.

"Yes, a good sign . . . She's going. . . ."

"Good, Maggie, that's fine," I put in encouragingly. "You have your own place to go to. You don't belong here any more. You have your own destiny. You must *go on*. . . . Amy, do you see her going? Getting smaller?"

"Yes, she's going—slowly. She's very small . . . way over there."

"Maggie, that's fine," said Johnnie. "Now you just keep going, and don't come back!" (A real old Army command!)

"And notice how you feel, Amy," I added. "Now say again, 'These things are mine.'"

"These things are mine. . . . These things are MINE!"

"Good!" We laughed. "Now, look, see if your mother is still there." Amy reported that her mother was gone.

"Good. And she will remain gone unless you call her back, and then she will come as a memory only, a pleasant memory. You are free; you are yourself."

"Yes, she will never bother you again," agreed Johnnie.

"Is there anything you want to ask about before you return to normal awareness?" I inquired.

Amy opened her eyes and stared at the ceiling, still in hypnosis. "Was she really here? Or did I just imagine it?"

"Does it matter, so long as she's gone?" I asked.

"It *doesn't matter,* so long as she's gone! And she'll *stay* away!" finished Johnnie.

There was not much more to this session. After bringing her back to normal consciousness I asked how she felt.

"Better—relieved! I was thinking about Mother's diamonds. I'll have them reset. They're *mine*—I can do what I want to with them."

Johnnie and I laughed again for her.

"I feel fine. I feel wonderful," ended Amy.

Several weeks later I saw her in the grocery store. "I'm okay. My mother is still there sometimes, a very small figure, and she never bothers me. I'm myself again."

A year later Amy told me that she did not see her mother anymore. She was happy, even though dealing with several domestic and financial problems. She felt strong.

As I said, this was my first attempt at what some have called "Depossession in the clinical setting." Neither Johnnie nor I knew how to help the deceased mother. We simply sent her out and away, perhaps to continue "just a-lookin' for a home" in some other woman, especially one who had "things" that might attract her. Maggie was not an "unclean spirit" nor evil in any sense, not even malicious—she was just selfish and uncaring, insensitive in death as in life. Later, alone with Johnnie, I looked at her and grinned, "Say—are we exorcists?"

In the months following this first amateurish "Releasement," a number of similar cases came to me. One of the first was by an odd chain of circumstances that once more took me by surprise.

I received a phone call from a lady who was concerned about her daughter, "Marta." She said that Marta had been with high school friends when one of them suggested that they go to her home for a "seance." Not knowing what was meant, Marta agreed, expecting some sort of teenaged fun. She described to her mother the circle of young people around a table, candles, salt, etc., and then chanting by the group. After a while the girl leader had Marta change her place and sit beside her, after which the chanting began again.

Suddenly Marta said she began chattering, just jibberish, and could not control what was coming out of her mouth. The other young people stopped their chanting, and then from Marta's mouth came clear words, "Tell Lorna Jassik that there is going to be a car accident, but she will not be killed." There was a pause, and then the message was repeated urgently, "Tell Lorna Jassik . . . but she is not to be afraid; she will not be killed."

Marta leaped from her chair and ran outside into the garden, crying. She insisted she had to go home at once. It was shortly after this that her worried mother phoned me, a second choice to the psychic friend she had been unable to reach.

When I am faced by a situation that calls for more wisdom than I possess, I always send an urgent request into the Higher Regions for whatever wisdom and power may be needed to alleviate the situation. I did this during the time that Marta and her mother were driving to my home. By the time they arrived Marta was self-controlled but nervous.

I explained that I wanted her to go into hypnosis and let me call back the voice that had spoken through her, but I assured her that I would not ask her to "channel" it again. I assured her that there would be no danger to her and that her mother would stay right with her. Then I induced Marta into a light hypnosis.

"I am calling the one who used Marta's voice without asking her permission. You had no right to push into her mind like that and frighten her. I ask you to stay out of her from now on!" I did not ask any questions. I just sent the voice away.

When Marta was back to full consciousness she said she felt clearly that the owner of the voice had been very sorry for having frightened her and had sent feelings of deep regret before withdrawing. Marta herself seemed to be greatly relieved.

I added that Marta had been given a precious gift, her psychic talent of receptivity; that it had been a scary experience this first time but that with more maturation and training it would become a controlled valuable talent, a God-given gift to be used for good; but that for the present she was simply to wait and let it grow, and eventually she would be shown what her next stage should be. I asked that a spiritual guardian be sent to protect and guide her during this growth period. (A few weeks later she told me that at first her guardian was with her constantly, helping her whenever she called him/her to assist with simple things, but that lately there had been no response. I smiled and reminded her that a guardian was not a sort of bellhop to assist with minor earthly problems but is a high spiritual being dedicated to *spiritual* protection and instruction.)

After Marta and her mother had gone, I could not get the episode out of my mind. Something seemed to be incomplete. I wondered if the voice had come from a being who was truly concerned for the safety of someone named "Lorna Jassik." Who was "Lorna Jassik?" Marta did not know anyone by that name, nor did I. I looked in the telephone directory.

Yes, there were two Jassiks listed. After thinking about the embarrassment of calling an unknown person with a message like this, I realized that my own hesitation was of far less importance than the delivery of the message which had seemed so urgent to the owner of the voice that had burst into Marta's consciousness.

So the next morning I called the first Jassik and calmly asked if Lorna was there.

"No, she's at work," answered the person on the other end just as calmly. Aha, there *was* a Lorna Jassik!

I called the work number and asked for Lorna. "She just came in. I'll get her," said the person on the phone. Next was a second voice, "This is Lorna."

Trying not to stammer, I introduced myself, complete with title "Doctor" and my location, and then began, "I think I have a message for you, but I'm not sure." And I told her the story as told above. She listened silently. When I finished I added rather apologetically, "I don't want to upset nor worry you but I thought at least you ought to know." She thanked me and agreed that she was glad to know and was not upset. She asked who the girl was who had received the message.

"You don't know her and she doesn't know you," I hedged. "We didn't even know whether you existed."

"Oh, I exist." laughed Lorna. I was relieved to know that she could laugh about it.

The next day the phone rang and a man's voice introduced himself as Lorna's uncle and asked about this message that

I had given to his niece. Again, with apologies, I repeated the story, adding that I just didn't know, but had thought maybe it might be important.

Without hesitation he said, "It *is* important. We are planning to drive several hundred miles tomorrow. What do you think we ought to do?"

Trying to keep my mind clear, I suggested, "Well, just be alert and drive defensively, and keep in mind that a drunk or a careless person may suddenly come out of a side road or cut across in front of you."

He thanked me and then asked if I knew whose voice had been speaking to his niece. I said I had not asked, but afterward I had wondered if it were Lorna's grandmother. "Is one of her grandmothers dead?" I inquired.

There was a slight pause before he said, "Yes." He thanked me again and hung up. Only later did I realize it may have been his own mother whose voice had come through.

I spent considerable time afterward wondering if I had done my part wisely. Perhaps I should have advised postponing the trip? Or had I taken the whole incident too seriously? I simply did not know. Nor did I ever know how Lorna and her uncle got along on their trip.

I did know that if more such cases were to be tossed into my path I would need to get more instruction.

## Next Step: More Learning

In California in 1985 I found a two-hour workshop offered by William Baldwin, D.D.S. and Ph.D. candidate, which gave me the techniques I needed to treat such cases more adequately for both the client and also the invisible personalities. Baldwin called his workshop "Depossession in the Clinical Setting"—i.e., not a religious setting but a health worker's setting.

Starting with this workshop, and adding several of Baldwin's tapes from previous workshops, I began a little home course in the recognition and treatment of cases of obsession and oppression—a sort of self-taught crash course in modern exorcism, one might call it. I procured and eagerly read an old book that I had first heard about years ago when I was in my early twenties, *Thirty Years Among the Dead*, by the psychiatrist Carl Wickland. He had performed hundreds of "depossessions" at the turn of the last century, using his psychically talented wife, Anna (with her willing cooperation), as the "channel" for the entities obsessing his psychiatric patients. [His book was first published in 1924 and reprinted in 1974.] Baldwin was influenced by Wickland's firm-but-kindly approach to the invading personalities and modeled his own approach after Wickland's.

I also read Annabel Chaplin's book, *The Bright Light of Death* (1977), the account of some of her cases of assisting personalities entrapped in living individuals to leave their unwitting hosts and go on "into the Light." Chaplin avers that she never in her life was in a "trance," but her description of her method, including taking a moment to "center herself" or to "quiet herself"—equivalent to placing herself into an altered state of consciousness—produces what many might call a trance. The words chosen are not important; it is the altered state of awareness that is important. In this quiet state Chaplin opened her natural psychic ability to perceive clairvoyantly what in ordinary consciousness she might have only vaguely sensed. Her approach to the invading entities, like Wickland's, was gentle but clear-cut and firm. It was a psychologist, Dr. Edith Fiore (author of *The Unquiet Dead*) who recommended Chaplin's book to Baldwin, and—like Edith—he was influenced by Chaplin's mild way of treating the invading personalities.

I read other books. (They are listed in the Bibliography.) I attended Dr. Fiore's all-day workshop on "Clinical Depossession." And all this time I was beginning what rather quickly became a considerable portion of my hypnotherapy practice: the releasement of obsessing souls from living patients. "Releasement" is Baldwin's word; I prefer it to depossession, disobsession, or exorcism, terms used by various other therapists for this process.

It was an easy step to begin to do "Rescue Work" with wandering entities who had not invaded living persons: work with so-called ghosts, poltergeists, and invisible presences, most of whom need help to escape from their unhappy situations. I felt that my new occupation was one of the most fascinating in the world, and was valuable to others as well!

## Terms and Definitions

What shall we call disembodied souls like Maggie? Her physical body was buried but some part of her was seen and recognized by her daughter and was felt to be alive and able to understand conversation, even to resist suggestions. Some of the therapists doing releasements speak of the "spirit" of a deceased person which can be contacted and which clairvoyants can see. Others save the word "spirit" to mean the divine incorruptible spark in the person, "which is housed in the soul as the soul is housed in the body" (to quote from *Mary's Message to the World*), the word "soul" being used to mean the mental and emotional and perceptive portions of a person which persist as a unit after the death of the physical body, housed in a body of invisible "astral" substance.

Maggie as seen by Amy was in her *astral body* (the usually invisible organized body of emotional energies that survives death along with the mind and its *mental body*). The *state of hypnosis* expanded Amy's ordinary powers of perception to include *astral vision and clairvoyance* so that she could see astrally. If her mother had been willing to speak, Amy could have heard her *clairaudiently*. As it was, Maggie did become willing to send her thoughts *telepathically* into Amy's mind so that Amy was aware of what her mother was thinking: thinking of all the cherished "things" that Maggie had to leave and now wanted to regain as her own again through co-occupying her daughter's body. But that meant pushing aside her daughter's own "soul" (personality, spirit), even pushing it clear out of her daughter's body—unethical selfish acts, although Maggie had not bothered to consider the ethics.

For myself, I like the term *psyche* to mean that mental/emotional/spiritual part of a person that survives death, but I admit that it becomes boring to use the word too often. *Personality* is almost as good, as is *soul, mind,* or *consciousness,* with the implicit inclusion of perceptiveness and emotion. I shall use these terms interchangeably, and also *spirit,* in the sense that Baldwin and members of the Spiritualist Church use it—as the living mind housed in the usually invisible astral body.

I say *usually invisible* because persons in hypnosis and those who have a natural talent for astral vision (also called clairvoyance or second sight) can see the astral forms as if they were physically visible. ("Second sight" is a term also used to mean precognition, the awareness of future events.)

Among the gradually increasing number of hypnotherapists who do Releasement work at present, it has become accepted to use the all-inclusive word "entity" for souls that are being contacted and assisted. Each of us is an entity, of course, as is each other individual being.

When hypnotherapists speak of an entity, however, they usually mean the soul of a deceased person or other invisible being that is entrapped in a living person or is causing problems in other ways.

## Normal and Abnormal Pathways of Souls After Death

When clients are regressed to a previous life and come to the death experience terminating that lifetime, therapists may continue the regression past the physical death and on into the after-death state. Similarly, when we contact earthbound entities—souls like Maggie, for instance—we can ask them to recall the circumstances of their physical death experiences.

Normally, after the physical body dies, the psychospiritual part—the mind, the psyche, the soul—finds itself floating above the body, still conscious of itself and aware of the people and activities around the dead body. This stage may be brief. The now disembodied consciousness, usually feeling free and light and greatly relieved, senses that it can go wherever it seems to be drawn, for instance to a Light—perceived to be alive and sentient, a Being of Light—which welcomes the personality with understanding, kindness, and love.

Most souls find themselves going to a state that is peaceful and beautiful. People who have had out-of-body experiences during a time of life-threatening danger or illness, or who have actually been pronounced dead and been resuscitated later, most often have reported visiting the beautiful realms. Only an occasional such person reports a chilly, lonely, or horrifying "near-death experience" (NDE).

There are stages after death, not always in the same order, in which the soul *reviews* the activities, thoughts, and words of its entire life and evaluates them as to their spiritual value and their impact on other persons, and thus *judges itself* as to the worth of the life just past, seeing both the successes and the weaknesses. Another stage is the *cleansing,* often described as the feeling of being embraced or surrounded by light.

A soul that is still very heavy with negative emotions and undesirable habits such as rage, cruelty, greed, etc., may be too negative to be attracted to the Light, and will turn away, not perceiving it, and go to a "place" (a vibrational frequency, a "dimension") that is likewise dark and heavy, appropriate to its own present nature. Its environment will change and brighten as the soul changes its negative traits to positive ones.

Like a mixture of substances suspended in water, the "heaviest" souls after death sink to the lowest astral levels, the "lightest" ones float to the upper levels, and the rest find appropriate levels in-between. This is really a self-determined matter for each, determined by the life-patterns *before* death. All such souls have followed what is for each one its normal path.

Other souls, however, do not follow a normal sequence after death. Multitudes who die do not have a clear idea of what occurs to the consciousness after the body dies, and find themselves bewildered upon discovering that they are still aware, still "alive," although their body is dead and they can not re-enter it. They remain in the vibrational vicinity of the earth-plane, able to see and hear living persons but invisible and inaudible to the living—a very frustrating situation. Not knowing where to go or what to do, most such souls start to wander, either aimlessly or else to some chosen place or person. We call these souls *wanderers.* (Perhaps

Lorna's grandmother was one of these, unless she had come back purposely from a higher level to the earth-plane in order to warn her granddaughter of danger.)

Some wanderers remain in the area of the body—which may now be buried—or in some other specific location, and become known as *ghosts,* seen or felt occasionally by living persons who are psychically sensitive. Others may seek amusement or try to attract the attention of the living by managing to make noises or even move objects around, to the consternation of the persons in the house. These are called *poltergeists*—"playful spirits."

And many wanderers eventually find a "place" that seems lighter or warmer than the chilly darkness of the earthbound state in which they have been, and they move into what turns out to be the body or aura of a living person, and become *attached entities* of that person, often without either the living host or the invading souls being aware of the relationship.

Several degrees of closeness of such attachments have been identified and named by therapists:

First may be *temptation* of the living person by an aspect of the wanderer—not really an overwhelming compulsion but *the thought of doing or saying something that is contrary to the basic personality* of the living individual, i.e., out of character—a temptation due to the presence of a hovering entity.

*Influencing* or *shadowing* are the terms used when the disembodied entity is affecting the host person mildly or intermittently, as with mood swings, irrational moments, sudden inexplicable fears or depressions.

*Oppression* is the word used, or *harassing*, when the entity is affecting the host's personal feelings and habits more noticeably and frequently. A clairvoyant may see the entity attached to the host's aura or within it.

*Obsession* is the condition, remarkably common, in which the entity may invade not only the psyche but also the physical body of the host and meld its own personality traits and former bodily feelings with those of the host, often to the confusion and bewilderment of the latter, who may be aware of persistent pains, sudden changes in emotions unlike his normal feelings, unfamiliar attitudes, or even unnatural traits and talents.

*Possession* is the condition in which the invading entity takes over the body of the host completely, pushing out the host's own personality (soul) and expressing its own words, feelings, and behaviors through the host's body, as Maggie was apparently trying to do to Amy. Complete possession is rare, but is sometimes spectacular when it occurs. Cases of a person suddenly going berserk, for instance, may well be cases of sudden complete possession. Possession may alternate with obsession.

I have seen personally only one instance of complete possession so far. It occurred without warning in my own therapy room (as described in detail in a later chapter).

# What Conditions Make
# Such Invasions Possible?

Let us assume that a group of people, such as battle casualties or a group killed in a plane crash, are all deprived of their physical bodies at the same time, and their souls find themselves conscious but without a means of communication with persons still in living bodies.

These souls may feel stunned for a little while, but some are soon aware enough to see their bodies (they seem to be floating above the scene) and they watch what is going on, usually with more or less impersonality toward their former body. But, as they so often tell us, "I didn't know what to do; I didn't know where to go."

Those who see the Light and move toward and into it find the normal pathway into the "next world," the astral world. The others wander away. Some may be attracted to persons who are smoking, drinking, or using drugs, if they themselves have been users of those substances. They feel that they can satisfy their hungers through the bodies and senses of the living; and so they move into the smokers or drinkers or drug users.

Others find and become attached to a living person whose aura is weak or "open," as after an accident, an illness, an anesthetic for an operation, a sudden physical shock or pain, or an emotional shock such as fear or grief. The aura in health is a strong defense, a protection for the psyche within the body, but in weakness it can be breached by an invading soul.

Still other disembodied psyches in this group find living persons who resemble themselves in some way, either psychologically or in environmental conditions. The similarity draws them into the host. A soul released from the body by a heart attack, for example, may enter a living person whose heart is feeble, making the condition still worse for the host. A soul who died filled with anger from any cause is attracted to a living angry person, entering and increasing the host's anger.

Still other souls may find themselves drawn to living persons whom they admire or who may give them a safe "home," or whom they even feel they can help and protect (although almost always such a selfless motive on the part of the invader contains a self-serving element somewhere).

One more class of invaders is that of souls who have had a close relationship with the living person in some past time, either in the present life or in a past existence. Either for love and friendship, or else for hatred and revenge, such souls may find themselves teamed up in an obsessive relationship. Maggie and her daughter Amy provide a good example of obsession—not quite the complete possession that Maggie was apparently trying to establish.

After all these reasons for the formation of an obsessive relationship have been tallied, one more is simply that the living person happened to be there at the time when the wanderer happened by. No one seems to be totally invulnerable. Living persons who work in the health profession are vulnerable to obsession by deceased souls because they are caring people and souls feel safe in them. Children, whose auras are not yet fully protective, are also vulnerable. And it was an invading entity who remarked that the unborn child *in utero* is the most vulnerable of all.

# What Can We Do to Prevent Obsession or to Get Rid of an Entity?

In general, we need to keep our aura clear, clean, and strong with healthy habits of all kinds—physical, mental, spiritual, and emotional. Asking deliberately in prayer for spiritual protection is fine. Visualizing a protective capsule or bubble of light surrounding one's body and aura is good. Monitoring one's inner thoughts and feelings is essential, too, lest corrosive angers or fears open the aura. Meeting the daily vicissitudes with calmness and strength, making a habit of positive attitudes of mind and heart and positive habits of speech—all these help to keep the aura strong and clear. If the presence of an invading entity is suspected—as after the death of a close friend or relative—then the person can talk directly to the deceased and assist the obsessing soul to leave and move into the Light. More will be said about this later.

But what about dealing with an oppressing or obsessing entity that is already attached to the host person? The process of expelling an invader used to be confrontive and angry, a sort of power struggle between the exorcist and the invader, whether the exorcist (therapist) was the host or a professional healer or clergy person. Some who felt themselves shadowed or harassed or otherwise negatively influenced by something not in accord with their own character have suspected an obsessing entity, and by meditations and prayer have been able to perform their own personal exorcism. In one case that I contacted, however, the entity had been expelled only as far as the outer portion of the woman's aura and still clung there, no doubt waiting for an opportunity to get deeper into the aura or even into her body. It said it had come from her parents and intended to return to them if sent out of my client. It was told that *that* was not an option; and, reluctantly, it allowed itself to be drawn into "a place *of* the Light but not *in* the Light," as the condition was described to us by one of the discarnate beings assisting. Each case needs to be evaluated individually and treated according to what is felt to be the wisest approach.

More will be said on this subject in the last chapter.

*chapter 2*

# BACKGROUND, DEFINITIONS, AND METHODS

During the past century a good many religious and philosophical ideas have changed or been rejected in the landslide of the materialistic sciences. Electromagnetic and gravitational forces were studied in the so-called "hard sciences" but the other types of forces—i.e., mental, emotional, motivational—were neglected. When I was a medical student in the middle and late 1930s, my medical school, Tulane, was one of the very few that offered any course in psychology or psychiatry, the attitude of most schools being, "Doctors take care of the body; priests, rabbis, and preachers take care of the soul." Even this remark might be uttered with a slight taint of sarcasm sometimes, implying that the work of doctors was of greater importance, for who knew whether the soul even existed?

Then the tide began to turn, and one of the comments being passed around in the middle and late 1960s was, "Have you heard, the psychologists first lost their souls, and then they lost their minds—but now they are about to make up their minds that they have minds."

Looking back through old school books of a century ago or reading the lyrics of old hymns and popular songs, we note the casual reference to the soul, the acceptance that at death the soul "takes its flight to worlds unknown," that the soul of a dying child, "covered with flowers, is rising, rising."

Through the ages the belief has persisted in many cultures that the disembodied consciousness or soul remains aware, and can even enter and take possession of a living person's body and dispossess that person's own mind. In a few groups this belief has been taken for granted and has persisted, while in the secular society and even in a good many religious denominations the concept of awareness after death seems to be largely ignored or disbelieved. At the funeral of a lovely young woman I heard the minister say, "If she were here, she would be happy to see all of you and your gifts of flowers." He assumed that her consciousness was far away. Perhaps it was actually present, invisibly. A good many souls when regressed to a past-life death have reported staying near the body until after the funeral.

Gradually in these modern times more and more therapists, especially hypnotherapists, are coming to be more open to the once-common assumption that "deceased" psyches—discarnate entities—can and sometimes do invade living persons. Sometimes the change in therapists' attitude is due to the spontaneous complaints of clients and sometimes to the suspected presence of an invading entity from various clues presented by the client, who herself may be entirely unsuspecting.

When I was in high school I held the tentative belief that the Gospel stories of casting out unclean spirits must be merely the Biblical way of describing epileptic attacks. A considerable proportion of the Gospels is given to stories of the casting out of "unclean spirits." Then, still in my teens, I heard of so-called "earthbound souls" who did not progress to the next dimension after death. According to what I read, these discarnate souls, many of them unaware that their bodies were dead, continued to hover in the earth-plane and were drawn to other psyches similar to their own, through whose physical bodies they might find gratification of former habits. The books (Rosicrucian and Theosophical) also discussed "elementals" and other nonhuman entities. At that time I put most of those ideas aside with a puzzled smile and a raised eyebrow—but kept the ideas on my mental "neutral shelf," for future reference in case further evidence came along.

By the time I began serious experimentation with hypnotic regression work in the mid-1950s I had learned the important art of not judging any idea too hastily no matter how far out it might sound. I did have occasional lapses, as, for instance, when a lovely white-haired woman—the widow of a minister and herself a lay counselor, lecturer, and healer—diagnosed my chronic fatigue in the thoughtful words, "I think this may be oppression by an evil spirit." My disappointment in her was profound. How could an intelligent, educated person like Mrs. Eggleston hold such medieval ideas!

My chicken came home to roost a few years later when relatives and friends made similar comments to me: "With your scientific education, your modern training, how can you possibly believe in stuff like this?"

I think that almost the same sort of change occurred in the attitude of psychiatrists and psychologists toward the concept of multiple personalities: first the doubts and questions, and later the acceptance, which caused doubts and questions in the relatives and friends.

# Comparison with Multiple Personality Disorder

We hear much these days about Multiple Personality Disorder (MPD), now called Dissociative Identity Disorder (DID). In other circles we also hear more and more about Spirit Attachment. I believe the areas overlap. Only the differing theories have prevented the discovery so far of how great is the overlap: the questions asked in the two fields are not the same questions. Important questions to ask any "alter personality" are, "Are you a true part of this person? Were you invited to enter her, did you invade her, or were you created? Have you ever had your *own* physical body? Think back to the last time when you were in your *own* body and tell me what was happening." In the case of an obsessing entity, this last request will bring forth a death experience. Other questions will bring out the details of such an entity's whole life history.

The accepted treatment of multiple personality syndrome is to identify each of the alter personalities within the patient and work to integrate them all eventually into one, the basic personality. The process may require several years. (Braun, *The Treatment of Multiple Personality Disorder,* 1986). The treatment of spirit possession and obsession is to call out and identify all the various spirits (souls, psyches) within the patient—the ones claiming *not* to be an intrinsic part of the client—and to release them, freeing them and also freeing the host. I find that this process can rather frequently be accomplished in one or two altered-state sessions, although it is good to follow with a session or more of "energy work" such as Therapeutic Touch (using clearing energy through a therapist's hands to restore and heal the client's aura). This clears the residue. It would seem to be reasonable for therapists to ask some of the initial "releasement questions" early in the treatment of cases diagnosed as MPD (DID) so as to release any obsessing entities before beginning the process of integrating the alter personalities, which are separate facets of the patient's own personality.

Multiple personalities are usually found to be defense mechanisms of a person who was severely abused as a child. Invading entities, on the other hand, may enter a living person at any age, even before birth. And obsession seems to be an amazingly common condition among ordinary "normal" people. Therapists doing Releasement work (Baldwin, Hickman, and others, including me) estimate that 70 to 80 percent of their clients have obsessing entities in them causing various physical and/or psychological problems, none of these responding to medical or psychiatric intervention. Dr. Edith Fiore, one of the pioneers of Releasement (Depossession) work, estimates that the percentage is closer to 90 or 95 among her many clients.

## "Splinter Personalities" from a Past Life

Sometimes what is taken at first to be an invading entity turns out to be a personality (sometimes called a "shell" or a "splinter") from a past life. Far from being passive and dormant, such partial personalities, when negative, can hinder the present person just like an obsessing invader. These belong to the person's real self but are not "created" alter personalities as in cases of DID. When positive they can protect and assist the present psyche. Baldwin gives several interesting examples of such past-life personalities that  penetrated into the present to accomplish what that past-life psyche felt was a good cause. That is the crux of the problem: The past-life personality, although aware of the present circumstances, may still be judging and trying to compel the present personality to operate according to its own past-time values and conclusions.

As Baldwin says, "It is inappropriate for the past-life personality to be active, interfering, or dominant in the present time. It rightfully belongs in another era. Some form of emotional residue activates the personality and this [needs to be] processed to completion."

### Case 1

A young client of mine felt that an entity was in her, admitting that she saw herself as "jealous, selfish, possessive, dishonest, wanting to control," etc. Her husband also thought she had an obsessing entity. An entity was indeed found and released, but many of the problems of mood and behavior remained, with no second entity to be found.

When asked to "Take us to the *cause* of these symptoms," the subconscious mind brought up a past life of the client as a minor overlord of an area in old Greece. He was devoured by discontent and anger, wanting still more power, wealth, prestige, not wanting to feel "like a nothing—like a peasant."

"I cheated the peasants; I did not see that they got fair prices; I took a cut for myself." There was no guilt, nothing but lusting for "more of everything."

I conversed with the overlord as if he were an obsessing entity and finally commanded him to go back and remain in the past, allowing this lady (his future self) to live her life in the present without interference and to develop spiritually as she desired to do. This method worked very well.

Accustomed to commanding others, he was able to accept commands from others who had gained his respect, as apparently I had.

## Case 2

A second case, also of a young woman, is somewhat similar. She had always resented being female, looked down rather scornfully on women in general, and was strongly, even emotionally involved with conservation policies of the area. Tall, slender, dark-haired, she said she was always surprised to see in the mirror that her eyes were blue. She had borne children but had only moderate maternal feelings. She felt that she had been Native American in a previous life.

In regression she went back easily to a life as a Native American man who had almost always incarnated as one, because "here I am strong; this is my country." Once or twice discarnate counselors got him to agree to incarnate in other places; and before this present life he was urged to be born as a "white" because of his former scorn and hatred of whites.

He had accepted this urging, but added, "I was embarrassed when I found myself in a female body." He was fully aware of his present life and body and wanted to keep on controlling all thought habits and attitudes of this present white lady, keeping her an Indian man, scornful of whites, angry at their wasteful ways, their attitudes toward nature, etc., etc.

I pointed out to him his own narrow-minded attitudes (e.g., that "women are not bad, just weak" and that "they need to be protected and controlled").

"Some women are weak," I admitted, "but some are strong. Some men are strong, some are weak." I pointed out his own weakness—that he said he had become addicted to alcohol and had helped the whites to find passes over the mountains and assisted them in other ways in order to obtain alcohol. (The client told me after the session that he had become angry at my lecturing him in this manner, even though my tones were mild.) Finally I got his promise that he would retire into the past and let his present self learn and mature in ways suited to the present, bringing only his old *strengths* into this present female self.

I used to try to figure out the profound enigmas of space, time, and philosophical problems that this sort of conversation implies but discovered early that it was beyond my present capability. I only present what we obtained with this young woman. A second regression cleared up still more of her ambivalent attitude and she seemed more at ease with herself and more positive in shifting the stern nature-morality of the Native American into the modern setting of conservationist activities. She told me she felt more satisfied after the second session. Her autocratic, male-chauvinistic former self was apparently keeping his promise to retire into the past, although some of his traits did remain to tincture the present personality. This, however, is almost a "normal" past-life effect.

Not all such *Splinter Personalities* are limiting or obstructive. In several instances among my cases the past-life personality has aroused the profound respect, even the reverence, of the present personality. I remind the client that this is what they once were, and therefore can become again; that the awareness of the past self can be an inspiration and encouragement for the over-burdened, struggling present-day self.

In one case the client, a physician, learned that his present fear of loneliness had come from a past life as a Native American man, Straight Eagle, who had gone on "many Vision Quests until I had overcome the Great Loneliness."

Then why, I wondered, did his present self feel loneliness?

"It is possible that the loneliness I felt as Straight Eagle was *this* loneliness now," he said thoughtfully.

This was the first occasion in which causality had been assigned specifically to a "future" life that happens to be the *present* life but is considered by a *past-life* personality to be causal for himself! Straight Eagle was called "straight" because his tongue was always straight: he always told the truth or what he perceived to be true.

I do not allow myself to be distracted into a detour by such an instance, for my work is in therapy, not philosophy or research. We hear repeatedly that "time is an illusion." For my present stage of evolution and for the purpose of this book, I just accept in simplicity what is told to me. Yes, perhaps Straight Eagle, long ago, did indeed overcome the great loneliness for his future self, and when his future self learned of Straight Eagle's victory, the future (present) self's loneliness was diminished. And now his life is changed; he is no longer alone or lonely, though his responsibilities have increased. He is mature and strong, a worthy karmic descendent of Straight Eagle, his former self.

I do not ask such positive past-life personalities to go back to the past, for they can be like spiritual guides and helpers in the present.

## Talking to the Invisibles

Symptoms of spirit-attachment may be subtle. At times the host-person may say wonderingly, "Whatever made me do that? That's not like me." Or his family may notice a change in his personality, especially after an operation or other period of stress. After a death in the family, a family member may continue to feel clearly aware of the presence of the deceased and feel little or no grief or loss, and may even begin to exhibit certain traits of the deceased. In such a case the psyche of the deceased may indeed have entered the living relative, bringing its own thought-patterns and habits.

When the therapist has called the entity and is talking to it through the vocal apparatus of the hypnotized client and asks how and why it entered the client, the entity's reply may at first be, "He was just there," or, "I don't know."

Further questioning may bring out such comments as:

- ❖ "She was vulnerable and I wanted to protect her."
- ❖ "He was on drugs and I thought I'd get some kicks through him."
- ❖ "She knew where she was going. I wanted to get some fulfillment through her."
- ❖ "She was weak. She needed me to make her stand up for herself."
- ❖ "He was mad. I was mad, too."
- ❖ "He was easy. He had been sick a while. He was open."
- ❖ "When he got his head hurt, that's when I went in."
- ❖ "She was lonely; she needed me. I came in to comfort her."
- ❖ "He was creating a launching pad. I think I helped him."

When many such answers are tallied up, it seems that a few of the most important reasons allowing the entrance of an invading entity are the following (to repeat the earlier list):

❖ Similarity of mood (e.g., anger, loneliness) or of circumstance.

❖ Openness or weakness of the living person's aura from illness or shock.

❖ Addictions to drugs, nicotine, sex, eating, etc.

❖ Desire to finish some unfinished task through the host.

❖ Desire to remain close to a loved person or to harass a hated one.

❖ Desire to protect or assist a weak or threatened person such as a child or infant.

Such reasons as these last sound like unselfish reasons, and some of them may really be so, but the end results are not often what the entering soul desired. As one female entity who was found obsessing her granddaughter said, "I went in to protect her as a child because she was vulnerable; but it didn't work out the way I thought it would."

## Spirit Attachment, Though Common, Is Not Healthy

There are a few definite reasons why the condition of oppression/obsession (and of course possession) is almost always disadvantageous to both the invading entity and the host:

❖ There is no *conscious* communication between them.

❖ The thoughts, feelings, and behavior patterns of the invader pop up into the consciousness of the host at unexpected moments and produce confusion, bewilderment, and fears of going crazy.

❖ The invader saps the bodily energy of the host, because the astral body of the invader has no physical energy.

❖ The obsessing entity seldom is able to leave the host and move freely, and thus finds itself imprisoned in the host, as if by a strong magnetic force.

❖ On a more metaphysical level, the invader is trapped not only astrally but spiritually, unable to progress on its own spiritual pathway as long as it remains in the host, while distracting the host from *his* individual path to a greater or lesser degree.

For all these reasons the training we releasement therapists received at first was that every obsessing entity, without exception, needs to be expelled from the host person. A few examples began to turn up, however, in which the obsessing entity did perform a beneficial function for the host. Each case needs to be evaluated individually, although in general the old rule is still applicable: If a soul is in a body not its own body, it should be released, for its own good and that of the host. The original soul is the only soul—in almost all cases—that has a right to that body.

Another rule we releasement therapists were taught early or discovered for ourselves is that angelic beings, masters, teachers, and true spiritual guides do not invade their pupils and disciples; they respect each person's privacy and free will. They do not coerce or take advantage of a person's moment of weakness or vulnerability. There are a *very few* instances in which this rule is modified with the consent of the living person or by his/her invitation. (Examples of all these will be given later.)

*Walk-ins* are a different class. They are souls who take over a living person's body completely but *on a contractual basis of mutual consent*. When a living person's body is dying, or when the person wishes intensely to die, the discarnate psyche of another may approach the soul of the first and offer to take over the body and release the original resident, who thus makes the transition of death without incurring the karma of suicide and leaves the body to be occupied by the walk-in. The walk-in therefore has the task of healing and restoring the body as well as completing the duties and some of the karmic situations of the first soul. It was Ruth Montgomery in her book, *Strangers Among Us* (1979), who first named and brought walk-ins to public attention. I have encountered only a few in my practice, several of them well-balanced and self-confident but others still struggling with the problems which caused the original owner to despair or caused the body to become almost untenable.

In one unusual case the original owner of the body changed his mind and wanted to return and was trying to evict the walk-in—a turnabout situation! In this case it became plain in a hypnotic session that the walk-in was the proper tenant and that the original owner of the body was a selfish lower type of soul trying to break his contract. With the combined talents of our meditation group we were able to send on the original resident to the Light and establish the new tenant firmly, freeing him from the harassments of the would-be obsessing original owner!

## Types of Entities Found Invading

The *earthbound souls of deceased human beings* (called *dybbuks* in the Jewish Kabbalah) are by far the most commonly found kind of obsessing or oppressing entity. Such human entities include as many various types of human souls as were once in living bodies: old or young, strong or weak, recent or ancient, familiar or foreign.

Not only a deceased person's mind but also a portion of the *mind of a living person,* as mentioned, can become an obsessing entity. We speak of such a condition when we say of a person, "He just seems to be obsessed with her."

A *past-life personality* or *shell* (as some have called it) may shadow or oppress a living person, coloring their present attitudes and distorting some of their behaviors just like an obsessing entity. The symptoms are similar and usually hinder the present personality.

*Thought-forms* created by the combined thinking of many people over the years, or else created deliberately by persons who use the intentionally focused power of thought in a magical way, will take on a life of their own and may affect and obsess living persons. They can be treated as invading entities, although they do not have the spark of soul.

*Animal souls* may occasionally be found as obsessing entities. In my practice they are rare.

*Elementals,* discarnate living beings of rather low intelligence and often on the negative side, may be encountered. They have never had physical bodies of their own. Those I have found were relatively mild.

Discarnate *dark beings of a demonic nature,* the lesser or minor ones being captives of the stronger ones, may also be found as invaders. The *minor demonic types* are usually rather easily persuaded to turn away from slavery to the negative old nature, and to perceive the kernel or spark of light within themselves. The *major dark ones,* malicious and often highly intelligent, are seldom amenable to the usual techniques of Releasement.

The above is a partial list. Cases illustrating these will be given in subsequent chapters.

# Methods of Releasement/Depossession

With such a wide spread of types of entities to deal with, it is not surprising that therapists have developed a wide spread of approaches to the goals of rescuing wanderers or expelling parasitic entities from their clients. Most offer therapy first to the invaders, releasing them, and then to the client who was the host and who now is free from all but his own problems.

A number of therapists follow the old confrontive attitude of the religious exorcisms, assuming all obsessing entities to be evil or at least unclean, assuming that most or all of the entities are hostile or dangerous, and taking a very authoritarian manner toward them. Sometimes this approach works, but often only after a great deal of energy has been expended by the therapist.

Sometimes it is not the approach needed. In at least one instance, the second therapist called found that the entity was "terrified, just panic-stricken" by the efforts of the first therapist, who had ordered it out of the client "in the name of the Father, the Son, and the Holy Ghost." It turned out to be simply a harmless lost soul seeking refuge and needing direction and assurance.

The other extreme in Releasement attitudes is the "soft touch, soft talk" approach in which "gentle persuasion" is used in conversing with the invading entity. It is remarkable how often this approach is successful, even with hardened, embittered souls and demonic types. Compassion is an almost universally acceptable instrument for successful releasements. A good motto to remember is Dr. Hazel Denning's: "The meaner and nastier a person is, the more he is hurting."

Somewhere between these two extremes is the challenging mode in which the therapist is the challenger, the obsessing entity being kept on the defensive by questions or verbal thrusts, the therapist still keeping firmly a compassionate mind-frame. Such means are useful in many cases but not in working with strong dark beings, whose own verbal thrusts can be devastating to the "merely human" therapist and throw him or her off balance, allowing the dark being to take the initiative.

Even for fairly powerful dark ones, however, gentleness and compassion often produce that fateful turnaround from viciousness to weeping and then to willingness to change.

"What was it, honey, that hurt you so much long ago?" I asked one embittered female entity. There was a pause, then silent tears, then stifled sobbing—and the hardened entity was ready to tell her story and to be comforted and helped.

One more type of therapeutic means requires mention, that of *Remote Releasement,* or Depossession *in absentia.* Eugene Maurey (*Exorcism,* 1988) uses a pendulum technique to locate and diagnose the obsessing entities in a person whose name has been given to him, and to perform the releasement in his home, never conversing directly with the entities. His method has well-documented success. Dr. Irene Hickman (*Remote Depossession,* 1994) uses hypnosis with a colleague who channels for the entity that is in the absent client. She too has had well-documented success. I perform such channeled releasements routinely when the client is an infant or child, or when the client is geographically distant or has a handicap which prevents him or her from channeling the entity directly. Such a handicap may be simply great fear or other strong emotion, such as grief. In these cases I enlist the help of a coworker, who goes into hypnosis and, as the channel, permits the entity in the absent client to speak through her voice, as Dr. Wickland's wife did many decades ago.

# The Author's Method of Releasement

I try to check for entrapped entities at the first or second session with almost every client who comes to me, with whatever complaint. I discuss with the client the possibility that her problems may not all belong to her but to some other consciousness that has been influencing her. Nearly all people would be willing to believe that some other influence is to blame for some of their troubles! But this by itself would not be sufficient reason to suspect or diagnose an obsession. In case a client may be made anxious and nervous by the very mention of a possible not-self-consciousness within their own mind or body, this first little conversation, therefore, is held in a lighthearted but common sense manner, with examples, and ending with some such remark as, "Well, in any case, if it is all right with you, I would like to check and see."

Then, with the client in light to moderately deep hypnosis (the depth need not even be as deep as for most simple regressions), and telling the client that a certain finger is the "yes" finger, which will twitch or rise when I ask a question to which the answer from the subconscious level is "yes," and also a "no" finger (touching the fingers as I speak), I then ask, "Is there any consciousness, any mind, any entity in this person" (calling her by name) "which does not belong to her, is not a part of her own being? Please answer through the fingers on the count of three: one, two, three."

If the client already has a "yes" and a "no" finger, I use those instead of designating others. A few seconds may elapse before the fingers respond. The manner in which they respond is significant: a quick response means that the invading entity is eager to speak with the therapist and will probably be very cooperative. A hesitation or only a tiny twitch of the "yes" finger may indicate that the entity is fearful or timid, that it is not sure of what this is going to lead to. In such a case I usually follow Dr. Baldwin's approach and assure the entity, "Don't be afraid of me. I want to help you." More assurance may be needed, especially when the entity is the soul of a person who died by betrayal and cannot trust others, such as a child who was killed by abuse.

When the fingers do not move at all, I used to think the fault was in me or was just a block of some unknown type. Now I have discovered, as Baldwin did before me, that in almost every case it is because the entity does not want to be found and is trying to hide from the therapist, pretending not to be present, not permitting the "yes" finger to move and reveal its presence. But the truthful subconscious mind of the client will not falsely move the "no" finger. Therefore neither one moves.

In such an instance I speak to the entity, "Please don't be afraid of me. I believe you are here. Is there an entity hiding from me?" This question often brings a "Yes" movement, even if small. Then I thank the entity for letting me know of its presence, and we continue from there.

When the entity is unable or unwilling to speak through the voice of the client (or the channel), much can be learned merely by asking for finger movements in answer to questions framed to be answered by a simple Yes or No. Nearly all entities of whatever type *can* use the voice of the client or channel by placing its *thoughts* into the mind of the client or channel, who then speaks the thoughts aloud. If the entity believes it cannot do so or for any reason refuses to, still much can be learned through the finger movements alone.

Routinely I program each new client, with his or her consent, to go into the altered state when my voice speaks the cue-words, "Rest now." This, I explain, is merely a little shortcut, a time-saver which can be canceled out at any time the client desires. Meanwhile it is convenient in case the client wishes to receive hypnotic assistance over the telephone.

On the subconscious and superconscious levels we are all—living and "dead"—in close connection with one another, regardless of space and time differences. The state of altered consciousness enables one to access these other minds and become aware on a *conscious* level of their thoughts and feelings. Not at all complex, it seems to be very simple and natural to all who are involved: the client, the entities, and the therapist.

## Nested Entities

The condition that Baldwin used to call *piggy-back obsession* and now calls *nesting of entities* is remarkably common.

Imagine that an old alcoholic who died and whose soul continued to haunt bars had been obsessed by the soul of another drinker who had died before, and who, in fact, had increased the old man's addiction and hastened his death. Then suppose that the two-in-one had managed to invade another customer in the bar (one with a strong taste for alcohol, in all probability)—and obsessed him. The customer, leaving the house, might have had an irresistible urge to stop as soon as possible at another liquor store, perhaps to the person's own astonishment at feeling the sudden strength of the urge. From then on, the guest would be entertaining not only his own desire for alcohol but also the thirst of the old alcoholic plus the thirst of the other in him, the one "nested" in the old man. This is a sketch of the type of doubling-up of entities that occurs quite easily over the years and lifetimes. The symptoms are the same as outlined for what may be called simple obsessions, in which each invading entity has no other inside of it.

When an obsessing human entity is stubborn, harsh, mocking, cruel, or even exhibits emotional coldness, saying, for instance, "I don't care," when its harmful influences are pointed out, then we suspect that it harbors a nested negative entity within it. Questioning, we ask it to "look inside of yourself and tell me what you see." If it says "Something dark," or "Anger," or a similar negative thing, we call out that thing, using the name given it by the entity it inhabits, and speak to it as if it were (as maybe it is) another entity, but this time obsessing the first one. Once that nested one has been called out and released, the formerly harsh, cold entity is abruptly revealed to be an ordinary troubled human soul, glad to be rid of the evil influence that had warped him or her. Releasement of this human soul is then usually quick and easy.

Baldwin first and I also have sometimes discovered several to many "layers" of nested entities within one client. I have not tried to keep accurate count but usually ask the client to answer through finger-movements whether any obsessing entities remain after the first ones discovered have been released.

When an entity has others nested within it, the client's "yes" and "no" fingers may hesitate, hardly knowing whether to say, "Yes, more than one invader" or "No, only one." Whenever I see this hesitation I take it as a clue to ask the invader to look inside itself for others. This hesitation may occur even when the nested one is a harmless little soul like that of a lost child or an aborted infant. If the nested one is a dark one, however, its influence will have been apparent in the host-entity's negative traits, and because of this host-entity, therefore also in the client.

Does all this sound complicated? Actually it is rather straightforward, especially if we pause during conversation with an entity when we begin to suspect that it contains one nested within it, deal with the nested one first, and then with increasing ease with the obsessing entity that contained it and successively with any others, layered like onion skins. In theory a systematic deepest-first releasement seems most reasonable, but whatever sequence is most natural in each case should be followed, remembering that some of the "onion layers" may represent nonhuman entities nested within human souls. (See later chapters on nonhuman and dark entities.)

*chapter 3*

# HUMAN SOULS RELEASED

In hundreds of sessions, literally hundreds of trapped entities have been released during the years of my active work in this field. It is impossible to relate more than a few of the interesting stories of these entities' lives and deaths.

To illustrate some of the various types of personalities that have been freed and the various conditions of the sessions, I selected—almost at random—from the many notebooks in which they are recorded. These condensations do not reveal the personal feeling that the original verbatim scripts provide nor do the written notes give the vivid tones of voice of the entities' words.

## Eve

This case is so simple and direct that it is almost a classic type. "Eve," a lovely highly educated lady who had done remarkable things with her self-hypnosis, had not been able to rid herself of a fear of high places, a fear which had begun only a few years before. I explained to Eve that perhaps it was not really her own fear—maybe it belonged to a consciousness that was fearful and that a releasement might help. I was prepared to learn that the supposed invader might be anyone—perhaps a person who had committed suicide by jumping from a high place.

Because this was the first time that Eve had attempted to channel she was somewhat apprehensive and a bit tense. For this reason I deepened her hypnotic state a bit more than usual. Somewhat abbreviated, the conversation went like this:

"Is there any soul or consciousness in Eve's body or aura," I asked, " that is not part of Eve herself? Please answer through the fingers on the count of three: one, two, three." (The "yes" finger rose.) "Is there more than one such entity or consciousness that does not belong to Eve?" (The "no" finger rose.) "Thank you for letting me know that you are here. I'd like to know your name. Put the thought of your name into Eve's mind and she will speak it for you. Eve, just say out loud the very first name that comes into your mind, no matter what it is."

Eve: "Alice."

"Thank you," I said, "for cooperating and letting us know who you are, Alice. How old are you?"

Alice (speaking through Eve's voice) : "Old . . . dead for years . . . died in '65. Heart failure and lots of things wrong . . . seventy years old and tired."

"Go to the moment when your soul leaves your body. Tell us about that."

"It is a release . . . I felt strange, lost. I saw people looking at the body and crying. They were not looking at *me*."

"No, they couldn't see or hear you," I agreed, "but you could see and hear them. What did you do, Alice—did you stay close to your body?"

"I stayed for a while . . . then—I don't know . . . I feel light and pleasant, warm, comfortable. . . . I see the sunshine. . . . I feel happy . . . drifting."

"Did you know that you were in Eve's body?"

"Yes. She's my granddaughter. She loved me. I entered through her eyes, at the cemetery after I died."

"And really it was not to her advantage nor to yours that you entered her; but you didn't know that. Her body belongs only to her. You should have gone to the Light—but you didn't know. When you entered her you brought into her not only your love but your fears as well. Did you have fears that you brought into her?"

"No . . . Well, I might have."

"Eve now feels afraid of high places. Were you afraid of high places?" (A leading question, although I seldom use leading questions.)

"Yes," admitted Alice.

"And you brought into her your fear. How do you feel about making her fearful of heights?"

"I'm sorry." Alice's voice was very low.

"Alice, why don't you use this marvelous little whisk broom like the one that Eve used when learning self-hypnosis and sweep away your fears and your tiredness and everything else you want to get rid of? And *think* yourself strong and well. Thoughts are very strong where you are, even stronger than they are for us here on the earth-plane. Think yourself younger. You are seventy; how young do you want to be?"

"Twenty-five!" Her answer was eager.

"Then *think yourself* to be twenty-five. Stand up straight, strong and young and beautiful! Now watch for someone coming to meet you. . . . Tell me when you see someone."

"I see a figure—a man; he is tall and slim," she said.

I spoke to the man.

"Have you come to take Alice home, or do you need help yourself?"

"I've come to get Alice," he replied. It seemed rather non-committal.

"Alice, hold out your hand," I suggested, "and take his hand. How does it feel?"

"Cool," was her answer.

"Do you like a cool hand?" I was checking on this supposed guide.

"No, but his eyes are kind."

I was still not quite convinced that this guide was appropriate for Alice if his hand felt *cool* to her. I invited another guide to come, "a high, wise helper who wants to help Alice."

"I see a woman coming," Alice reported.

"Thank you for coming, Lady. Hold out your hand to Alice. Alice, how does it feel?"

"Warm. And her eyes are gentle."

"Lady," I addressed her, "hold out your other hand to the first guide and all three of you go home to the Light, the higher dimension. And I invite any other souls who have heard my voice to come and follow these three. . . . What do you see, Eve?"

"Only shadows coming," she said.

"Alice, do you have a message for Eve as you go?" I inquired.

"Be happy," said the grandmother.

"Eve, do you want to say anything to your grandmother?"

"I love you," whispered Eve, with tears coming.

"Then good-bye, Alice. When you think of her, Eve, your thoughts and your love will reach her; she will know. But when she sends you thoughts and her love, you may or may not know consciously, because we are heavily veiled down here on the earth-plane. . . . Good-bye, Alice; I have enjoyed meeting you. Tell me when she is gone, Eve."

After a brief pause Eve murmured, "She's gone now."

A recent telephone call to Eve confirms our expectations: she has had no more acrophobia since this session and proudly told of driving over one of the more adventuresome mountain roads that used to frighten her.

# Joe

My friend "Joe," a hypnotherapist in late middle age (now deceased), was a reformed alcoholic who had been working with alcoholics for twenty years. He had written a book for reformed alcoholics. But he said he had never gotten over a craving for alcohol. He wanted to find the cause of the craving and also to check up on possible entities within him.

With Joe in hypnosis, I asked for any entity or consciousness in him who was not a part of Joe himself to please come out and talk with me.

An entity came at once, calling himself C.B. In answer to my question he told me, "Joe was about thirty-five when I went into him, at the Lodge (the meeting place for Alcoholics Anonymous). I was the first one to die in that Lodge. Joe was shocked. I had cancer but was in the Lodge for alcoholism. I was real sick for a long time with lung disease. . . .

"Joe was good to me; got me in the Lodge. I thought he'd be glad to have me (come into him). . . . I was a heavy drinker and a *good* gambler. I wouldn't let Joe gamble. I didn't want him to turn out like me—broke. I kept him afraid to gamble." (C.B. did not seem to perceive that if he were a *good* gambler he would not be broke!)

The spiritual guide who came to escort C.B. into the Light looked "like a picture, like 'Little Boy Blue,' only his clothes are white. He's kinda pale—long brown hair—nice-looking, lotta love in his eyes . . . a nice person."

A hardened, sullied adult entity may regress back to the innocence of childhood as he sheds the earth-heaviness and returns "home." In this instance it was not the entity himself who appeared as a child but his guide, a being he could trust and love.

After Joe returned to normal consciousness he said that he remembered C.B. very well. C.B.'s craving for alcohol had apparently been added to his own. C.B. thought that Joe, as a good friend, "would be glad to have me," a typical attitude for obsessing entities who feel friendly. They have no understanding of the mutual disadvantages.

Joe's craving was markedly diminished after C.B. was gone.

# Ted

Sometimes a parasitic entity may try to convince the therapist that the relationship is a real benefit to the host; and in some respects, perhaps it may actually be so.

In one case the host, "Ted," was a blind man in a responsible professional career and the trapped entity was a young male paraplegic, "Tim," who tried to persuade me, speaking through the host, that he was the source of the blind host's remarkable clairvoyant seeing.

"Ted is my legs and I am Ted's eyes," he told me.

For a moment I was at a loss, not wanting to expel the entity if that would take away the only sight that Ted did have. It occurred to me to ask Ted (in hypnosis) if he had a guide or master. He said yes, and told me the name of his master.

I asked the master if he would please tell me what to do. He said (through Ted's voice), "Louise, let me handle this.

Tim is not Ted's eyes; Ted's vision is his own. Tim, come on down, move down in Ted's body . . . on down . . . farther on down. . . . Let him go, Ted . . . clear down into his feet. . . . *Let him go, Ted!* . . . Now, Louise, you can take it from here."

All this time I had been sitting silent and passive except for writing down what was coming from Ted's lips.

When Tim was turned over to me, I reminded him that "thoughts are very powerful where you are. Just *think yourself well,* come clear out of Ted and stand up on your own strong legs, with your head up, your shoulders back . . . ," thus using the powers of mental/emotional forces to assist Tim to transform his astral limbs, still paralyzed simply because he had *expected* them to be, into straight, useful, healthy astral limbs. This type of healing is almost always swift and complete for disembodied souls. (For bodies that are still living it is a slower process but still powerful: "mind over matter.")

I thanked Ted's master for his invaluable assistance. Both Ted and Tim were free now. Ted still had his astral vision and Tim had useful legs again!


## Dolores

Occasionally an invader feels that it is helpful to the host in psychological or social ways. Such an entity was Dolores, who said (through the man she had entered) that she was a seamstress in an English factory and had died in 1844. Dolores was a "child-soul," self-centered, cheerful, lacking both foresight and hindsight, and socially insensitive. She described herself thus:

"I didn't have much religion . . . just enjoyed living . . . was carefree . . . didn't have much responsibility. I wasn't married. I got sick—something inside of me was wrong. I had a lot of pain. Might have been pregnant, I don't know. I enjoyed sex a lot. . . . There were no doctors. I just died . . . went into 'Ben' when he was twenty-one; I chose him because of his energies. He needs to be *himself.* He wasn't much fun—too serious. Maybe I'm not serious enough. It was interesting to watch him. He went through a lot of conflict and felt strange whenever he was having fun."

"Maybe you helped him have fun," I suggested.

"True. But he's helped me, too. . . . He's a sourpuss—don't enjoy nothin'. Too responsible. But he seems to have *purpose.*"

"Maybe that conflict was due to *you,* Dolores."

"True. It's like we are opposites."

"Now, Dolores, what would you like for your new life outside of Ben?"

"A pretty dress!"

"No, not anything earthly like that. What characteristics?" (She seemed to consider.) "Are you ready to start growing up now?"

"Yes. Watching Ben was interesting; I was watching what he *feels* and goes through. It's easier to understand others this way, when I'm inside him. It's hard to do when you are in a physical body. . . . And he experiences me but doesn't know it. . . . He's trying to learn so much it scares him. My feelings are so different, and he feels them; and his *heart* is drawn toward it but his *mind* doesn't know how to put it together. What he was taught by society is so different from these things. . . . He's showed me a side of life I didn't know. I didn't relate to others or understand others. He showed me there are *two sides: enjoyment* and *responsibility,* and you have to get them together. . . . Ben helped me to learn to *think.*

"He doesn't trust his feelings," she went on. "I trust my

feelings. I feel good about myself. It makes Ben feel strange; he feels he shouldn't feel good about himself."

She began to talk about "people in churches—they look like they *enjoy* suffering, women more than men. They say, 'Think *this,* feel *that.*' They can't get the two together. Ben's changed his attitude toward women, and that's nice."

"Have you changed yours toward men? Men are more than just toys for you to play with, you know. They are human beings just as much as you are. Are you seeing deeper into men now?"

"Yes. I think more about the *qualities* of men than I used to. There are men who are good. It's like watching *hearts.* Women seem to do it easier."

"Maybe in your next life you may choose to be a man?" I hinted slyly.

Dolores paused, then sighed. "That would be an experience! It would be an experience to see why they act as they do."

"Before you go, Dolores, do you think you could make a gift to Ben of some of your joyousness? As you say, he is too serious."

"Yes," she agreed at once.

"It has been fun talking to you, Dolores."

"Thank you," was her final word as she went into the Light. "Good-bye, and thank you."

In this example it did appear that the obsessive relationship had been of genuine help to both parties in several ways, even though a definite problem in certain others. The host, after being released from Dolores and several other entities, thanked me repeatedly with big carefree smiles. I wondered if the gift from Dolores (the name means "Sorrows"—not at all appropriate for her) was already taking effect in Ben!

# Annie

This intelligent vigorous young woman had been having difficulties in the movement class she has been taking. On a recent hike, a companion commented on her "funny" gait—an odd movement in walking of which "Annie" had not been aware. She did know that her right hip had given her problems for many years— a condition diagnosed as "ideopathic sinovitis," which means that the doctors didn't know what the cause of the inflammation was. Her right knee also gave her trouble. She said that her right leg felt "like a club."

With only this much information we decided to find out first of all whether all these problems were her own or belonged to an obsessing entity in her. It was no surprise to me when her "yes" finger indicated that there was such an entity present; in fact, there were "three or more," said the "yes" finger.

Following the general formula of calling out first the strongest entity present (although I do not know how the strongest one is selected!), we found old Cleo, who described himself this way:

"I'm an old man—gray beard, seventy-five or eighty years old. I entered Annie when she was being born . . . don't know why I chose her. I was gnarled with arthritis, hands like claws, had pain and stiffness in my body. I was shrunken. It was in Finland. I had no family, was just alone in the cold, in a little cottage in the snow. I cut wood, sold it; not sure anyone paid anything for it. I see a big pack of wood on my shoulder. Maybe I was just surviving. Got reindeer meat for food. I set lines in the woods; the reindeer tripped on them. No visitors. I'm all alone. . . .

"I got banished from my village. The people of the town

were throwing things at me. 'Dirty old man, get away from the children!' They said I had been hurting the children. It's about the boys. They said I corrupted them. We smoked and drank together. . . . I didn't do anything that everyone else didn't do. I slept around with the teenage girls in the village. The other men slept around with them, too—oh, yeah! But I didn't have a wife. The wives knew that their husbands were sleeping around—everybody knew. Everybody pretended they didn't."

I asked, "How did the girls feel? Did they feel everyone was hypocritical?"

"They thought it was great. The girls thought they were special, important."

Asked to review his life, Cleo saw himself banished as a young man after being stoned out of the village, and going on a ship to "a blue–green sea—the Mediterranean"—where he had found a woman and lived the life of a pirate. Years later as an old broken man he went back to Finland to die, broken because "I never did anything good." He admitted voluntarily that he stole, robbed, cheated. . . .

"You have honesty, Cleo," I told him; "that is a good start. And you have perseverance. Now get rid of the self-centeredness, greed, cheating, and lying; brush out the arthritis, the gnarledness. . . . Are you doing all this?"

Suddenly smiling, Cleo exclaimed, "I can stand up, way tall!" No longer was he "shrunken." And when he had also cleaned up his feelings and thoughts he said he had become "a chubby blond cherub." (This type of transformation back to the innocence of childhood has been encountered every now and then as hardened entities "clean themselves up" preparatory to going on into a realm of astral peace.)

"Now clean up Annie's body, fix up everything that you brought into her," I instructed him.

"I've cleaned out her hip, but the knee is stuck. It's not

loosened. The knee is not me; something else is in the knee . . . but the bones ( in the hip) are all shiny now!" He smiled.

As releasements usually go, Cleo should have been ready now to go at once into the Light. It turned out that there was another difficulty. Although Cleo could see a light, it was only "a little pin-hole. I can squeeze into it . . . got my arms through . . . pretty tight around the shoulders; they are too wide."

Asked to discover why the shoulders were too wide, Cleo murmured, "A lump in my chest—like a piece of fat; heh, looks like a piece of tofu, but it's guts—no, a piece of brain—no, a *big fat cow's tongue.*"

By questioning we found that the "big tongue" was a symbol of "all the awful things I've said to my wife: 'You make me sick. You're repulsive. You disgust me. You're not worth the time of day'. . . . She says nothing."

"Go into her mind," I instructed. "contact her thoughts."

"She's shrinking into a puddle on the floor, with pleading eyes. I've destroyed her. Nothing there but black oil with eyes on top." (Tears came; Cleo said they were his wife's tears.) "Talk to her," I suggested.

"That was the only language I knew. I learned it from my *mother*—my mother talking to my sister. . . . No, she didn't talk to *me* that way. I'm her favorite, yep."

"So you grew up and talked like that to your wife, a female? Talk to the puddle on the floor as your mother used to talk to you."

"'You're my favorite'. . . . But I don't mean that. She's not good enough; she deserves it (the things I tell her)."

Firmly I stated, "Now I am canceling out those bitter things that you said to her, and the things your mother said to your sister."

"But if I'm wrong, I won't be her favorite! I *can't* tell the truth, she won't love me any more!" he wept. "I'm a bully; I pick on everyone. I haven't told her."

"You are a bully to your wife now, as your mother was a bully to your sister."

"She drove my sister crazy, drove her into a mental institution and she died."

"And you drove your wife crazy; you drove her into a black puddle and she died. It's time to get rid of that attitude!" (Cleo nodded.) "Cleo, you do have honesty to look at yourself closely. Take that lump out of your chest, throw it on the ground, give it a push with your foot. You don't want to keep it. You say it aches? It is melting away now into clear, pure water, flowing over the black puddle, calming and soothing and comforting. The eyes are closing in restfulness. When they open, there is hope in them. The eyes are looking at you, hoping. What do you say to the eyes?"

Cleo's answer was a whisper, "I'm sorry . . . I'm sorry." Then in sudden astonishment, "A whole body has formed up! I wish I hadn't . . . Look at her! I never noticed before. She's gorgeous!"

"What do you want to say to her now?"

"'Well, you are *some dame!*'" He said that she felt vindicated now, and he felt relieved. He saw the light above him now as "a big manhole. I've been in the black slime of a sewer. I'm looking up (through the manhole) at blue sky."

The rest was simple and easy from here on. Cleo saw a cherub coming "just to take you to heaven," but said his wife would have to wait. "It's not her time yet; she has to regain her joy."

We were told that we could not help her further today, so I bade Cleo good-bye and thanked the cherub for coming.

Then I called the next strongest entity in Annie. This was a seventeen-year-old girl, Gladys, who had entered Annie when Annie, too, was that age.

"She was pregnant; so was I. That's why I chose her. I was not married. The baby's father was the blacksmith—he raped me—a big, fat, gross, oily! . . . Nobody knew. My family didn't notice the pregnancy. I wore a big apron. I hadn't told yet. I was thinking about it when I was out picking asparagus. It was in the plains of America. The tip of my prairie boot got stuck under a tie of the railroad. I see my bonnet, basket, petticoat . . . I didn't notice the train coming. My foot was stuck. The train ran over me.

"My last thoughts were: 'I can't get out of this! Maybe it's better—nobody will ever have to know.' I had a feeling of peace. . . . But when my soul left my body I thought, 'I'm not done yet. I need to finish this. Can't do it here—must find somewhere else to go.'" That was when she sought and found Annie and moved in.

Gladys also took into Annie her sadness, helplessness, fear, and feeling of incompleteness. I explained this to Gladys.

"Nobody ever told me," she said. She willingly began to clean up her feelings, but she rejected the visualized whisk broom that I offered her. "I'm using a sponge. The broom was too stiff. Part of the stuff is wet. I really need a hose."

So I agreed. "Here is a hose flowing with healing water. As you wash clean, the bad things are carried away."

She sighed, "Yes, it's better."

At first she could not see any light. She said a "doughboy" was in the way. I asked the doughboy to stand aside.

Gladys, having cleaned herself up, was ready to go. "I guess I have to go out the other way, through the foot." She said she had entered "vaginally somehow. I might have tipped things (in the pelvic region). Everything needs to go back to its right place. I sort of knocked over the furniture. I'll wash down the walls: there's stuff hanging down. I'll loosen up that old groin . . . huh, huh, it's pretty tight."

When she was through I reminded her, "As you go through the foot, fix up her knee."

"Good idea," she said. I commented that her own knee was all right now, too.

"Yeah. Yeah, I'm kinda washing the muscles and tendons and all. I'll flatten the arch a little . . . needed some rehab here," she chortled. "Yep, have to work now 'cause I didn't get to finish the other work."

She "went the other way" to get out of Annie. "I didn't know there was another exit. Hee-hee, the end of the tunnel, and no train coming!" She laughed. Then when I asked if she saw someone coming to meet her, she suddenly began to weep.

"It's the *conductor*! He is *so sorry* !" The tears belonged to the conductor, she said. "He stopped too late." (She may have meant the engineer. People used to confuse the two.)

"See, someone did care about you. He came. Now are you ready to go, Gladys? You'll have a fresh start. Good-bye. "

Then I returned to the doughboy. He talked freely, saying that his name was Peter, that he was Scottish, laughing when I asked which army he had been in (soldiers were called "doughboys" in WWI ), informing me that he was seven years old and "not that kind of a doughboy - I'm a lard bucket."

Proudly he admitted having a keen sense of humor. He said that he found Annie when she was digging snow tunnels and making a big snow bear. Like him, she was seven years old.

"I tunneled in, in the snowstorm and got in her butt, 'cause her dad made such fun of her. He said, 'Do you have a license for that *trailer?*' She felt awful and confused and betrayed. She was the only one nice to her dad, and he made fun of her. I got in her fanny and made it feel really *cold* in there, so it matched the cold words and felt the same inside as outside and was not so confusing any more. Then she did have a trailer—it was *me!*"

He paused and began to chant, "Peter, Peter, pumpkin-eater," and then suddenly began to cry.

"I'm so skinny! I didn't have any food. I'm hungry. It was in an orphanage . . . in England . . .1920 . . . I'm Scottish, I had a plaid scarf. I starved to death . . . just a pile of bones."

"What were your last thoughts, Peter, as you left your body?"

" 'It's not fair. I deserve more.' "

"When your soul had left your body, what did you do or seek?"

"A safe place, a big cushion to snuggle up in. I just wanted to be at peace and sleep. I wanted to be full, fat, *succulent!*"

"How did you make yourself so?"

"I *ate* all the awful things Annie's dad said to her." (tears) "He was so *big*! I protected her. I thought she could 'stuff' it all in there. . . . It made her walk funny, like a pregnant elephant."

"Peter, thoughts are very strong where you are. Just think yourself healthy and clean and look for the Light."

"I can't go. I'm too mad at her dad. He thought it was okay to use words instead of fists. He thought it was terrible if men *beat* their wives."

"Were you with him or with Annie in a past life, Peter?"

"No."

"But if you don't get rid of the anger you may have to be with him in a future time."

"Good! I could teach him a thing or two."

"It wouldn't be a good relationship, if he were to be your father, for instance. Let the anger go, so you won't have to be with him in a future life. . . . Use the water in the hose, Peter, wash it over yourself. It is healing water."

"I smell better. I don't smell like lard now."

"Wash away the starving, the loneliness, the 'It's not fair.' Those things are canceled out of you now, too, Peter. We won't try to get them out of her dad today. Use the hose with the healing water at the 'mad,' too."

"Will Annie be all right if I go? Will she be protected?"

"Oh yes. Now I invite someone who cares about Peter to come. . . ."

"It's Fibber McGee, the dog!"

"Grab the fur on his neck and hold on tight. Fibber will take you to your home. Thank you for coming, Fibber."

(Fibber's thought): "You're welcome."

This was one of the several instances in which a loved animal came when I asked for "someone who cares about this soul to please come." One time it was a horse, the only friend that the man had during the years before his death.

It is to be noted in the case history of Annie's releasement that old arthritic Cleo claimed responsibility for making her hip stiff with "ideopathic sinovitis"; that Gladys with her knee mangled by the train was responsible for Annie's knee problem and for making her right leg "feel like a club"; and that Peter, "eating all the awful things Annie's dad said to her" and making himself a "lard bucket" in her "fanny so that she walked funny, like a pregnant elephant," was responsible for the odd gait that her friends had mentioned. Annie herself is not overweight; she is tall and well-built and keeps herself in good condition; but Peter was very earnest about trying to protect her from her father's verbal abuse while feeling safe and "succulent" himself in her body.

Annie did not have a second session. She felt that would not be needed. Recently she told me, "My shoulder and hip are both okay now since Cleo is gone, and I have more fluidity in my movements. I do yoga consistently. My knee is fine, now that Gladys is gone. And my body shape has changed—I have no 'rear end' since Peter is gone. Gladys said she sort of 'washed things in the pelvis,' too—and she gave me the courage to make the decision to search for the child I gave up for adoption when I was seventeen, twenty-eight years ago." She was laughing softly as she told me over the phone, "He is six feet tall, an engineer—and he wants to visit us! He only has to wait for some of the paperwork to be finished up. . . ."

The session with Annie had been therapy first for the entities trapped within her, as is usual in Releasement work. Only after the obsessing souls have been helped to become free and to go into the Light is the client the recipient of therapy, and by this time may not even need any more.

## Jim

This case, like the preceding one, shows clearly how releasement therapy is first of all for the obsessing entities in the client.

Jim, a respected lawyer in his fifties, had complaints of insomnia, lack of energy, and stress. Standard medical treatments had not helped much and now he was starting herbal therapy and was also referred to me for hypnotherapy. His sleep pattern was to fall asleep normally but awaken at 3:36 a.m. and be unable to return to sleep for an hour or two; then to sleep late in the morning, and to struggle against sleep in mid-afternoon when he still needed to be alert in his occupation.

In hypnosis he went back first to a childhood experience in school that made him feel unfairly treated. When I asked his mind to search for any other cause of his problems, he found that drinking more than two beers would cause insomnia: "I'm allergic to alcohol"; and that his job and its stress also contributed to sleeplessness.

Checked for "any soul or entity in Jim who is not Jim himself," Jim's "yes" finger rose at once. When it also said that there were two or more such entities in him, Jim laughed. He was in hypnosis and had been only half believing in all this far-out business but had been willing to go along.

I asked the first entity to tell me its name. Jim said that the name "Harry" came first, but almost at the same time came the name "Robert." I explained that the subconscious mind usually speaks first, without thought; so I spoke to "Harry," asking how old he was.

Jim said, "Well, I got forty-three and then twenty-six. But *he's* not going to tell the truth."

Suspecting that two entities were trying to speak at the same time, I learned, through questions, that Harry was forty-three and Robert was twenty-six, and that there were still other entities in Jim besides these two.

Harry's story was first: "I'm red-headed, no part in my hair; I'm rugged, somewhat overweight . . . I'm *engaging*—I like to jest and laugh—*heartily*! And I like whiskey! I appreciate Irish bars."

Asked to see, without pain or emotion, what happened the last time he was in his own body, he hesitated, "The last . . . is being . . . in an auto accident. I was coming around a corner, walking. It was a 1919 Studebaker that got me in the leg."

Jim interrupted the narrative here: "I don't know if I'm making this up or not."

"You're doing fine," I assured him. "Just keep going. Harry, what year was it when you had the accident?"

"Nineteen twenty-seven—in Ireland." He said his last thought was, "Oh! Well, that bumper got me in the left leg!"

He said, "It was above the knee. I don't remember dying. . . . Whoo! I was making a right turn around the corner and the car came along and the bumper hit me. 'Goddam, I got in an accident, didn't I!' I died right there in the street, on the cobblestones. That bumper *flattened* me to the ground. I hit the right side of my head. I got knocked down in the brain—and I come up and I can see me lyin' there, and my left leg is killin' me—and I'm out of my body . . . and I'm flyin' . . . I'm flyin . . . woo-oo, what a ride! Rock n' roll!"

Jim spoke again as himself (though still in hypnosis): "But people don't know about rock and roll yet!"

I explained, "Harry, in the state you are in, past and future and present don't make much difference. Now I need to explain some things to you: Jim has a right to his own body without anyone else being in it. You have been using his energy and he feels tired without knowing why. And you have been trapped inside of him and haven't been progressing on your own spiritual path. You have had fun with him and have enjoyed the sense of humor together. . . ."

"We been buddies for years. We've had a good time."

"Yes, and that has been good for you both. But it is time for you to leave and when you go you can leave him some of your good humor." I suggested that he brush out of himself sadness, sorrow, alcoholism, and so on. He interrupted me:

"Well, I tell you what. I'm not too proud of my life. I drank a hell of a lot of whiskey. I didn't apply myself to anything. But I'm not a bad guy. Old Jimmy here, he's a go-getter." Then with sudden insight he exclaimed, "*That's why I got into him*! He'd do okay on the work and I could just ride along! . . . I'm tired," he finished.

"Harry, finish brushing out the things you don't want to keep, like the alcohol addiction. You'll be given a chance to do better. Now look for a light. . . ."

"That car knocked the lights outa me! Oh, yeah—let me

tell you how it is: When ya come out of your body, they *raise* ya, and ya see your body—and then . . . have you ever—? No, I don't suppose you have—ya kinda *hover* like a . . . like a spaceship over your body—and it *lifts* ya, and you can *fly* and *soar*! . . . And the Light ye're talkin' about is the Truth . . . and you can *fly* to the Truth. But flyin' may get boring after awhile."

"Oh, you won't fly forever! Someone is coming to escort you to your own right place, much better than this down here on the earth-plane. And you'll keep the friendship with Jim. Leave him some of your jesting, too. He needs a little bit."

He asked, "Where did *you* get 'wiz'?"

"I've been learning lots in these past years. Do you know, Harry, that this is the year 1990 now? And you have been stuck down here since 1927!"

"I won't argue with you. You want me to go so you can help Jim. You're helping *him.*"

"And helping you, too, just as much as Jim. It will be much better for *you,* too. See or feel someone coming for you."

"Well, but you see, the thing is—" He broke off suddenly. "It's my mother, I think! She has that blue dress on again. . . . And she has her hair all fixed up! . . . I kinda took care of her. I oughta go with her now." He said he preferred not to call any of his old buddies to go with him. "Oh, no, oh, no, they drank too much. Just good old boys. Just because they drank, they weren't bad. But I'll go just with my mother now."

"Thank you for coming for Harry, Mother," I said.

"She wants to thank *you,* Ma'am, for finding me." He and his mother left, and Jim no longer saw them.

Then it was Robert's turn, but I glanced at my watch and saw that time was passing fast. When I mentioned Robert, Jim (still in hypnosis) laughed, "Ha, you're going to *love* him! I see a ship, a fourmaster. Robert sails. He is in seventeenth century clothes, twenty-six, a real handsome fellow: ruddy-white skin, black hair pulled back in a bun, sharp features, bold. He's the captain. English . . . he's English, all right—a damn pirate!"

I spoke to him. "Robert, it is time for us to stop now, so I ask you to remain quiet in Jim until I can talk to you next time he comes. Just round up your personality into a comfortable little ball and stay quiet within him. . . ."

"Oh, Madam, you ask a difficult task! When a ship is sighted I might go off on my own. You wait until my heist is *over*. There's no time *then*; we're too busy! . . . We'll go now." He did promise me that during this interval he would not kill nor injure anyone, and that when I called next time he would come to us. It sounded as if he felt free to leave Jim and return to him.

Robert was ready and waiting when Jim went into hypnosis at the next session. It was Jim's own rational mind that did not believe he was present: "I cannot see or hear him. There is a handicap." The handicap was only in Jim's own conscious mind, not in his subconscious awareness, for the conversation with Robert continued easily, through Jim's voice.

Robert said that he had been in his ship—one that he had simply boarded in full daylight in Plymouth Harbor in 1614 and used as his private vessel. When I asked him gently if he was "what people call a pirate" he paused quite a moment before answering "yes." But Jim was aware of Robert's feelings that he was no ordinary "pirate," for he felt that he was superior to the others, had a sense of discrimination—never attacking "just any ship" but selecting only those with treasure, and that he had "a sense of honor."

It was in 1617, he said, that southwest of the British Isles the ship was struck by a storm astern: "Water came in through the back . . . the water caught me . . . forced . . . forced—the *force* of the water was like it just *burst* me out of my heart, out of the ocean—and down, sucking my body down. It caught me in the right side and forced me up to a corner of the ceiling of the galley, and *pushed* me through my body, through my heart . . . I was free of the ship . . . I rose out of the water and up. . . . It was dark. . . ." He shuddered.

"Was it cold, Robert?"

"Not so much cold as dark."

"How old was Jim when you found him?"

"Seven. He needed . . . he needed a father." He suddenly sobbed.

"And you felt you could be a father to him?"

"No—just a . . . a friend." (I did not ask whether the sobs belonged to the seven-year-old child or to Robert.)

I told Robert that he could "just pretend that all the dark, heavy things like anger, hate, jealousy, regrets, selfishness, greed, egotism—that all of those are like a filthy old overcoat, and just shed it from you and throw it away! You keep the wisdom you have learned but get rid of that heavy dark overcoat." He indicated that he was doing so. "And remember, Robert, that gentleness and humility can be strengths. Look inside yourself now and see the bright things there: courage, independence, and wisdom. . . . And now think: Did someone ever love you? A parent, a dog, a woman?"

"Yes—a woman—Rachel."

Remembering her, he could see the Light, "like light from the sun in the clouds . . . when the sun is setting . . . I'm going off the ship . . . to starboard . . . into the Light! Yes . . . and Anna, my little daughter, is coming. She looks at me, and takes my left hand."

He went with little Anna into the Light, "and blue takes its place," added Jim, when the light had withdrawn. He did not explain the color, and I did not inquire.

Then I asked about the next entity in Jim. The fingers said there was none. There was a little uncertainty from the fingers, "yes" and "no"—that one entity wanted to come out but another wanted to remain hidden. After awhile I asked if one or more of them were ready to go into the Light.

"Yes."

"Are *all* of you willing to go?"

"Yes."

Jim spoke, "I see a woman—in a carriage. She's in a black dress. Dark circles around her eyes . . . angelic look. She's looking out. . . ."

I spoke to her. "Lady, Jim sees you. Why don't you change the color of your dress to a beautiful light blue? And make your eyes bright and clear, and smile? Look for the Light, Lady. That's the right direction."

"She's changing—her eyes are bright. . . . The horse and carriage are moving into the clouds, silvery-lined, beautiful clouds. The horse's color has changed from gray to dappled white. She goes with *majesty*."

I did not ask more about the lady's story, for time was now short, but we felt that she was safely on her way into the Light. Questioning Jim's fingers told us that he was now free of all invading entities and that this work was enough for today. The superconscious mind, answering through Jim's fingers, also said that there was no other important reason for Jim's insomnia.

On returning to full awareness, Jim apologized, "I don't know whether my thoughts of being conscious were a handicap. I tried to go deep for you." I laughed, because he had been so deep in hypnosis that at times his voice was barely audible.

And then a remarkable sequel occurred. Jim, the down-to-earth, left-brain type who had no previous experience of this sort, sat up on the cot and, gazing across the room, began to describe in detail how Robert had obtained his ship. He described the town of Plymouth, "up here, above the harbor," and told where the owner of the ship was—"in a house right *here*. He's middle-aged, has white knee-high stockings and knee-length pants, and he's rounded [gesturing to show a round belly] and he's really upset about something. Something about the barrels isn't right. They contain white powder—sugar? No, I don't know what it is. . . . Robert knows where the crew is and where the owner is. He and his crew just board the ship in midafternoon. Only two men are on board as guards. One just shrugs and thinks, 'Why should I fight and die for what little pay I get?' He tells the other guard, 'Come on, let's go,' and they just leave. Robert and the crew have to get the ship out of harbor while the wind is right. They just sail off, tacking back and forth."

When I expressed amazement that Jim was now "reading the Akashic Records," no longer expressing Robert's individual words and thoughts, he explained to me, "I just tell what I see." To him it was as simple as that, and he seemed amused at my interest in his sudden exhibition of psychic sensitivity.

Jim felt that his early-morning wakefulness was probably from Robert's influence. As captain, Robert was a light sleeper and may have had a habit of waking to check the ship mentally during the night. Jim had been specific that the time of his own waking was 3:36 a.m. Undoubtedly there was a reason for such pinpoint accuracy but I had not remembered to ask the questions that would have explained it. If a question is not asked, the client seldom offers information voluntarily because of the slight drowsiness of the altered state. After returning to full awareness, however, the client may fill in many details which were not verbalized during the hypnotic state. In Jim's case the surprise was that he relapsed spontaneously back into an altered state and was "reading" what he saw, world memories (Akashic Records, the Memory of Nature).

A month later I phoned Jim's home to check on one or two points in my written account. His wife answered and reported that although both of them still had restless periods in the early morning (as also do a good many other people these days) and still had "strange dreams—not nightmares," Jim now slept "definitely better than before, is a *lot* more restful than before, and he feels such a relief—has no anxieties anymore; the pressure is off." Laughing, she added, "He is easier to live with now, and it was a joy to live with him before. I don't know how much more of this I can stand!"

(Dr. Winafred Lucas included Jim's story in her two-volume work, *Regression Therapy: a Handbook for Professionals* [1993]). I want to express my appreciation to her for allowing me to use it here. Jim himself gave me full permission to use his real name, though I have chosen to use only his first name here.)

*chapter 4*

# RELEASEMENT IN ABSENTIA, I.E., REMOTE RELEASEMENT

Gradually more and more psychotherapists are finding the concept of Spirit Releasement extremely useful as a therapeutic approach and are becoming open to new and nontraditional ways to use it. One of these I have already mentioned: that of performing releasements without the presence of the victim/client. Drs. Edith Fiore and William Baldwin seem to be the first of the modern therapists to use and teach Remote Releasement.

Necessity has been the chief factor in my own use of remote techniques for releasing entrapped entities. When the person I suspected of being obsessed was a child or was someone living at a distance, it simply seemed sensible for me to ask a coworker or a relative of the supposed victim to be a channel for any invading entities. As hypnotists know, time and space in the altered state of consciousness are far more malleable and far less important than time and space "as we know them" in ordinary waking consciousness. And so I began what is now called Remote Releasement in those cases that needed intervention without the physical presence of the client.

But what of obtaining the permission of the absent client? For babies and children, I felt that the permission of a parent was sufficient. For older persons, permission by telephone or letter was enough. But in cases when the person suspected of being obsessed was not aware of my suspicion, what should I do, especially if he or she might be amazed (or worse) at the idea of this work?

As several other therapists have also decided, I felt that in cases that seemed clearly to need such intervention, I could ask my coworker in hypnosis to contact the Higher Mind of the absent one and ask the Higher Mind if we had permission to release any parasitic entities. If the answer was no, we would abide by that, at least for the present session. At a future one I might repeat the question, possibly rephrasing it. If a second no was given, I might ask the reason; but in any case we would do no work along that line for that person.

Very seldom was the answer no, for the Higher Self of every person is wise, compassionate, perceptive, and always desirous of whatever is *spiritually* best for the lower self. When the client's Higher Self said it was all right for us to do a releasement, even in an unknowing person, we went ahead confidently.

In one case when the answer was a no, we were told firmly that the person was not yet ready to deal with so great a change as a releasement would cause in the person's internal psyche; it would only confuse and start questionings. In a different situation concerning a man, when I received a no, I objected, "But he is a friend of mine. If I am a true friend, won't I want to prevent him from making a serious spiritual mistake, either by telling him of the danger or else doing work for him in his absence?"

The answer was an emphatic, "No! It is not your responsibility. He has free will. If he leaves the 'Right-hand Path' [makes a spiritually unwise decision] eventually he will return."

Sadly I felt that perhaps the "eventual return" might be in a future lifetime. I accepted the channeled decree, however, for it came from a high source, Nan Taylor's master. (I had not yet learned at that time that I could have called the man's Higher Mind.)

As mentioned earlier, Eugene Maurey performs all his "exorcisms" remotely, using a pendulum over a chart to decipher the characteristics and needs of a person whose name has been sent to him and the characteristics and strength of the entities in that person. Then he follows a verbal formula, asking Higher Beings to extract the parasitic entities. His book, *Exorcism* (1988), gives his technique in detail.

Dr. Irene Hickman uses by choice the remote method of releasement for the cases she describes in her book, *Remote Depossession* (1994), although she has also performed re leasements directly. Dr. Hickman's reason for choosing the remote method is to keep the personality factors of the host-person from possibly influencing the results, her goal being to provide reliable material for research projects, noting the condition and complaints of the subjects (clients) both before and after the remote releasement.

As Baldwin points out, when we do a releasement directly, the client herself is the "channel," for the entity is already there; whereas with a Remote Releasement a third person is the channel, receptive in hypnosis, and the entity in the absent client is called to come and speak through the channel.

In my own practice I have found so little difference either in technique or in results that I do not think of one case as "direct" and another as "remote." It is only because some people reading these chapters may still wonder about the feasibility of Remote Releasements that I make a separate chapter for some of my own cases.

# "Half-Remote Releasement" by Telephone (Geographically Remote)

A sort of "half-remote" releasement technique was also the result of necessity. As mentioned earlier, with each new client I routinely ask permission and "cue" her to enter the hypnotic state thereafter at the sound of my voice as I speak two or three certain words (such as "Rest now") and have also programmed her to respond from the subconscious level through an ideomotor finger answer, one finger having been programmed to be the "yes" finger, another the "no" finger. Then sometimes sessions need not even require an intermediate channel, courtesy of the telephone system.

## Elsie

One of the first such cases that I attempted in this manner was that of a first-grade teacher, "Elsie." She telephoned me from several hundred miles away, telling me of irrational fears, inability to think clearly, and feelings of desperation because her schedule for the children had fallen far behind in some subjects. These symptoms were of fairly recent onset.

Since she had previously been cued to go into hypnosis at my voice, I suggested that she make herself comfortable with the phone receiver propped to her ear and the mouthpiece near her lips; I spoke the cue-words; she went into the altered state; and we went right into a suspected releasement.

Her "yes" finger moved, she told me, at my question, "Is there any mind or consciousness in Elsie that does not belong to her?"

I thanked the entity for letting me know of its presence, and asked it to put the thought of its name into Elsie's mind; and she said the name "Ephraim" came. After this, however, there were very few verbalized answers to my questions; almost all were finger-answers which she reported to me. It became a game of "Twenty Questions" several times over!

In this way, however, we learned that the entity, Ephraim, was a forty-year-old mentally retarded man full of terrible fear. There was something about a wolf—no, maybe not a wolf but a big dog. It was coming, it was threatening and growling, it was leaping. Ephraim tried to protect his head with his arm, and the dog's teeth sank into the arm. Eventually the dog managed to reach Ephraim's throat, and in a panic of pain and suffocation Ephraim died. He continued to experience the fear and the mental dullness of his earth-life and brought them into Elsie when he found and entered her. Undoubtedly he sought someone like her because he felt he would be safe in a gentle person who cared for children—feeling, as he did, like a hurt, frightened child himself.

I followed the usual formula over the telephone, and Ephraim finally saw some light; he even saw someone coming toward him—a kind-looking man; but the man's face began to change and become blank and then even rather unfriendly.

With my limited knowledge at that time I did not know how to ascertain for sure whether this was another lost soul looking for help or actually a guide for Ephraim. Therefore at a later session with a friend as channel I checked up on poor Ephraim and learned that he had gone Home safely. Elsie and I decided that he had so often seen friendly faces change into cold faces on sensing his mental limitations that he seemed to see this change in the face of his guide even after his death.

I did try to get Ephraim to think of himself as safe and clear-minded, but perhaps I might have offered more help toward self-confidence, and so on. It seemed that the session was getting long over the telephone, I suppose, though the greatest hindrances were in Ephraim himself, so close to the earth-scene that his mind was still dim.

A letter from Elsie a few weeks later reported that her mind was clear again, that she had lost the fears, and that her schedule for the children was coming along much better.

## Different Channels, Similar Reception

Some readers might wonder if the personality of a channel could be influencing the received information noticeably and distorting it. Of course that is always a possibility. My own conclusion is that *almost anyone in hypnosis can channel, if willing to do so and willing to let the received thoughts come into the conscious mind and then right out through the mouth, without internal censorship.*

This last point is important because at times the thoughts that well up or pop into the channel's conscious mind are not the sort of thoughts she would care to express in her normal personality! When curses and insults come into her conscious mind or sneering putdowns of the therapist, the channel feels hesitation and sometimes even revulsion, for she is aware of her own self (except when she "lets herself go away").

Even the reverse can be true. One of my most advanced young channels became miffed by a certain entity who came, unasked, and almost ordered me to get to work and put forth the valuable things I could offer the public. Some of the things said were overwhelmingly complimentary but given in a manner that made "Lili" say afterward, "I don't like Randolph. He is *rude*. I don't like it when he talks to you that way. I don't want him to use my body to talk to you like that." She snorted disdainfully, then added, "And you were laughing!"

Yes, I had been inwardly laughing, trying hard to stifle my mirth and not let my voice give any telltale quaver; but in hypnosis, as sensitive as she is, she perceived my giggles. Undoubtedly Randolph, the would-be advisor, perceived them, too. I am sure he meant well, but his attitude was that of a Prussian commander; and I could not help laughing and wanting to remind him that "honey catches more flies than vinegar."

So that you may, if you wish, compare the material received through several different channels, I present a number of cases and identify the channel. The three whose work is given below are all my students, ladies in their thirties to sixties.


### Wayne

The subject, "Wayne," was a young man who had been having mood swings and feeling frustrated in several aspects of his life. When I had mentioned our Releasement work he was willing to have us see what we could do remotely to help him. He was living near Denver; we were over the mountains, some three hundred miles away. Lili, the channel, was about the same age as Wayne and had known him a few years earlier.

After the usual induction and a brief deepening of the hypnotic state I said, "I am calling any entities attached to Wayne Durham. Let the strongest one speak first, please."

In a high-pitched childish stammer the words came from Lili's lips, "Doc-Doc-Doc-Doctor Frey, I-I-I-I'm not the strongest but can I come? I-I-I-need to—"

"I want the strongest one first, honey. I'll talk to you afterward. What's your name?"

"Casey."

"How old are you, Casey?" I sensed that this was a little girl.

"I'm-I'm-I'm four."

"I'll talk with you after a while, Casey."

"But-but-but you won't be sorry. I-I-I-I need to tell you 'bout Wayne. W-W-W-Wayne's so soft and so nice. He's really special, and protects people and is so nice—but he has funny things that I want to help him with. He has stars in his mind; they won't go away; they scare him."

I decided to let Casey talk. She seemed to know something important. "What makes the stars?"

"I don't know; I've never seen 'em; but it's scary."

"Are they because of some drugs he has taken?"

"What's drugs?"

"They are something like medicine, pills and things, like maybe LSD."

"He's been sick. He takes medicine. . . . I've been sick, I had stuff in the back of my throat. I was hot, hot, HOT! And they gave me medicine. It was right *here*" (Lili put her hands to her throat ), "right *here*."

"Is that what made you die?" I asked.

"Did I die?"

Instantly I realized I had made a mistake. "I think your *body* died, Casey."

"Oh-h-h-h . . ." She seemed thoughtful, not alarmed. "It was right *here* and the medicine made those kind of stars."

I realized by now that Casey needed to come first, even if she wasn't the "strongest" entity.

"Casey, think back to that day and tell me about it, without any pain or sadness."

"I'd been sick for a little while. They locked the door and wouldn't let anybody come in. Mom stayed. They passed things in the door to her, food and things. My body was so hot, *hot*! They wouldn't let me have my kitty-cat. The medicine tasted terrible. It seemed somebody said—I can't remember—somebody came to the window, somebody different that I didn't know—and told my mother that there was somebody who could poke something in my throat and pull out that flim—plim—flim?—growing in my throat. Doctor, can they *do* that?"

"Yes, honey, sometimes they can—the phlegm, or the flim. Was it diphtheria?"

"Dip-theria! Yes! That's what they said. . . . Wayne is so nice. How can I help him? I was in a room where he was. He was so sad. I just wanted him to be happy. I stayed there too long; I outstayed my welcome." (Apparently she was quoting someone she had heard.)

"Was this in a hospital where you met him?"

"Was a hospital." (Or perhaps, "What's a hospital?")

"Was Wayne a big boy?"

"Oh, a BIG boy! He wasn't a daddy, but he was *big* enough to be a daddy."

"Well, Casey, now you can be free to go. Look for a light."

"Oh, it's light all around. . . . Before I go, can I tell you something? There's this funny lady and she wears a mask—like this, see? Are you looking? Like *this* [Lili put her hands across the lower part of her face from the eyes down], and when she talks, her words make stars in his mind, and I *want her to quit*! But she wants me to stop. She talks, and the words come out different from the holes in the mask. . . . Sometimes she talks, and Wayne's heart goes like *that* and drops on the floor. I pick it up for him and try to put it back. Can you help Wayne?" (She had held both hands together like a closed heart, then opened them like a heart split almost in two.)

"We are trying, honey. We are doing all we can to help him. And I think you can help him, too, even more after you go."

"Can I? How?"

"Well, did your mama ever talk to you about angels or about Jesus?"

"Yes, Jesus—and Santa Claus—and Easter Bunny."

"Well, it's Jesus we want this time. When you feel that Wayne needs more help, you can ask Jesus to help him. And you can always send Wayne thoughts of your love."

"Oh, goody! Wayne has a lawyer daddy and a lawyer mommy, two lawyers. And you are a doctor. I don't have a lawyer daddy or a lawyer mommy."

"Well, if you want me to, I'll be your doctor mommy."

"Will you? Oh, goody! I'll go now, Doctor Mommy. Bye!" And she sent a huge smack of a good-bye kiss in my direction. . . .

It is possible that Casey visited Wayne "in spirit," after she had already died; we could have found out more by questioning but did not take time at this session. It is possible that she was invisibly in a room where he was hospitalized or when he was visiting a friend who was a patient. Casey thought the year was in the late sixties. If any such questions seem important after a session like this, Casey could be asked to return and answer more specifically and from a more mature age level. But such contacts, I feel, should be made only with a worthwhile motive, not for mere curiosity. My present understanding is that usually they require extra energy from the entity called back. At the least, such an interruption is a distraction from the entity's astral-life activities.

After receiving Casey's big happy good-bye kiss tossed from Lili's lips and fingers, I proceeded to ask again for "the strongest entity" in Wayne. But it was Lili's own voice that spoke.

"Louise, Louise, there's a circle around Wayne and I can't get through it."

I asked for several of the "Bright Beings" to please come—Jesus, Buddha, my own Spiritual Advisor—and "if it is permissible to get through this circle, we ask your help in doing so."

Lili was shaking her head. "*He's* drawn a circle *around himself.* He's looking for protection; it's his own circle, filled with his *own symbols.* He's hiding, like a turtle. . . . I can't go any farther. It's to protect himself from *everything.* He retreats from pains. He's been given extreme talents but he is *choosing* not to use them, so they are fading. . . . His *coping skills* are dissipating, and the more he feels it, the more he retreats. He could build steps and climb over it. It's not a tall cylinder. There's a hole in the top. It's not material.

"Some entities are here," she continued, "but we can't go against the Laws, we must not *invade.* If he steps out [of the circle] you could program him for strength, willpower, courage: the basics in all four types, physical, emotional, mental, spiritual.

"He has recurrent shortages in the brain," she finished, "possibly from the former LSD, and feels he is losing control. His girlfriend plays on this." (Aha, the funny lady speaking through a mask!)

I had been listening and writing down what she was saying. Now I said, "Recently I learned about another type of entity, called Technicians, who can repair damaged brain tissue from alcoholism, etc. I'll ask permission from Wayne to ask a Technician's help, too. . . . Are the entities still here?"

"M'hm."

"I am speaking now to the entities who are in Wayne Durham: Please remain quiet until I can have a session with him and then I will ask you to come and talk with me. Meanwhile, gather your own personalities within yourselves and do not let any of your own traits influence his feelings or behavior. Do you understand me?"

"M'hm."

"Are you *willing* to do this?"

"M'hm." And with this we terminated the session, even though the only real accomplishment was helping little Casey. I sent Wayne a typed copy of all this so that he could study the received material with his conscious mind and make changes in that hindering over-protective "circle."

As time passed the relationship between the "funny lady" and Wayne fell apart. If she was in him, we were unable to reach her at this session. Perhaps Wayne's clearer understanding of her devious ways and words helped him to free himself from the stars and heartbreaks.

Lili has clear memory of the details of a session for a few days afterward but then the memory fades like a dream. Later she learned how to control her own awareness so that her consciousness could either remain in contact with the proceedings, as she did during the latter part of this session, or she could "go away" and let the other entity almost literally take over her body, as she did for little Casey.

## J.R.

Another case in which Lili was the channel involved an entity, J.R., whom I had contacted previously in another state in the young woman he was obsessing. A pirate, he had been firmly opposed to leaving her and was suspicious about going "into the Light." He had agreed to remain passive within "Sally" until I could talk to him again. Finally a few weeks later Lili and I got together for a session.

"Now, J.R., I am keeping my promise to you. When I

contacted you before, I didn't have time enough to let you decide about going to the Light. Now I ask you to come and tell me how you are doing these past weeks." There was no answer. "I am here to help you."

"I'm here. I went into a tunnel—not black, just gray. I didn't find a light."

"Did you look for one?"

"No."

I explained again about the changes at the death of the body—how the consciousness may leave and enter another living body, and how the relationship is not to the advantage of either. "And if there are dark things inside of you, sometimes you can't see the light till you get rid of them."

When he still didn't answer I went on: "J.R., there was another pirate who was lost like you, and he remembered that he had loved his little girl and didn't want her to know that her daddy was a pirate. Whom did *you* love most? A little child, or a woman? Or a dog?"

"Me mother . . . Ah, she was the best lady in the world! We lived in a port. Me father was a sailor. We lived there till she died. I was nine."

"Oh, you were still just a little kid?"

"A BIG kid! I ran away and hired on as a cabin boy. I never saw my dad again. Don't know what happened to him—'dragon o' the deep'. He sailed—never came back. A thousand things could'a happened."

"What of your family? Did you have brothers and sisters?"

"Ay. I don't know what happened to them. After me mother died I ran off. What was there to stay for?"

"You know she is waiting for you."

"Only if I be lookin'."

"Don't you want to?"

"Nah. I'd rather have adventure."

"You've had a long time for adventure. Your mother

would love to see you. . . . There are two things to look for, J.R.: first, look inside yourself and see any dark things that may be there, like anger or cruelty—lots of pirates are cruel, you know."

"Don't you be lumpin' me in with the rest o' the group!"

"No. But your feelings may be either from plain egotism and arrogance, or else from a sense of your own individuality, J.R.—and *that* is okay."

"I got nothin' else to say." (He scratched his head.)

"Everyone has some dark things," I went on. "Why don't you just push them out of you now. . . . I don't have to know what they are. Just shove them all out of you. Then look inside yourself and see the bright things! Love for your mom, and adventure—you can keep that. . . ." There was still no answer.

"And now look for the Light. Now the adventure really starts! J.R., I promised you that this time you could make a real decision. Sally and her friends and I all care about you, and now Lili does, too. We all hope that you will choose to go to the Light. The very hardest thing to give up is pride, isn't it? But think about your mother and about making *her* happy. . . . What year did she die?"

"It was 14-something—I don't remember. The queen was Elizabeth."

"Elizabeth I. Now the queen is Elizabeth II, J.R., and this year is 1985."

"Hm . . ."

"How did your body die, J.R.? Without pain or fear, tell me."

"I got the melting-flesh disease. Me nose fell off and me lips and fingers. . . . I stayed in me cabin. Even the cabin boy didn't want to come near me. I'll no be takin' that with me, will I?"

"No; not unless just enough for you to repay any karmic

debt that you owe, and the counselors will help you decide about that. Was your disease what we now call leprosy?"

"Ay."

"Now do you see the Light?"

"I be seein' 'um—but I can't go over."

"Why not?"

"You keep a-talkin'!"

I laughed. "Okay, J.R., you are free now and you can go to the Light. Run, if you want to. Do you see your mother coming?" I missed hearing the next few words but heard his last ones, "Be seein' you, lady."

When Lili came back to full consciousness she reported that she felt like scratching her head, face, and body, and was thinking, "Lice!" She also had the impression that the mother was unwell, burdened with many children, and was not able to give as much love as the children needed, and that the boy's love was that of a child and was forgotten in later years except as a warm memory seldom recalled.

Lili also said she saw J.R. *crawl* cautiously and suspiciously towards the Light to try to peer behind and see if there really *was* adventure waiting!

Sally, the young woman J.R. had obsessed, had felt reluctant to let him go, feeling that he was a familiar and rather friendly presence. I explained to her that she could still send him thoughts of happiness and friendliness, "but please do not call him back. . . . If you wish to look him up after you pass over, that will be up to laws like 'resonance' and 'polarity' to determine. But for now you can always send your affection and good thoughts to him and they will be received."

I have not heard from Sally since this remote releasement except through a third person—that Sally was feeling better but still had some problems. I wonder if she let J.R. return.

## Cheryl

When I was asked by a hypnotherapist friend in Santa Fe, New Mexico, if we could have a releasement session for a friend of hers, "Cheryl," I arranged with Charlene, a nurse and hypnotherapist herself, and we met for the remote releasement of Cheryl. Charlene's fingers said that three or more entities were in Cheryl, who had been having fears and mood swings, including sudden rages at times, unlike her normal personality.

The entity who came first said his name was Barney. He said his skin was dark brown; that he was a dock worker; and his boss "Captain John, as good as any—he was all right." Barney was nineteen. When we contacted him he said he was hiding, but the dogs found him. He had run away, a mob chasing him, accusing him of having killed a woman.

I asked him directly, "Had you?"

There was a long pause, then, ". . . Maybe. She wasn't dead when I left her."

"You left her when she was dying?"

Little by little the story emerged. The young woman and her father sometimes walked on the dock, and Barney thought "she made eyes at me." On this day she managed to make arrangements to meet him in the woods, where she talked with him, asking his help in getting away from her father on a boat. "We talked—and . . . I . . . just took her. She didn't object too much." He said that he knew about the baby she was going to have. (We did not ascertain whether the baby was the result of incestuous contact with the girl's father and she wanted to escape from him, or whether it was the result of a liaison with another man and she wished to escape her father's wrath when he discovered it.)

Barney admitted that the lady changed her mind and wanted him to leave her alone. But he kept on, and in the struggle she was injured; he became frightened and left her there. When she was found she accused him of raping her and of being the father of her child. Neighbors formed a mob to capture him. "I hate people. I hated the white woman for telling lies about me. I hated myself for what I had done. . . . The dogs chased me and found me. The people came and drug me back—tied me up—burned me—called me 'black son of a bitch' and 'nigger-nigger-nigger'."

After his death Barney wandered around a while, then found a woman into whom he entered, feeling safe there. Asked whether this was the woman he had raped, he was uncertain.

There was a long pause before he said, "Maybe . . . she doesn't . . . I don't know. . . ."

I pointed out that he was taking advantage of this woman, making her feel his anger, hate, and rage, and taking her energy. I asked him to come out of her. "Are you doing this?"

"Thinkin' about it. . . . Is she a *good* woman? Does she tell lies? If I leave, *she* would be better? Where would I go?"

I explained about the "better place" and asked Barney to recall someone he had loved and to look for the Light. Apparently he was a nonvisualizer.

"I don't see it but I feel something warm . . . No face there." I suggested that he hold out his hand to the warmth. "I don't think anybody will take it." But then he felt an arm around his shoulder—"my mother's! She says, 'Son, I've waited for you a long time.'"

I asked Barney what he would say to the lady he had raped.

"I'd tell her I'm sorry. I didn't mean to hurt her. I'd tell her to give up *her* hate, too."

I called the young woman (I felt that she must be wandering, earthbound) and reminded her that she and Barney had, in effect, killed each other.

"I'm sorry, too," she said. "There was a time we didn't hate each other—there was no reason we needed to hate."

But forgiveness was not quite complete, for she added, "Sometimes I still feel hate. . . ."

She seemed to wander off and no longer responded to my voice.

In Cheryl there was also little Petie, almost four, who had fallen over a log as he played with his dog and had drowned in a creek. When I asked for a guide his granddad came for him. Petie called his dog and could hear Bingo barking but could not see him. (Probably the dog was still in a living body but was aware of Petie's call.) Petie asked me to thank the nice lady who had given him the "warm quiet place" that he had found after seeing his body in the water.

A third entity in Cheryl was the soul of a fetus that had miscarried. It told us that spiritual counselors had insisted before its conception that it needed to come back to the earthplane for more experience and learning.

"I thought I wanted to be born—but I didn't, so I wanted to go back—but I didn't make it back (to the spiritual plane)."

"You mean that you felt your first decision was a mistake?"

"Yes, a mistake—my mistake and their mistake, too!" The infant soul said that no one killed its body, "I just wanted to go back." It was seven months along when the child's soul left it. "The baby's body died, and it was just a body. I left. . . . The lady died."

Charlene as channel, feeling the baby's feelings and knowing its thoughts, and I as facilitator, both had the distinct impression that this little soul did need more earth experience to tone down its flippant don't-care attitude and its casual way of making decisions that it shortly changed its mind about!

After typing out this session and sending it to my friend in Santa Fe, I received back some weeks later a note, "I've thought of you so often and all you did for us and my friend Cheryl. She's *much* improved and was grateful for your prayers and your friend's, too." The word "much" was underlined with a dark sweep!

## Jack

This session with Charlene was for a doctor friend of mine, "Jack," who had an alcohol problem along with a chronic depressive attitude toward nearly everything in his life. He had helped himself to a degree with self-hypnosis but could not overcome those two main problems. He willingly acquiesced when I asked him on the phone if he wanted us to see if a remote releasement would help. Several entities had already been released with Jack himself on the long-distance telephone.

Charlene placed herself in hypnosis, and I asked for the strongest entity in Jack to come and tell us his name.

"My . . . name . . . is . . . Fred," came the answer very deliberately.

He said he was "old"—aged forty-five but felt old both physically and emotionally. He had drunk alcohol since his teens. "Not especially unhappy" but "always felt sad." Thought that if he drank he would "have fun, a lot of fun, but I always felt sad . . . sometimes drank too much. People said, 'There's nothing more disgusting than a drunk that cries.'"

Asked if his parents had been happy together, he said they hadn't acted so. Asked if they loved him, he said, "I always wondered." He could recall no time his parents showed him affection since he was "little and cute. I'd sing. People thought I was cute."

On the last day of his life he "had about decided to do something about the drinking. I was pretty sober; had told a friend I'd go to an AA meeting with him. . . . It was really funny, really funny: I started walking out to meet my friend and saw a car coming—the light changed—I didn't stop—and the car hit me. You know what was so funny? The fellow driving the car was drunk! Sort of poetic justice . . . I never killed anybody but I never made anybody happy either. . . . Nobody ever made me happy, either."

Fred looked at his injured body. "It doesn't look like it could go to any meeting. The head is all squashed, the brain. It's had it." But he went in spirit to the meeting, was interested in some of the things said and asked questions, which were ignored. "Nobody listened. I thought that nobody cared about me."

I explained, "But they didn't know you were there. They did care about you. Find your friend. Contact his mind. What is he thinking about you?"

Fred grimaced and then relayed the thought, "'Well, we'll never know whether Fred would have made it or not. Maybe he wouldn't'. . . . I might have. . . . Nobody seemed to care. I needed a drink *bad*. I didn't understand why they didn't answer me."

Fred said that Jack was always open to invasion by souls like himself. "If people want to come he doesn't try to stop'em—just says, 'Come on!'" And even though Fred was tempted to return to a pleasant time in his childhood, a picnic with his mother, he vacillated: "I think—I think I need to stay here. Jack needs me. I help him. He's lonely, too."

"No," I assured him emphatically, "with your loneliness in him he is twice as lonely. And you are drinking through Jack's drinking! True? That is selfish of you. You are not helping him. Be brave! Go back to the time when you decided to change. That determination was good! Pretend that the alcohol addiction is a black chunk in your heart, and pull it right out, and the loneliness, too, and the feeling that nobody cares. You don't want 'em, do you?" He shook his head. "Your alcoholism made you and everyone miserable. Just chuck it out of you, and that low self-image and all the other things you want to get rid of. Clean yourself up."

After a long pause Fred began to smile. "Y'know what it looks like? When fog closes in on you, you feel awful. This is like a *nice* fog, not closing in, and you feel good, light. . . . It's not in a city any more, it's on a meadow—where my mother and I had the picnic. You know who I'd like to see, don't you? . . . I see someone . . . not my mother . . . I thought it was going to be my mother."

"I thought it might be, too; but this means she is still alive in her physical body. If you saw her she'd be 'dead,' like you. But you can visit her if you want to."

I asked for a guide who cared about Fred to please come and find his mother with him, and I asked the mother's Higher Mind to be receptive as her son came to visit her.

Fred's eyes filled with tears. "She's sleeping. . . . I think she knows I'm there."

I suggested that he put a dream of himself into her sleeping mind and assured him that he could send her his love any time. Then I committed him to the care of the guide and told him good-bye.

Charlene, the channel, said there was no other entity in Jack but only a potential space, an empty, lonesome feeling that needed filling, but not by searching *so hard* for happiness. "Perhaps the answer is to relax and accept, take the affection offered, not looking for ulterior motives. Be content with the love he does have, and fill the empty space with loving concern for others as well as for himself."

Jack is still alone but is no longer drinking. He seems to have stabilized himself, with the aid of a canine friend and treatment to detoxify and rehabilitate himself.

## "L"

Mary, the channel for this case, is an artist, talented also as a channel. One of our nurse friends asked us to do a remote releasement for one of her patients, "L," whom she suspected of harboring an entity.

After Mary had placed herself into hypnosis, I asked for protective light to surround us, invited our spiritual advisors (as I always do), and then asked that we be given an answer through Mary's fingers to the question, "Is it all right for us to do this work without the man's knowledge or consent?" "Yes," said Mary's finger, unequivocally.

Therefore I called the strongest entity in L and asked the name.

"Paul. I'm thirty-six years old. It is 1907. L was seventeen or eighteen when I entered him. He was in an accident and had a small concussion. It made him more open. I entered his mind. . . . I didn't influence him so much as just strengthen what he had. I wasn't ready to quit when my time came. I have good drive. L had a lot of drive and ambition. I wanted to accomplish my unfinished things through him. I needed to fill up something empty in me. . . . I needed to know I was a success. My small business wasn't enough for me. I had great plans. There was a big emptiness inside of me."

"You mentioned 'when my time came.' Was it really your time, or was it a true accident?"

"I chose it. I took my life. I was depressed . . . but it was a big mistake. . . . I was in my place of business. . . . Business had not been good. I couldn't take care of my wife Sally and my children as I wanted to—three children and another on the way. . . . I can't accept that I'm a failure." (Mary said afterward that she saw the wife when Paul was speaking: a haggard worn-looking woman, rather unkempt.)

"I'm sitting at my desk with my head in my hand—I reach into a drawer . . . pull out a gun . . . aim it between my eyes . . . pull the trigger. . . ."

"What was your last thought?"

"*Sadness.* I feel that this isn't the way—but I can't *live* with the failure. . . . I'm just hanging over the body, drifting, looking around. . . . I don't know what to do now. I feel an emptiness in me—a need to fill that great cavity in me. I make the decision that I must continue—to try to fill this need. I'm attracted to this one (L). His needs are the same as mine: a great driving ambition to be a success—to fill the need inside. So I merge with this one. It's interesting that I'm not really fond of this one."

"No, and now you find yourself trapped in him and stopped in your own spiritual evolution. You said this was in 1907, and today it is 1987—eighty years that you have been stagnant, Paul. Did you think of your family as you pulled the trigger?"

"Oh, yes, of course. I knew how they'd get along *with* me, and that was not good."

"So your act was not entirely selfish. But it was a mistake. So, Paul, push out of yourself that excessive ambition, that idea of earthly success. Had they made you become hard, self-centered? Driving? Maybe in these was the reason for that emptiness. Were you always trying to get '*my* will, *my* way'?"

"I was told that it was good."

"Put out your loneliness, the feeling of failure, the frustration, the hopelessness."

"I'm trying but they're not going. They're *useful.* . . . Who is God? I don't know God. I don't know if what you say is right."

"Ask the Bright Beings here. The Silver Rule is, 'Don't do to others what you don't want others to do to you.' And the Golden Rule is even more beautiful, 'Do to others what you would like them to do for you.' Do you understand? It brings you a different type of life. Just put out the anger, the envy, the jealousy. Ask the Bright Ones if all this is true."

There was a brief pause. "They just smile. . . . Yes . . . yes . . . *That's* why I didn't succeed!—I missed some happiness that was there for me. My sights were on the wrong goals."

He took a deep breath. "I feel there's something inside that's better, light as a feather . . . but . . ."

"Put out the emptiness, too," I reminded him, "and let light fill the place where it was. Now do you feel lighter?"

"M'hm."

"Paul, I'm so glad. You'll be leaving L. Are there any others in him?"

"Minor troublemakers that come and go. His own darker nature attracts them; he's vulnerable all the time. He could use some help."

"Should we do more for L, today?" (The fingers said no.)

"Then, Paul, hold out your hand. I think someone will be coming to meet you."

"Oh, yes, it's Sally! She's young again and fresh."

I said good-bye to Paul and his wife. Then I returned to L, asking if there were any more instructions concerning him. The channel answered, "Surround him with light. Golden light is best. Have all in the group send positive thoughts. That will bring results. He'll resist overt actions. Have the nurse record any changes; this will give all of you faith. You'll be amazed. There's no need for anyone to go through life negatively. It's always okay to send positive thoughts to others."

"Is it Mary's Higher Mind speaking?" I asked.

"It came from above," replied Mary.

So Paul with his suicidal despair was gone from L, but L still had his own darker traits to deal with. And our nurse friend has a clearer idea of how to deal with them.

## Tim

"Tim," a Vietnam veteran, was in another city when we did this work for him. He had given permission for a woman relative to go into hypnosis and channel for the entities that he felt were in him. At this session his grandmother was also present. Tim had many troubles with alcohol, drugs, rages, and totally irresponsible behavior.

Five entities were released from him in this session, with one or more still remaining at that date. Three of the five released were a trio of Puerto Rican youths who had died in a gang fight in New York. They were "mean ones," sullen and uncooperative. After much persuasion, explanation, and finally an ultimatum from us either to go on up to a higher state of learning or else each one would go alone to a visualized room described as being lined with mirrors where there would be no companions, they held a long confrontation among themselves, one or two choosing to go up, the leader stubbornly refusing to do so. Finally—almost to my astonishment—they all decided to go "up to a higher life." This is a very brief report of what was almost an hour-long argument among the four of us!

The fourth entity gave his name as John and said he had been killed at twenty-one in Vietnam by an explosion. He said he entered Tim because "he was just there." He kept sighing deeply because he was "just *sad*—at the *death everywhere,* the screaming, fire everywhere. . . . And I'm *angry!* At *everything!* . . . I felt pain . . . fear . . . disgust . . . *hatred!* . . . hatred toward the government!" He said he didn't hate the Vietnamese: "They are just people." He insisted that before the government sent him to Vietnam he had been a different sort of guy—"just . . . happy." He had friends.

I asked how he had changed. *"They* changed you!" he snapped harshly.

"Yes. Do you want to change back?"

That set him off. He began shouting, yelling, "I can't—I can't—not after all that! I *can't* change back! Don't you understand? *You weren't there. You don't understand . . . you can't . . . nobody can! Ever!"*

Through the channel's body he thrashed, screamed, and wept, pounding the cot.

I let him weep a while and then interrupted softly, "John, in World War II people were asked to give their dogs to the army to help out in the war effort. These pets and house dogs were trained by the army to be killers. After the war the dogs were given back to their owners—but they were still killers. There were many accidents, and some dogs had to be destroyed. The families protested so loudly that the army promised to 'rehabilitate' the dogs, to *untrain* them as killers and *retrain* them to be pets before sending them back. Then the dogs were *no longer killers.*

"What one elderly World War I veteran told me is what I have felt, myself, for many years: The service needs to be sure that its veterans are *untrained* from being the killers it *trained* them to be, before discharging them back into civilian life again. The Army, Navy, and Air Force need to see that *men* are rehabilitated as well as dogs. This old veteran said that his entire life had been affected by the military experiences. He still had nightmares of the war, even from 1918 when he was a teenager.

"Some of us civilians do understand more than you veterans may think, John. The relatives of men in the field suffer, wives and mothers and sweethearts suffer even if they are not 'there'. Civilian doctors know, too, John. We read the terrible accounts of war casualties in the medical journals, we see the photos. . . ."

John put his hand to his forehead. "My head hurts."

I placed my hand on his forehead and continued to talk softly, visualizing aloud that his pain, hate, rage, etc. "are coming into my hand, up my arm to my elbow, then into the air and out through the window, dissipating harmlessly in the outside air and not bothering any living thing." He became quieter. I asked that calmness, strength, and peacefulness come into him, "and become continually stronger as I remove my hand. I am drawing out all the rest of the negatives like helplessness, rage, hate, pain. . . ."

"Is there anything else you'd like to say, John?"

His lips moved. "War"—he murmured. "*It must never happen again.*"

"Son, I know. You want to stop war, and you can't I can't, either, John. We are not God. But you are *one,* and I am *one,* and there are hundreds of thousands of us working against war. We each do what we *can* and just have to leave the rest to the Higher Powers, praying that they may penetrate the self-centered minds of those who profit from and perpetuate war. Do you think you can do this, John, and go on now to the Place of Learning and become wiser and stronger so that you can do more when you come back in your next life? And live longer in your next life?"

"I'll try," he whispered. He was very quiet. Soon he saw his deceased grandmother coming toward him. "She's holding out her hands and smiling." He went toward her and took her hand. I bade him good-bye with my blessing and they went together into the Light.

After the lady channeling for Tim's entities returned to full consciousness she told me that "John" was the name of a fellow soldier Tim had mentioned as having had bitter rages in Vietnam. He had finally pulled the pin of a hand grenade and had blown up both his superior officer and himself. Evidently he had been driven into frank insanity before death.

Tim's living grandmother had sat in on this session and afterward said, "That was Timmy, pounding his hand like that! He used to say, '*He* made me do it!' That whole scene was just the way Timmy is!"

"No," I corrected, "I think Tim was right: it was *John in him* who made Tim do it."

As soon as John was safe I asked the fifth entity in Tim to come out. This was Andrew, whose name I had learned from a previous entity. Andrew did not want to talk. He closed his lips tightly, thrusting out his lower lip.

I chuckled. (It is often best to tease and jolly an entity out of its mood, if possible.) "I think you are going to be one of those stubborn ones, are you?" (No answer.) "Are you a little kid? How old are you?" (Still no answer.) "Come on, honey, tell me." (No answer.) "You're a little fellow, right?"

Sullenly Andrew said, "I'm eighteen." Then he refused to answer several more questions.

Needling him a little on purpose, I hinted, "Are you mentally a little bit retarded?"

"No! I'm not *retarded!* I'm *smart!*"

"What caused your death. Andrew? Tell me."

He said it was "drugs—heroin—anything I could get." It was "in the war—Vietnam." He had known both John and Tim, friends of his. He admitted that he still craved drugs and tried to make Tim get drugs so that he could feel their effects through Tim. Tim, however, was fighting against the drugs except for liquor.

"If Tim is your friend and you are trying to *force* him to get drugs, that's not very nice of you."

"I don't care!" He put his hand to his head.

"What's the matter, Andrew? Are you craving drugs right now, son?" I placed my hand on his forehead, as I had for John (a touch technique that I seldom used at that time) and kept on talking, using imageries as for John, that "all craving and addictions are coming out of your head, out of your mind, out of your brain cells, into my hand. . . . Let it all trickle out of you into my hand, all anger and craving and anything else you want to get rid of," and so on. "They will go out of my hand and vaporize outdoors as a harmless mist . . ." He became quieter, his breathing calmer.

In a little while he saw someone coming for him: "It looks like an angel." I wished him a happy journey into the Light and said good-bye.

Addictions of most kinds, whether emotional or physiological, are seldom controllable through conscious mind willpower and determination alone. It is true that a few people can succeed by these means. For most, however—even addicts of coffee, cigarettes, or sweets—the cooperation of the subconscious mind is required. For drug addicts in the agonies of craving, it seems that every cell in the body is screaming for the drug. It is a condition that needs understanding and help from those not addicted, not mere self-righteous admonitions. The Twelve-Step Programs have helped innumerable unhappy addicts. Releasing any obsessing entities who are drug-addicted helps, although Tim in this case probably needs more assistance. As mentioned, one or more entities still remain in him. He still has problems with alcoholism and irresponsibility—whether because of the entrapped entities or not, we do not yet know. My guess is that one of the entities remaining is alcoholic and one is a very young child.

### Erin

An excellent example of a false memory due to an attached entity is reported by Scott Herner of Scandia, Minnesota, in

Dr. Irene Hickman's book, *Remote Depossession,* pp. 81, 82. With her permission I quote it here:

The case is that of a little girl, Erin, who until the age of about five had been "very pleasant, bright, happy, always getting along well with her sisters. She had at about five begun to talk of having been abused but could recall no details of actual abuse. At age seven, Erin developed headaches located from the top of her head and down the left side.

"The changed pattern of behavior included vehement noncooperation, obnoxiousness, being annoying and mean to her younger sister—even to hitting her frequently."

Scott Herner, the therapist, with an associate as channel for the remote work, located three attached entities in Erin, one of them the cause of her headaches and left-side pain and her abhorrent behavior. It was this first entity who named the other two, the last being a small boy, Joe, who refused to go with the others to the Light.

"Joe petulantly stated that he 'wasn't going anywhere.' Further questioning brought the response that he had been very badly abused even while very young and had been beaten to death when he was four. He commented that he didn't think it was fair to die at such a young age. He had joined Erin when she was about five. Scott (the therapist) told Joe about the Light and that he could have his own body there. When the call was made for anyone in the Light to come for Joe, Grandma Annie came. Then Joe was willing to go.

"Erin's body was [then visualized] filled and surrounded with Light. The very next morning Erin was a changed child. She even told her mother that she felt different. She is much happier and quieter. This report was sent about five weeks after the depossession. During these five weeks the new attitude and behavior had continued. She gets along well with her sisters with no hitting. Her aunt also remarked about the marked change in Erin.

"The most significant part of this, I feel," adds Dr. Hickman, "is that Joe, who had been abused and beaten to death at four, had joined Erin when she was five. Erin began at that time to talk of being abused herself, without being able to come up with any pertinent details. *This raises the question as to whether children may have felt abused because of an attached entity rather than from their own personal abuse. Could this be [a] reason for what has been called false memory syndrome?*" (Emphasis mine.)

## The Mind of a Living Person May Become an Obsessing Entity

One of the cases Baldwin mentions is one in which the entity within his client was the mind of a little girl living in a distant city. She said (through the client) that she had come, while her body was sleeping, to be in this woman who was supposed to have been her mother. The child's mind would return to her own child body when the period of sleep was over. The client had had herself sterilized after two children because, being angry at her husband, she did not want a third child. The soul of the third child, thwarted in getting the mother it had chosen, accepted a different mother and was born to this second-choice woman; but during sleep the child was astrally visiting the woman she had wanted, her first choice for mother.

Instances of similar psyche traveling have been reported among the still-living elderly who are very ill or incapacitated in nursing homes. Their minds may visit other living persons as obsessing entities, often causing the host to feel their illness or weariness or pains while they, the obsessing minds, enjoy the activities of relative health and vigor through their hosts. In cases of this type it seems that the entities can come and go rather freely and are not imprisoned either in their own bodies or in the bodies of their hosts. It needs to be pointed out that the obsessing minds are not usually aware that they are troubling or hindering their hosts; they are not malignant, merely unaware of the effects of their intrusion. Still, friends may be speaking accurately when they say of someone, "She just seems to be obsessed about her father's being in the nursing home," or, "He is simply obsessed with fears since his wife went into the hospital."

## Tom

An unusual example of the mind, or a part of the mind, of a living person obsessing another is that of "Tom," a client of mine who suspected that he was host to one or more entities and asked to be released from them *in absentia*. One of the women I trusted served as channel, and through her we received a situation that perplexed me considerably at first. When I requested the strongest entity in Tom to come, a haughty personage came who said he was Ramus (his English spelling of the Eastern name), a "ruler." "Why do you bother one such as I?" he asked, pompously.

He said that he was the leader of "a group of herders"—apparently a nomadic tribe—and he felt that I was totally wrong in insisting that he was inside of anyone else.

He admitted that maybe someone else was in *him,* however. At times he saw this other, a man, standing and watching as his dancing girls performed. "It is true that no one else can see him." He said the stranger never approached the dancers.

The idea that perhaps this visiting male might invade his harem of women through his own body, however, plunged him into a dark anger: "I WANT HIM GONE! I WANT HIM GONE!"

It had not been difficult for me to perceive that his attitudes towards women were quite similar to those of Tom himself. I theorized that this similarity had drawn Tom's dreaming or fantasizing mind to the tents of Ramus in India and had built up a strong connection between him and Ramus—into whose body this part of Tom's mind might well have entered at times so that when I called for the entity within *Tom* it was Ramus who came at the call, invading Tom periodically or because of the remarkable similarity between the men's attitudes.

After giving Ramus a little lecture that women were minds and hearts as well as bodies and suggesting that he begin the "adventure" of finding out what the dreams and hopes, the likes and dislikes of his several wives were, I ended, "Here is a sword of liberation, Ramus, a sword made of light—not a sword of destruction or killing. Take it and hold it out horizontally and draw it down gently between you and Tom, and all the ties between the two of you will be severed and fall away. . . . You may keep the sword, if you wish; but remember, it is not a sword of destruction but one of freedom, to cut chains and fetters."

The young lady channeling said afterward that he did keep the sword. She said that he agreed with a sort of mental shrug to the stipulation of treating his women more understandingly, as if saying, "Well, if this is the only way I can get rid of *him.*"

Ramus insisted that he is alive, dwelling in India. Therefore this was a case of obsession by part of the mind of a living person—whether it was Tom's mind in Ramus or the other way around, or alternating. We therapists are still learning how mobile and unfettered a mind can be while at the same time the same mind can be limited and fettered by its own list of fears.

## Gina

In April 1990, I had a long conversation with the lady sitting next to me on an airplane. Exchanging information about ourselves, I mentioned my work with hypnosis and releasements, and instantly she began quizzing me about the symptoms of obsession. She felt that her little daughter needed a releasement. Shortly before the child was born, the child's grandmother killed herself—just a few days before the grandfather returned home, dying of cancer, from the hospital. The mother, at term in her pregnancy, was undoubtedly wrenched by these events, and the unborn child, at the very least, sensed and responded to the mother's emotional turmoil; at worst, the child was open to invasion by entities.

Wanting to help the little girl, who was now five or six, I asked the mother if she would like for me to see what I could do with the assistance of friends after I returned home. With gratitude she said yes.

When, a few weeks later, a coworker channeled for the child, "Gina," we found one entity, a man of middle age who had slept away, heavily drugged to ease the pain of far-advanced cancer. He found himself looking down at "this person on the bed—looks like an old person. . . . A nurse comes, says, 'He's gone now.' But I'm not gone, I'm *here.*"

He said he was not ready to go—"should have done more, needed to help my family more." So he stayed in the earth-plane near his family by going into the infant Gina to help her breathe: "She needed me." He took into her his own restlessness, discontent, desire to run away, etc., not realizing that all his traits, both positive and negative, would influence her with him in her. Before leaving, he warned that Gina's ears should be examined, that there was a deep infection in one of them.

The man's mind also told us that there were entities in Gina's mother. The first we found was a high school girl who had drowned when her boyfriend's car failed to make a turn on the way home from a party and went into the river. "They couldn't see me, 'cause I wasn't in the car. I don't know why they couldn't 'cause I *was* there." She didn't want to leave Gina's mother until I reminded her that it was selfish of her to stay and be a parasite in anyone. Then she was willing.

The other entity in the mother was a child whose name when spelled phonetically was "Tinka." She had died in 1915 in Syria, her chest hurting, her body hot. She was leaving her sick body and "it felt good. I was going to go, but Mama screamed and cried and yelled, 'Don't go! Don't go!' I wanted to go but I couldn't" (crying hard, frightened, barely able to talk). "I don't want to go if Mama doesn't want me to, but I do want to go." (Weeping hard for several minutes before being gently quieted.)

"I stayed with Mama a long time, till she left me." (This means through death, usually.) "I looked for a place to go, for somebody who wanted me. This lady needed me. I don't know . . . she just needed me. Somebody had died and she was sad. That big girl (the other entity) didn't help her much. I didn't mind staying."

When Tinka saw someone coming for her she smiled, "She's running—she's running. It's my Mama! She's saying, 'I'm sorry, I'm sorry!' But now we're together again."

*chapter 5*

# RESCUE WORK AMONG
# THE INVISIBLES

Does it sound more intriguing—or more scary—to speak of ghosts, or of "entities within" a person? In actuality there is very little difference except to the individuals directly affected by these invisibles: those persons living in a haunted house or close to a haunted cemetery, for instance, or those obsessed or oppressed by entities trapped in their bodies or auras.

In dealing with all these lost, confused entities the approach is similar and the attitude always needs to be one of wishing to help the disembodied soul (whether or not it thinks it wants help).

When a location is suspected of being haunted or has the reputation of being the site of unexplained noises or feelings, we may suspect that a discarnate entity is staying there for one reason or another. (Or it could be only that the old "vibrations," old residues of former negative energies, have remained attached to that location and there is no soul, no "entity" needing release, only the old memories needing to be neutralized (Denning, 1996.)

At a workshop in California in 1992 I called all the souls who had lost their bodies in or near the large hotel since it was built there in Marina del Rey. My coworker in hypnosis saw a group of spirits coming at our invitation. I spoke first to the children and youths in the group. Several of the children had drowned. The oldest, a lad of fourteen, had drowned farther up the coast and his consciousness had followed his body as it washed down to this area. He had taken over the leadership of the dozen children, herding them as they amused themselves watching visitors and tourists, they themselves unseen, of course. The leader disclaimed indignantly that they ever caused any "trouble," such as poltergeist activities. I asked for a wise high spiritual guide to come for the children, and they followed the guide into the Light.

Then I spoke to the adults, helping them in the same way. Some had died of heart attacks in their hotel rooms; a few had committed suicide. All were deeply grateful to be remembered. Others who had died here no doubt had already gone; these were only the souls that had remained earthbound.

Then I asked for any souls whose bodies had died during the past centuries at that location, including Indians, Spanish, and French. Only one came, as seen by my coworker. He, a Spanish soldier, had been there for "a long time"—i.e., nearly three centuries (earth-time), kept back by the guilt of having killed a fellow soldier. (His story is related in a later chapter.)

Discarnate invisible entities are around us all the time, everywhere. It is not necessary for us to wait until we hear of a haunted house or see a ghostly form. Psychics tell us that there are multitudes of such wanderers dwelling in the invisible vibratory levels of the astral plane, imperceptible to most of us living on the earth-plane. Intelligent entities on the other side informed Dr. Wickland that a long line of entities waited for their turn to speak through Mrs. Wickland, the channel. Even some free spirits not earthbound, who wish to come voluntarily and give information, like the poetess Ella Wheeler Wilcox, had to wait their turn as well, so few were the psychics available back then who could channel messages from the other side.

When we assist earthbound souls who have not become snared in a living person's body or aura, we call it "Rescue Work" instead of "Releasement." I believe the term began with the London group of psychics who helped soldiers killed during WWII. The techniques are just the same as for Releasement work. The only difference, it seems, is that many of the wandering entities still feel lost or confused, whereas most of the entrapped ones think they have found a warmth or a lighter place and are safer than before.

## Most Suicides Remain Earthbound

Among the earthbound wanderers are many, if not most, of the psyches of those who have committed suicide. The picture of the post-death condition of such persons given by Annabel Chaplin in her book, *The Bright Light of Death,* is symbolic—a dreary, head-in-the-mud stagnation. For many souls it is not accurate in the literal sense, unless for those that Chaplin saw. As with all other things, much depends on the individual circumstances of the person who killed himself or herself—although in nearly every case it seems that there comes a realization very soon that this was not the best way to deal with the situation—that a better way could have been found, that suicide did not solve the problems after all and certainly did not obliterate the person's feelings of emotions and suffering, nor awareness of others' reactions to the suicide.

While I was visiting a couple of elderly friends in 1985 they told me that their young medical doctor had killed himself after various troubles that ended with a divorce in which he lost the custody of his children. His death shocked all of "Dr. Sid's" patients and friends. My two friends felt so deeply and emotionally about it that I asked if one of them would be willing to channel for Dr. Sid. I felt that he probably needed assistance on the other side and perhaps we could help him.

With the husband in hypnosis I called Dr. Sid by name, telling who we were. He came, sad and cast down. When I asked what the last straw had been, the one that broke him, he said, "The loss of my family." What he had not realized at the time was that his death would be a still further shock to his children and make them feel they had lost their father even more completely than by the divorce. In one's distress, however, one seldom pauses to think and reason things out. The emotions and pain carry one away into acts that may later be bitterly regretted. It was so with Dr. Sid. He was desperately sorry for his deed but did not know what to do.

Without attempting to do more than to assure him that many people mourned his death—for his patients had loved and trusted him—we asked if someone would come to help him find the path from this earthbound trap into the next dimension. A friend of his, previously deceased, came at once and we were happy to know that Dr. Sid was on the way home.

# Wanderers

Sometimes clairvoyant or psychically sensitive people have felt or seen an entity in my house. Several such instances have resulted in the rescue of the entity, with the help of the living person as a channel in hypnosis.

## A Man and His Horse

The first time this occurred was during a meeting of a small group of women who had all taken the ESP course from Nan Taylor and had continued to meet, discuss, and meditate together. Two of the group said they had perceived a man standing inside the front door as they meditated. I felt that perhaps the stranger was forlorn and could use some help. It would not be courteous to order him away without knowing what he wanted. With one of the ladies in hypnosis, I called the man, and we got his story: A loner with no friends but his horse, he had been thrown off and killed, his head hitting a stone, when his horse stumbled on a loose rock. Now, not realizing that he might call his horse, he was simply wandering aimlessly. I asked him to call his horse—and he immediately saw it coming, felt it nuzzling his shoulder, and the two friends were united. I felt it safe to ask "Brownie" to be the guide and take her master to his rightful home, trusting the intelligence and wisdom of the animal whose love and faithfulness drew the two together.

## Lisa

A second instance that occurred in my house was a few months later. A young woman had come to help with secretarial work, most of which was located in one certain room. Before long she came to me, asking, "Is there an entity in that room? I got the coldest chill!"

"I don't know. I did carry a little stick of incense through every room except that one. Shall we find out? Would you be willing to channel?"

With "Bettie" in hypnosis we got this story:

"My name is Lisa. I'm lost . . . my last day alive? Oh, it was a long time ago. . . . Something fell on me—big, heavy." Her body began to jerk.

"It's all right, Lisa. You are safe. Just see, observe, and without pain tell me."

"A big tree fell on me. I'm grown, I'm married. This is the New Land—forests all around. We are clearing the forests. The tree was not supposed to fall on me. My husband was chopping it. I saw it coming. I pushed the children away. Oh—pain!"

"The pain is easing, Lisa, it is fading away. You gave *your* life for the children."

"But their tears!—they are so sad. He's just standing there with a terrible look on his face."

"Where is he now? His body is probably dead but where is his soul?"

"I don't want to see it. I don't want to see John. He chopped that tree and it fell on me."

"Oh, Lisa, do you really think he would do that to you *on purpose?*"

"He wasn't very nice to me. He didn't beat me but he wasn't very nice."

"Contact his mind as he stands there 'with that look on his face.'"

"He's thinking, 'What have I done?' I guess he wasn't mean; he didn't mean to. I guess he just didn't know how to chop it right; it was just ignorance. Yes, I guess I misjudged him. He's thinking, 'Who will take care of the children?'"

"Who did?"

"He married again soon. He was the same to her as he was to me."

"And what did you do?"

"I screamed and cried, and tried to put my arms around my son, my daughter. They didn't respond. They cried, and cried, and cried. . . . Then I went for a walk—in the forest—for a while. It got darker and darker. It's lonely, the darkness. I don't want to stay in the darkness. I don't want to be lonely!"

"Then you need not be lonely any more, Lisa, or in darkness. But you need to put out of you those dark things like anger, resentment, and fear and envy. . . ."

"I'm feeling lighter."

"Now look for the brighter things in you: your love and faithfulness? Joy? Laughter?"

"Laughter! I can laugh again! I used to laugh with the children. . . . Will I see my children?"

"I think probably you will."

"Oh, they're coming!" (weeping) "My children are here! They say, 'Come with us.' Oh, I thank you so much!"

"Before you go, tell me if you can see John."

"He's still standing in the shadows. I don't want to go away and leave him there."

"All right, you and the children wait right there. John, will you please come and talk to us? John, I hear that you were not very nice to your wives."

"That is true. I'm ashamed."

"What do you wish had been different?"

"I'd have more love in my heart, less selfishness."

"I'm glad that your honesty and frankness make you see that."

"I don't deserve to go to the Light."

"A lot of people feel that way. Are you judging yourself? We are told, 'Judge not.' Just push that insensitivity and selfishness out of you, and loneliness—"

"Oh, *loneliness!*—yes—and *pride.* I was too proud to let them know I loved them."

"See, you do have lots of bright things in you: you loved them, you were a good provider—"

"Yes, I worked hard for them."

"So come out of the shadows and be with your family. They are waiting for you. Now you are all together again! Good-bye."

Often I have wished that I had asked for the date and place of these early rescues. Not being a researcher primarily, in the sweep of the drama of rescuing these pathetic souls, often I ignore such mundane things. This seems to have been in early Colonial times in America. A researcher would be interested in all such points.


## John

A third entity who came into my house was perceived by a woman who was one of a small group taking my class in regression techniques. She felt a presence near the end of the sofa; she said the presence came still closer until it seemed to be right beside her. She was somewhat disturbed.

I asked if she wished to channel for the entity. She feared it might take too much time from the class. Inasmuch as the entity had intruded so conspicuously, however, I felt that perhaps this was something of an emergency, or else something that the students needed to know. I asked the lady to place herself into self-hypnosis; and this is what the entity told us little by little as I questioned him.

He saw fire—fire everywhere. This was Boston Harbor; he had been on a ship, and—with anguish he confessed it—he had been careless and had started the fire, first on the ship, then it spread to oil on the water, then to the pier and the port, spreading rapidly until everything began to burn. He was escaping in a small boat with another man until the enormity of the disaster caused him in his anguish to jump back into the burning water himself. Since then he had been wandering for a long time. Sometimes he still saw the fire, but often he was in darkness. His brother Giuseppe had been among those killed in the fire. . . .

The name "Giuseppe" gave me a thought: "What religion do you have, John?" When he said "Catholic," I said, "I ask Mother Mary to come please and stand here, looking at you. Do you see her? What do you see in her eyes? What is her expression?"

"She's smiling. . . . She says, 'Come with me.' She *cares* about me!" He was weeping.

"She will take you to your own proper place, John. She knows you are sorry for your carelessness. I imagine you will want to make it up to all those whose lives were cut short by the fire, won't you?"

"Oh, yes," he agreed instantly. The thought of being able to make restitution gave him a feeling of new purpose and worth. He became calm and gravely happy. Giuseppe came without my calling him and greeted his brother "with forgiveness in his eyes."

When there is great remorse and guilt, it often seems that ordinary philosophizing and programming are not enough to relieve these, and the power of a Bright Being is required.


### Ephraim

A fourth and somewhat different rescue occurred when my coworker Lili was giving a demonstration of channeling for a number of other ladies in my home. I wanted, for one thing, to check on Ephraim, the mentally retarded man whose throat had been torn by a dog. When I was contacting him earlier, he saw a guide coming, but it seemed that the guide's face had changed from friendly to unfriendly. This had perplexed me. I did not know for sure what it indicated and wanted to find out Ephraim's present situation.

Therefore I worded my invitation, through Lili, "I am calling the Ephraim who is mentally retarded. Will you please come and talk with us? If you still have fear, let it release you."

Ephraim, as you may remember from chapter 4, used finger answers almost entirely. Now the "yes" finger was bobbing up and down.

"Are you willing to talk to us today?" ("Yes.") "Will you tell us your full name?"

"Eph'am Hiram Manatha. Eph'am Hiram Manatha," was the very distinct pronunciation. He called it "Effum."

"Manassa, do you mean? Do you lisp and say 'Manatha'?"

*"Manatha!"* he corrected firmly.

"Thank you for coming, Ephraim."

"You're a nice lady."

"Another nice lady is here, too, letting you use her mouth to talk. Tell us about yourself. Do you have a family?"

"M'hm. Daddy's *big—great* big."

"Do you have brothers and sisters?"

"M'hm, lots! I have John and I have Harold and I have Mark and I have Lucius and I have Toby and—" I could not write down the names as fast as he said them.

"Do you have some sisters, too?"

"M'hm, I have Sally and I have Martha and I have Sarah and . . ." There were more.

"Which is the littlest one?"

"Me!" he boasted. (Lili afterward told me she had seen two sisters smaller than he, but he was treated as the "littlest one" and wanted to be in that favored position.)

"Does your daddy love you?" (Sometimes a retarded child may be favored *or* rejected.)

"I guess so." There was a hesitation, a doubt.

"Does your mama love you?"

"M'hm."

"Now go walking on the years like a path, Ephraim, and tell me important things that happened to you."

"What's a year?"

"It's the time from one birthday to another birthday. Tell me about an important time."

"The time my brother set the mule on fire!" He roared with laughter. "It ran round and round! It got bloated and made a lot of farts and my brother set the farts on fire. That's funny! It ran all around the barn! . . ." He was cackling almost hysterically.

"Did the mule get all right?"

"Well, he never did that any more!" he giggled.

"Now you are older, Ephraim. What is another important event?"

"Hm. Well, my sister Sally got married." He laughed. "My brother rode the mule right into the house and upstairs." He began to laugh uncontrollably again.

"Where did you live, Ephraim?"

"Arkansas. Don't you live there, too? Where am I? Colorado? That's a long ways away. . . . I want to go home."

"Ephraim, go to the last day you were in your own body. How big are you now?"

"No different."

"See what happened that day."

"I got up. It was sunny. I ate some breakfast. Then I went outside. . . . I don't remember. Don't *you* know?"

"I know about *one* Ephraim, but I don't know for sure about *you*."

"I don't want to be here. I want to go home."

"Be brave, Ehpraim. Don't cry. Just see without fear or pain what happened that last day and tell me."

"I don't want to be here." He was whimpering. "Why am I here?" (lips tightly compressed)

"Come back, Ephraim; don't go away. We're going to help you. Why are you crying? . . . It's all right to cry."

"I don't want to be here. I want Mommy. I want Mommy." (crying) "I want Mommy, I want Mommy, I want Mommy, I want Mommy, I want Mommy. . . ." It was barely audible. (The ladies present said afterward that tears were in their own eyes.)

"She may be waiting for you, Ephraim. Now look at Ephraim's body. Just *see* what happened to it. Watch his body. I need to know so I can help you go home."

"I fell . . . I fell . . . in the mill wheel. . . . The body—it fell—and got crushed."

"What did *you* do?"

"I saw Daddy go down and the miller go down, and I called—but they didn't talk to me. Daddy went away and left me." (crying again). "He said that if I went with him to see it work, I'd have to stay right with him. I just wanted to see it work. Everybody else gets to see it work."

"*You* went and left *him,* Ephraim. He said to stay right with him. *You* left *him.* Go into his mind, see his feelings and thoughts as he looks at your body."

". . . I think he loves me. . . ." (very softly)

"Yes. And when he's leaving you, what is he thinking?"

"He thinks I'm gone."

"Yes; but you aren't gone, only he couldn't see you, Ephraim. You could hear and see him and you called to him, but he couldn't hear you, so you thought he had left you. But now you are going to have a wonderful thing happen, Ephraim. Look around for a light. Do you see it?" He nodded. "What color is it?"

"Bright!"

"Yes, and you feel feather-light. And someone is coming. Tell me when you see someone."

"DADDY, MOMMY! DADDY, MOMMY! DADDY, MOMMY!" He was yelling. "I love' em so much!"

"What are they doing?"

"Kissin' me!"

"I think I know someone who's happy. Don't you?"

"US!!" he shouted.

"Ephraim, your daddy and mommy will take you home. Good-bye."

Afterward Lili told us her additional impressions. She sensed that Ephraim was adolescent in body but only about five mentally. It was a black family in which none of the children received quite as much attention as they wanted and needed, but Ephraim was rather protected and babied by all the others and he enjoyed this situation. Lili said that when he slipped above the mill wheel, he simply sat down (in spirit now) while his body kept on falling.

Knowing all this was good and we were all happy for Ephraim. But not until I asked Lili's own discarnate teacher about the Ephraim who died from an attack by a large dog did we learn for sure that he, too, had "reached the Light." The teacher said the adult Ephraim's *body* had "reached full stature" and now that the body was dead, the mind had gone on. The teacher hinted that perhaps the mind, and the soul also, had not yet "reached full stature." I suppose we might have asked more questions but there were other subjects to ask about.

## Haunts and Ghosts

One may think about young Ephraim #2. He may have stayed around the mill for some time. He watched his father leave but did not go with him. Assuming that the dead boy's psyche remained in the vicinity of the mill, might sensitive persons coming to the mill have felt his presence at times? And if so, what would they think? And what might they have said about their feelings, or about the mill itself, and about the cause of their feelings? Would the feelings of a presence be due simply to superstitious fancy, or due to a ghost, or what? And if those uncomfortable feelings were due indeed to poor Ephraim's loneliness, believing that his father had gone away and left him, would the usual attitude of "exorcizing the ghost" have been the best way to relieve the situation?

Psychic researchers have indicated that in many cases perceptible hauntings and ghostly phenomena are due to the discarnate psyche of a once-living person that finds itself caught in a timeless round of re-experiencing a traumatic episode that left it "dead" and confused, and that often the knockings and clankings may actually be produced by the entity as it attempts to attract the attention of those in physical bodies and enlist their help.

Ephraim is an example of a "complete," albeit mentally retarded, "ghost." The Huna teaching of Hawaii is that usually discarnate entities are "complete", "normal" with both conscious and subconscious portions of the original psyche; but that in some instances one or the other portion may be missing. If only the subconscious portion is trapped as a "ghost," then it repeats endlessly and mindlessly certain experiences that it re-enacts, having *no ability to think or reason* or to ask why things are this way or how to get out of them. If the subconscious portion is absent, the conscious part may wander, "searching," "seeking," "looking"—but hardly knowing why, *having no clear memory* of the event that precipitated it into this situation. I have had little experience with such incomplete entities and shall merely refer readers to the interesting book by Max Freedom Long (see Bibliography).

# Poltergeists

Now suppose that young Ephraim had not stayed around the mill for any length of time but had eventually recovered his natural buoyancy and sense of humor and had started wandering around to find companionship. He might have found a house where he could feel at home and might have begun to make a good deal of mischief in his attempts to be noticed and to interplay with the inhabitants. He might have learned how to move objects around or make creaks and other noises that the occupants of the house could notice. Such a mischievous entity is called a poltergeist, a "playful spirit." Often poltergeist phenomena are reported from homes where an adolescent child, usually a girl, is living, but this is by no means a necessary requisite for such hauntings.

## Conrad

This type of problem occurred in my own home a few years ago. Within a period of several weeks almost every electrical thing I owned began to give trouble: electric clocks, two of them; two radios; the television; the vacuum cleaner; both of my elderly cars; and so on. I asked a psychic who had come to visit the area if she could shed any light on this situation. She had an instantaneous flash of "a small figure like a child, in the doorway between kitchen and dining area." She felt it was not really harmful but only mischievous. Asking her guide for more information, she received through automatic writing, "Yes, we have the contact: impish little fellow; name, Conrad. This little one means no harm. He enjoys watching Dr. Louise work, likes the feel of her home. This child passed over in 1956. He was in a fire. He has not accepted his own death. There was no religious upbringing; he has no knowledge of life, death, heaven, hell, or hereafter. That must be explained. You will need to bring his mother, Elvira, to him. She is on this side and is adjusted. She will take him to the Light as soon as he accepts he needs to go. When you hear his, 'Yes, I understand,' call his mother. She will take care of the rest."

Well, fine. But since I am neither clairvoyant nor clairaudient, how was I to hold a conversation with Conrad and know when he said he understood? "Oh, you'll see him. You'll hear him. You'll know," assured my friend.

"Maybe you're right, but my *conscious* mind doesn't see or hear. So how will I know?"

"Well, just sit down and call him to you and talk to him as if you could see him, and tell him what happened: how his body died in the fire and he is causing you trouble and needs to go to the Light. Tell him his mother is waiting for him."

That grand old motto again: "It can't hurt and it might help." Glad that my neighbors could not see, I did exactly as told, placing myself in waking self-hypnosis first, for the hypnotic state is a great catalyst. I did remember to ask Conrad (but only as he was already about to leave with mother) if he would fix up the many things he had managed to botch up while here. I wish that I had asked him first, given him a few days, and *then* released him! As it was, I had nearly two hundred dollars worth of repairs on various things. A few did begin to run again on their own, however—repaired by Conrad?

## Huberty

Although I had read about such phenomena in various books and articles, the very first poltergeist-type of activity I ever witnessed for myself was in Nurse Johnnie's home. Our ESP group was meeting there that day. Outside the east patio doors a porch swing was hung. Outside the south window grew a young aspen tree. People used to call aspens "quakies" or "quakin' asps" because of the way the small round leaves flutter with every breath of wind. This evening Jeanette glanced out the east doors and then stared at the porch swing. "Is there a wind?" she asked.

I looked out at the tree. "No, not a bit of wind."

"Look at that porch swing," said Jeanette. We all moved to where we could see. It was swinging rhythmically. No one was in it. No one visible, at any rate. Johnnie put her hand to her mouth. Some of us turned to take another look at the aspen tree. It was still.

"Whatever it is out there," I said, "we are stronger than it is. There are five of us here, and our guides. Let's put ourselves into waking hypnosis and tap into Universal Mind for all the protection, energy, and wisdom we may need."

One lady, a new member of the group, had been complaining about numerous family matters all evening since the meeting began. I had wondered secretly if Lana would make a congenial member, if this was her usual type of personality. Now, as we sat talking about whatever-it-was-out-there, she began to cry out, "He's right here! He's right in front of me! He's strong!" Her hands were fluttering in front of her chest as if electrically vibrating.

We had been discussing such things as the recent massacre at the McDonald's restaurant in California, and I had mentioned that since I knew some of Hitler's victims had been reincarnated as Americans, no doubt some of Hitler's stooges were now Americans as well.

"As soon as you mentioned Hitler," Lana cried, "here he came. Oh, he's *strong!*"

We grouped ourselves around her. In hypnosis we placed a visualized protective aura around her and commanded the entity, whatever-it-was, to leave her and move away.

We decided to use our meditation period to contact this entity, find out who it was and what it wanted. Johnnie was delegated to channel the entity while the rest of us received as many impressions as possible, and I guided by asking questions.

In hypnosis, then, Johnnie relayed that this entity claimed to be Huberty, the man who had killed the people in the McDonald's restaurant in California; that he claimed to have been a nephew of Hitler in his previous life, a boy of about ten who worshiped his uncle. He boasted, "He can do anything! He can kill thousands if he wants to." The boy himself had been killed by a bomb. He incarnated in America and this time died from a policeman's bullet through the head.

Now he was free, wandering, and he was attracted to Lana's home. "She's a magnet; she draws people." Lana has almost daily friendly visitors whom she feels but does not quite see. She holds one-sided conversations with them; she enjoys their company. When this one came, however, she did not recognize him as a visitor. Instead, her own personality began to change and become strident and sharply critical of everything and everyone. Huberty was "oppressing" her, although he was not within her as an obsessing presence.

In meditation one of the other ladies saw him now, standing at the far edge of the room. We had ordered him away from Lana but had not sent him clear away. Johnnie said that he was watching us, listening to us, in bewilderment and unbelief, as if he had never in his life met people such as we were. Francie gave him a real talking-to. He was

familiar with authority and behaved himself after she reprimanded him sharply for having shot up the restaurant and now
ordered him to keep his distance from Lana and the rest of us.

After Johnnie's conversation with him, he agreed to leave
but asked if he could come again. Johnnie hesitated a
moment, then said yes, if he would not cause any trouble.
Later she told us that the porch swing had been swinging
again the next day, this time as if two people were in it.
Huberty told her the second person was "a woman—but she
has nothing to do with this situation." After that we heard
no more about him.

This, therefore, was not truly a rescue. At that time we
did not know how to rescue such obdurate persons. We did
describe to Huberty the "Place of Learning". He did not
seem to be much interested. He was not attracted to any talk
about Light. He seemed to accept our insistence that he
would have to pay for the misery he had caused and he hoped
to avoid it. He may be still wandering.

Lana's personality, by the way, became as sweet and
pleasant as it was before the coming of Huberty. She became
a valuable member of the group.

## Home Is To Be a Sanctuary

One more aspect of our Rescue Work developed from this
fact that several times wandering entities had invaded our
own homes. Lana said that she frequently had such visitors,
as I mentioned—deceased relatives and friends, most of
them; but some wanderers were drawn by what they describe
as a warmth, a light, or a shining flower. Lana was described
by Huberty as "a magnet—she draws people."

My home was described as a "halfway house" to which
entities were drawn as by a beacon light, when they found

themselves halfway between earth and the next realm. Lili suggested that I ask her in hypnosis to *become* my house, for she felt she could discover important facts along these lines. Therefore when she had placed herself in hypnosis I gave her that instruction: "Now *become* my house and tell me what you find. Are there any entities in it?"

Without hesitation she replied, "Multitudes—multitudes. It's like there is another dimension inside here. There are people who are good but who are in the clutches of earth, *bound* by this dimension. There are some others who have sworn allegiance to the evil power itself. These come because it is summer and the dark forces are more active in summer, and because you have distorted the other dimension, have caused ripples. It is as if a vacuum had been created that sucked in a demon or two. They cannot eliminate you but they certainly can eliminate your help to these others by stopping you. They can attack you through your weaknesses. No human being is perfect and without weaknesses."

From a higher level than Lili's "being the house" came the statement from my Spiritual Advisor Master Ching that a home should be cleared, cleansed, and dedicated as a sanctuary, belonging only to the one living in it and free of all entities except "those who are *invited* as guests. All who enter without invitation are *invaders*." Although Master Ching knew I wanted to be of help even to those who came uninvited, he suggested that they come only in the company of a person who came by appointment—invited—and leave with that person. Then, after the dedication of this house and the grounds to the work that I am doing "for the Light," this would be the sanctuary it should be.

Similarly with my body: In privacy I should dedicate it in order to protect it from attacks whenever I should go away from the protection of home and grounds. His suggestions apply equally to all who are working in both worlds. We are all "causing ripples" and disturbing the *status quo* of the invisible worlds; and some entities are drawn to us hoping to "invade" us and find a nest or get help, while others are determined to block that help; but all are sapping the energy of the one whose home or body they invade. (Such invaders may seem to sap the life force of even flowers in a vase, causing them to wilt sooner than blossoms given to a friend from the same cutting.)

Since we received these explanations and suggestions I have gratefully accepted that my home is now my private sanctuary, just as each person's body should be his or her own private temple, occupied solely by the owner.

The entities lost and wandering need not be ignored nor rejected, however. Sometimes in a meeting of the ESP group I have suggested as a topic of meditation that we *invite* entities who are ready to move on to come and receive our help. Sometimes I lead the guided visualizations and give the souls instruction to look for the Light and move toward it. Sometimes other members of the group lead, some of whom are able to see the entities who come in response to the invitation. Virginia's attention was often focused on one or two entities who held her special interest. Johnnie often saw "crowds of entities, pushing each other to get closer to us. I told them there was no rush, that there was room for all and that all would be led to the Light. And then," she laughed, "the Light appeared *behind* them! They all had to turn around."

"The last shall be first," I quoted, laughing with her.

Master Ching urged us to do this type of work regularly, to assist as many souls as possible to find their way into the proper realm and try to clear out this crowded unhealthy low-astral plane of the earthbound. Master Ching's reason is thought-provoking, that before long "many will be dying

—thousands at a time. We are preparing for them. And there will be less chaos on this side if the souls still earthbound can be helped to move higher before the crowds of newly dead arrive." In the meantime Master Ching agreed to select an earthbound soul for us to assist whenever we could make time in our schedules. I have taken him at his word more than once and have never been disappointed at his choices. Two examples follow.

## Wanderers Selected for Rescue

### *The Young Professor*

During a class that I was teaching on Releasement, I was giving one of the students, Betty, the opportunity to release any entity within me as I lay in hypnosis. Finger movement had said first that no entity was present within me; then immediately my "yes" finger rose. Betty spoke to the entity and learned from him that he was a young male Ethiopian, a professor who had prepared himself to become a teacher and helper of his beloved country. Then he found himself included by the authorities in the class of undesirables who were to be herded to some location where they would be disposed of. Angry, disheartened, and weak, he dressed himself as a peasant but was found and forced into a long line of similar miserable rejects. Walking until he could no longer walk, he collapsed and felt one of the guards kick him repeatedly. He was left to die as the others went on. His dying thoughts were of bitter disillusionment: he who had loved his country and wanted to help her to new heights had been rejected by her and was dying like an outcast. Of course such feelings kept him earthbound.

Betty kept asking him to look for the Light, to keep his mind on the Light. I heard his weary voice coming from my mouth, "Oh, the light—the light—the light! That is for you people with white skins, not for us."

Since this was a class, I had kept my conscious mind more closely reined in than usual in hypnosis, and I murmured to Betty, "Call for someone to come for him." Betty knew instantly what to do. She asked him to look for a guide who would come for him, and almost at once he (and I) saw his mother, a large, majestic black woman in a long dress of black-and-red geometrical patterns and an attitude of self-assurance. She said, "Don't be foolish, son. Come on up." She seemed to be projecting to him mentally that his bitterness was accomplishing nothing and needed to be abandoned, along with any feelings of failure and anger. It was easy for him to go with her.

In contact with his inner emotional and thought patterns, I did not feel that this type of death was the result of his personal karma but was more likely to have been simply a case of being caught up in group karma. We did not ask, however.

## The Prostitute

Another time, with an artist friend as channel, we asked Master Ching to select one of the souls that we could help in the two hours that Kathleen and I had together. Through Kathleen's mouth came his calm voice, "An entity has entered this channel. There are many I choose to send to the Light."

Condensed, the ninety-minute releasement went like this:

"My name is Amiga. How . . . old-am-I? . . . I am a very beautiful lady, very dark, with beautiful hair. . . . Many men have *used* me."

"What are your feelings about that?" I asked.

"I am very sad . . . I'm glad I don't have that body any more . . . I shot myself. *That* wasn't life. I was forced into that life from when I was very young. . . . It was in the south, a Mexico country . . . 1840."

"Was there anyone who loved you?"

"No. Well, a little boy. I see him." (which means that the deceased boy had been attracted to her by her thinking of him and her love for him) "I took care of him sometimes—Paulo."

"Paulo, did you come for Amiga? Or do you need help, too? Are you lost?"

"It's very peaceful where I am, it's very nice. I want Amiga to come with me," said the child.

Amiga's eyes filled with tears. "How could anyone care for me? I'm so ashamed."

"You gave love, so now you receive love. Amiga, be brave. Smile at Paulo. Now kneel down and hold out your arms to him. The tears are washing out the sadness and it is being breathed out along with the shame and the feelings of being unloved. Now, you know that your *body* is dead—that you shot yourself? But *you* are not dead!"

"I do not understand."

"No, most of us don't. Our religions haven't understood nor taught us—"

"Ha!" she interrupted. "Priests!" (The channel said later that some of the men who had used her were priests.)

"People need to realize that they have four parts: the body, the feelings and emotions, the mind and its thoughts, and the soul."

"Even I?"

"Of course! Life is precious in the universe, and you and Paulo are children of the universe." (I carefully avoided religious terms.) "Now look into your heart and see the love there, and then go into the Light and up to the High Place."

There was a long pause, then Amiga said tentatively, "Will the High Place let me?"

"Of course. Don't disappoint Paulo. He came to take you to his beautiful home. But first stand in this warm little waterfall and let it shower down upon and through you, washing away loneliness and hate, dissolving away pain, sadness, grief, and feelings of unworthiness. . . . Just let the warm shower of the waterfall wash you clean. . . ." (I was using hypnotic suggestion here.) "And now you feel lighter. Paulo loves you! Did anyone else love you?"

"Oh—Grandmama loved me."

"And I'm sure she knows about you now. When you feel clean, look for the Light." (another long pause.) "Paulo, hold out your hand to her. Help her!"

"Oh, will I hurt him?" She feared even to touch him.

"Of course not!"

"Is this what it means, 'A little child shall lead them'?"

"In this case, yes."

"Then I'll try—I will go. But—" (There were more expressions of fear, unworthiness, uncleanness, etc.)

I then earnestly told her the story of Aldonza, the "dark savage alley cat" in "The Man of La Mancha," whom Don Quixote saw as beautiful and virginal and treated as such, giving her a beautiful new name—and the change all this caused in her. I also told Amiga about another soul I had met, another prostitute who had said, "I won't tell you my name; I'm ashamed of it." "Then may I call you 'Mary'?" I had asked. "Mary, the Mother of God?" she sneered. And to her, as to Amiga now, I had replied, "God sees the soul, clean and lovely. Don Quixote saw Aldonza's soul, just as Paulo and I see yours. Now, Amiga, go up to the High Place."

"If the High Place will take me."

"Just float up to where you can see into your past life, or

even a life further back, and find out *why* you had to suffer this kind of life."

There was another pause, shorter this time.

"I was a father—I was very cruel—cruel to my children. I enjoyed being cruel! They were little girls, and I *hated* them. I needed *boys,* to work. I hated everybody. I hated myself. I did not love anybody. Sometimes I wondered why I was so cruel." (We did not seek the answer to this question, at least for now.)

"Now go to the planning stage before your birth, when you are planning this new life as Amiga. There are wise counselors to help you make choices. You will be born as a girl"—

"A *beautiful* little girl—and I would suffer as I had made others suffer."

"Yes, and you learned a great deal. Did you learn the whole lesson?"

"Yes . . . did they find out where I got the gun? I took it from the general's uniform." (She was not supposed to touch the uniform, but saw the gun and felt that this would be her only chance to escape from this life. So she took the gun, but with strong feelings of guilt as a thief. Then in the small private room, in the general's presence, she shot herself.)

"I don't think that was very important. But look at the men who used you. Were any of them your former girl children?"

Amiga paused. "Maybe . . .good for them, if they got even!"

Laughing, I objected, "No—that's only hating and getting even, and hating and getting even, back and forth and getting nowhere. You have to start by *understanding,* as you do now since you saw yourself as the cruel father. Understanding leads to tolerance, and then to patience, and finally maybe even to forgiveness. This all leads to fairness and a balance is achieved. Are you ready to go now? You may see someone else coming."

"Yes—Grandmama!"

"I thought she might come! Now all three of you can go into the Light! Good-bye!"

"Gracias!" came Amiga's happy farewell. And the channel added, "I *felt* her presence go!"

Then Master Ching's voice came again, "Today's work was very good. A very sad little Amiga is helped, is saved. Thank you. Thank this entity (Kathleen) for letting Amiga enter her. All is past."

## Rescuing Groups of Disembodied Souls

After the great mudslide that buried several villages in Colombia, South America, some years ago, Nurse V. of our little ESP group told us that she had gone into private meditation and, leaving her body asleep at home, had traveled astrally to Colombia. She is the only one of our group who can do this and control the process. She attempted to help the persons who had been killed, reasoning that the people still living would be assisted as soon as rescue teams could reach them. Her intent was to meet the ones who had died—whose psyches had been so abruptly torn from their bodies. They would be in a state of shock or stupor. She felt that she did help many of these victims, although others "didn't seem to be ready, and some were still sleeping under the mud." The next day, back in her physical body, she felt drained of energy, nearly exhausted.

I wondered: Maybe there were points of technique that we needed to learn in order to avoid such exhaustion. In a later meeting we asked our Advisors about this subject.

"Remember," said one Advisor, "that on our side these events or 'catastrophes,' as you call them, are known about beforehand, and preparations are made to receive the souls that are [destined] to come over. Nevertheless, we miss some, or some are not ready. Any help that you on that side can give is always welcome."

Instead of trying to do too much, we were instructed, "Don't try to be nurses or doctors (helping one at a time). Just visualize a safe path or a road or highway and call the souls to get on the highway. They will be met by helpers and taken care of from there."

I like the images of those words: a highway, smooth and unobstructed; a homey little road; or even a clear footpath. No matter what the type of entity, one of those three pathways would surely be attractive, all of them leading toward the Light. Another meditation group visualizes a "Bridge of Light" and calls the souls to come and cross over it into the Light.

We remember these instructions when we meditate for the victims of earthquakes, floods, fires, and hurricanes, or famines or war zones. When we in physical bodies do this work, however, we need to remember that our earth-plane frequency of vibration is different from that of the souls passing over, and we need to ask for extra energy for ourselves. It was indicated that we might need extra rest or sleep afterward, as well.

About this time there was a tragic event in Saudi Arabia. The news media reported that many Muslims were trapped by an explosion in a tunnel while returning from their pilgrimage to Mecca. The temperature was 109 F. The lights went out, people became panic stricken, and crushed and trampled one another. An estimated fourteen hundred died, most of suffocation.

Charlene and I decided to see if the victims needed help. She channeled; I facilitated, calling "the souls who are trapped in the hot tunnel—calling the one who is strongest spiritually to be your spokesman and speak to us for you."

A man answered, saying his name was "Filoh"—spelling it out hesitantly when I asked how it would be spelled in the English alphabet. He said that many souls were together there.

"I ask you to listen to what I have to tell you and to have courage. There is something the souls need to know: We can't see nor hear you. Do you see us?"

"As if through a veil—misty," said Filoh.

"Yes, as if through a veil; and the veil is 'death'. Do you understand? You are on one side of that veil and we are on the other side of death."

Filoh's lips moved silently a moment. Then, "Yes."

"How much do you remember before things became misty to you?"

Filoh moved restlessly. "Noise—screaming—shouting—darkness—heaviness. Everything changed."

"Yes. And now all of you souls, listen: The noise, screaming, shouting, and heat and darkness are *in the past*. Your bodies are gone but you are alive. So stand up strong and straight, think your mind calm, your feelings calm, and think courage as you think of death. God, Allah, loves you. He is the Merciful, the Compassionate. Let there be memories only, of the past. . . . Filoh, are they listening?"

"They understand."

"Fine! We are not of your religion but we want to help you. Put out of yourselves heaviness and distress, any anger or hate, any pain and helplessness. Make yourselves shining and clean. You made your pilgrimage to Mecca and now you are going to the spiritual Mecca. . . . Filoh, please explain it to them in your own terms, if I have not expressed it clearly."

Most of the earthbound souls were ready to go. "All of you are faithful ones who were on your pilgrimage. You are God's children. But God has many children. God is merciful; his children are of all religions. Do you know this? . . . I ask for spiritual helpers to assist Filoh to lead them, if he needs help. . . . What do you see, Charlene?"

"Not even entity-types; just sparkles shining."

"Souls," I finished, "know that all religions are worthy of respect. Remember when you come back that we are all children of God. Good-bye. Happy journey."

"Allah be praised for your help," said Filoh. "We accept your help so graciously given. We go now."

Not all of the souls had been ready to follow Filoh. A woman's voice said that she was still looking to find her husband and oldest son; but she and others accepted that their family members, whether living or dead, were "safe in God's love," wherever they were; and she decided, "No one needs to look back, do they?" And so she led a second group into the Light.

That left only a few who did not want to leave the earth-plane. The man speaking for these said he had been born to perform a certain work, and that work was not yet accomplished.

I agreed that the change had been so sudden, so abrupt that it tore him out of the earth-scene. "But remember that we still here cannot see or hear you now. If you try to stay, you would be frustrated, ignored by everyone. The physical plane is for physical work. And you need to leave your work for others now and move on to the plane of souls, the heavenly land, and go to your own work there. You can still send love and thoughts to those who still live on the earth-plane. Do you understand? We are trying to help you."

"It wasn't supposed to be like this," insisted the man.

"Do you mean that your death was a true accident?"

"Yes," he said positively.

"One of your Muslim leaders said the explosion was the Will of Allah and that it was the destiny of each of the fourteen hundred to die at that precise moment, if not in the tunnel, then elsewhere."

"For some, perhaps," was his only reply.

"If it was *not* their destiny, then even so, as one holy teaching says, 'All things work together for good, *to those who love the Lord.*' All of you were on pilgrimage, all of you are those who love God. What else can you tell me, how this experience can be turned to good?" He did not answer.

I asked for a wise teacher of his own religion to explain the spiritual situation to this and the remaining souls, but there was no response. It was very quiet. After a moment of waiting, I asked Master Ching if he would give a message to these who felt that their lives had been cut short before their time.

With calm deliberation came Master Ching's message, "Nothing is lost; nothing is delayed; no harm is done. Time is not of much importance. You will go on—and learn—and come back, and do the job better for the experience."

I thanked him and said, "Souls, you heard this wise master. If you doubt, offer your doubt as a sacrifice to Allah, a gift to him. If you feel reluctance or regret to leave the earth-plane, offer those as gifts to him. Let his Light into your heart. . . . Let Master Ching's words be like a healing flow within you. Now are you ready to follow Master Ching or one of your own spiritual leaders?"

This time all were ready, "no little lost ones remaining," and Charlene said that all she saw was "just shining space."

"I saw just light and darkness, basically," she added, after returning to full consciousness. "A lot of souls had already gone on. Those remaining were still huddled together, filled with darkness and heaviness. It all happened so suddenly. They were good people. They were really grateful to be helped. When you said the word 'death' they suddenly understood and felt relief. But when you said, 'when you come back,' they looked startled!"

# What Each of Us Can Do

All through this chapter I have talked about channeling and contacting lost or wandering entities through hypnosis. That has been the way in which I have done this work, and it gives the satisfaction of hearing directly through the channel what the feelings and thoughts of the entities contacted are. It is a conversation between the contacted soul and me. The disadvantage is that a third person, the channel, needs to be present. Many are excellent, capable, and willing—but most are also extremely busy!

Some psychic persons, including some of my friends, are able to hold such conversations with invisible entities either in meditation or through automatic writing, or by asking their discarnate guides and teachers questions and listening with open minds for answers.

For most people, however, the psychic ability may not be sufficiently developed and the availability of a friend who can cooperate as a channel may be lacking. Many people do offer prayers for others who are in dire circumstances or in suspected distress or unhappiness. Depending on what their religion has taught them, these persons may pray for the "dead" as well as for the living. The prayers may be directed to God directly, to one of the saints, to angelic beings, or simply to "Servants of the Light."

For several years all of the friends who had assisted me as channels became so deeply involved in their own activities and problems that I found myself thrown back onto my own resources. I accepted the situation as a spiritual lesson that I needed to stand on my own feet and take full responsibility alone for the work I felt was mine to do.

During this period I began a series of morning meditations aimed at assisting certain groups of souls that needed help. One morning I might focus on the souls of aged people who felt that their usefulness had gone and that their continued living was a burden on their families, and who in their despondency wanted to die. I focused especially on those who did manage to commit suicide. In my meditation I called to their notice the "safe highway or roadway" that led into the Light, urged them to come and let themselves be comforted and helped home.

Another morning I would focus on the infants who had been rejected, their bodies aborted before birth or left exposed to die after being born. Using words like "a warm stream of love" instead of "light," I called these souls to come and let themselves be borne into the safe, warm Pool of Love. (When a friend did channel for these at a later time, she said that thousands of tiny bundles came floating at the call, most of them containing girl babies.)

At yet another time I would call all the lonely, miserable teenagers who felt that their families did not care about them and who in desperation had killed themselves. I felt their loneliness and desperation. Many of them believed that nobody would care, nobody would even notice if they disappeared; they felt worthless. And then there were those who had turned to drugs to deaden the feelings of desperation and loneliness and had killed their body accidentally by an overdose of something.

There was also the category of adults of both sexes who were overburdened by the demands of family and job. It seemed that there was never a dearth of groups of needy persons to try to help: toddlers killed by abuse; gang members in a rumble; victims of wars, floods, earthquakes, fires, famine, accidents. . . .

After a few weeks of more or less regular meditations of

this sort, I began to feel a deep weariness. Therefore I suggest that those who use a similar type of approach ask for additional strength and energy for themselves as well as for the ones they are wishing to assist.

As mentioned, my motto was, "It can't hurt and it may help." One disadvantage for me was that I had to offer my desire to the Higher Powers and not have any way of knowing how much, if any, effect my meditations and prayers had produced. This was only a self-centered wish, I knew, and I recalled the maxim of the Bhagavad Gita, to "Serve for the sake of the service and not in the hope of reward," and the Buddhist maxim, to "perform action without attachment to the fruits of the action." It is not necessary to know how much or even whether one has helped. To quote Gandhi, "Whatever you do will never be enough, but it matters enormously that you do it."

If you wish to become a helper in this work, as many do, I suggest that you begin by meditating at first for one or a few individuals whom you know personally or whose stories you have read about or heard about on television. *Quiet your own mind and emotions first of all; this is important.* Then call the person you wish to assist, and explain what happened and what the result was—i.e., that the person's body died. Be gentle but forthright. "Listen" for any answering thoughts that may come into your mind; they may be from the one you are talking to. Answer any questions that come into your mind as if from the other. The soul may not realize that the body has died.

Gradually, as you continue, you will acquire self-confidence and will feel at ease in calling to larger groups of souls and asking them to come onto the bright safe highway or the Bridge of Light leading into the next dimension, their home.

One psychic friend, a boy who was about twelve at the time, said that many who wanted to answer the invitation felt that they could not come because they were so "dirty"—loaded with the trash of unpleasant mental and emotional habits and of rejection and abuse. His mother, also psychic, agreed. She said that many souls needed to be given an opportunity, by suggested visualizations, to clean themselves up before coming into the highway and heading home. She likes the symbol of a pool of cleansing, healing light. Her son felt that some of the souls needed stiff brushes as well! Both agreed that many entities felt a deep sense of unworthiness and a fear of being rejected if they tried to come. We have included in our wording that the invitation is for *all* who hear us and are ready to go to the next realm, even those who feel most unworthy—the outcasts, the untouchables, the infants.

We have found that the greatest hindrance to this type of work is not in ourselves but in the deep-rooted rage and hate, based on either fear or a sense of superiority, that infects the places where wars are seething. Some wars are clearly visible, with all the fear, pain, violence, and blood that we hear and read so much about. Other wars are invisible, roiling in the hearts and minds of people who have been socially or religiously at odds with others in their country or neighboring lands for decades or centuries. These are the main hindrances, these long-term habitual attitudes of hate, often based on fear and perpetuated by all the subtle acts and words, the facial expressions, and little social slights that human beings know to make other human beings feel inferior, rejected, humiliated.

Although *individual* meditations and prayers are always welcomed by the Servants of the Light in trying to soften ingrained harshness and long-term negative attitudes—whether in small groups or large, whether racial, social, or religious—the meditations of a *group* of workers is recommended—"two or more gathered together"—and not just one time, but repeatedly. "Send Light, send Love, fill the leaders with love and compassion, send courage and patience and understanding to the people on both sides of the conflict," we are told. If we are in doubt as to the rightness of such meditations, we are told clearly, "It is always all right to pray for the soul of anyone, that it may have strength, courage, and love," and I always add, "and wisdom."

Such meditations for persons like Hitler may be difficult for us. But during the terrible Battle of the Bulge in World War II, when Hitler's forces were bulging forward into Belgium irresistibly, some Christian groups in the United States began to "send love" to Hitler as the person, not as a leader of those forces. And it was shortly thereafter that the "bulge" was stopped.

Of course no one can either prove or disprove any relationship between the meditations in the United States and the sudden change in the progress of the war in Europe. But that should not deter us from offering our meditations and prayers on the side of the Light, no matter where and toward whom it is directed. And that means we offer them with love, not anger or hate. In some cases it is easier if we envision the recipient of our love as the young hurt child he used to be, bruised and warped by life.

*chapter 6*

# BRIGHT DISCARNATE
# BEINGS

The purpose of this chapter—in the midst of a book about discarnate entities that invade human beings—is to enlighten readers about the ever-present availability of these Servants of the Light before I begin to speak about the nonhuman types of negative entities, some of which may seem troubling to readers new to these concepts. If one feels that one has to confront such negative entities and energies alone, some do seem frightening. This chapter has been inserted to assure every reader that no matter how lonely or fearful you may feel, you are never truly alone.

It may be true that sometimes one's prayers and meditations can evict a suspected invader only as far as the outside of one's aura, where it may remain as an oppressive or shadowing influence though no longer an obsessing one. In such a case, one may need to enlist the aid of a hypnotherapist or a psychic who has had training in Releasement work. But you are never totally alone. *Call* to the Bright Beings, *ask* for help, and put fear out of your heart. As Master Ching has told us, *"Fear is of Satan. Fear IS Satan."*

Keep your thoughts instead on the beauty, power, and joy of your bright helpers, the Servants of the Light. Paul enjoined us to think on "whatever is true, honorable, pure, lovely," and so on. That is, think on the positive things, not the negative ones. "Energy follows thought," we are told repeatedly. And so, gradually perhaps, we learn to trust the power and protection of our faithful discarnate friends more and more.

My Spiritual Advisor, "Master Ching," is present at my invitation right now. I feel his little smile, half of affection, half of amusement, for he has said repeatedly that he is "always" with me—and yet I feel that when I specifically invite his presence, he is "more" with me! Well—as I have often told my clients and students, although the Bright Beings are "always" available to us, they wait to be invited to contact us—they do not interfere in our lives unless we ask. And so I ask!

In 1980 I signed up for a series of six-week courses in ESP (extrasensory perception) with Nan Taylor, a young woman who had studied such subjects for twenty years and was naturally psychic to begin with. She offered "readings" as well as classes, a "reading" being the half hour or so when she withdrew her own personality and allowed the personality of her discarnate guide to take possession of her body and vocal apparatus, the guide then answering the questions of the client.

I had heard and read about "readings" but had never seen nor experienced one. At the age of sixty-seven I made an appointment with Nan for the first reading of my life. She drew up a chair so that I sat facing her, almost knee to knee, and explained that she would let herself go into an altered state in which her eyes would close, her head droop for a few moments, and then when her head rose and her eyes opened, the personality of her master would be there, looking through her eyes and hearing through her ears, and speaking to me through her voice.

"My eyes will look different," she told me. "My own mind hears, too, and understands, but the words pass right on through and leave no memory. When I come back into my body, I do not remember anything that was said until I listen to a tape or am told about it."

She said that the guide she had had until recently had been thoughtless about the fatiguability of her body and also about the propriety of various remarks and advice to clients and students in her readings and classes. I had been present at one such instance during a class, and agreed that some of her words had hardly been the type appropriate for a group of women of mixed ages. The guide had also become more and more "pushy" toward her, taking over her body at almost any moment and embarrassing her when she learned later from her husband of certain things she had said to neighbors during a little social call, for instance.

So Nan told us that she had sent that guide away and had prayed that a true master be sent to be her guide for the future.

The entity who volunteered to be this master was named Demetrius, a wise elder of old Greece or Rome. He seemed rather reticent about himself. Nan, after her unfortunate experiences with the former guide, was quite cautious about Demetrius. She even asked us, her students, more than once what we thought of him. We all assured her that he was an excellent coteacher and took over in class only to give us valuable information or counsel. And she had already said that she permitted him to do that.

In my reading, Demetrius commented that my master was "rushing you as fast as he dares, lest you turn in the opposite direction." I didn't know I had a special master! I considered Jesus, Buddha, and others my masters. And what did "the opposite direction" mean? I could not imagine that at this age I would turn away from the spiritual path that I had been following for many years.

"Lest you should wish to die," explained Demetrius.

Ah, that I could understand. Often when it seemed that life had become just too complicated or too rushed I felt overwhelmed. I had felt like saying, "Stop the world—I want to get off."

So I did have a special master? And my master knew of my feelings? Who was my master? How was he "rushing" me?

In class one day I asked if we might "see" our masters—and instantly felt abashed that I had been so presumptuous. Nan, however, took the request in stride, almost casually, and had us meditate to see our masters—our own as well as the masters of the other students. Then we compared notes, each of us telling what she had seen, heard, or felt.

Although I did not see any being, either for myself or for the others in the class, I felt or heard sensations that were not physical ones. Three of the other women, however, saw a master for me—and all three different! I felt, "My, we really are amateurs, aren't we!"

As it turned out, the Germanic man that Jeanette saw as my master, whose name Nan got as "William—Wilhelm?—Wilhelm"—was one of the temporary masters that Nan had spoken of for us. Wilhelm's work seemed to be assisting persons during a stressful transition period of some type. Mine was the selling of my old home and finding a new place to move to. Wilhelm's thoughts came to me at first in German, and I sagged at the idea of rejuvenating the little I knew of the language from college and graduate years. But Wilhelm quickly learned English. His impish sense of humor surprised me, from a German.

"I thought Germans were the scientific type," I told him.

"Nein, nein," I heard his thought, "Ich bin ein POET."

Oh, that made good sense. Wilhelm became a friend during the months of my seeking a new home. His signal to me of his presence was a flute-like tone in one ear, audible only to me. Once I asked him why his signal was sometimes low and at other times higher, sometimes in the left ear and sometimes in the right. "To get your attention," he said. Well, sure! As if I don't know that! It was the sort of answer my fun-loving dad would have given. And so Wilhelm and I chuckled together.

Wilhelm signaled me with a long flute-tone as I stood in an empty new house, looking it over as a possible new home. I felt that he was telling me that this was the one. Months later things did work out so that I was able to buy that house. It was exactly what I needed "for Louise to live and work in," to quote the hypnotic program I had sent into Universal Mind as a meditation or prayer.

And after I had moved in and felt fairly settled, there came a day when Wilhelm signaled again with a low, tender flute-tone for eight or ten seconds. I felt that he was telling me good-bye and I felt his thought, "Now you can go ahead on your own."

The master that Lanetta (Johnnie), one of the other students, had seen for me was a Chinese face. When she had mentally asked him if he was my master, he had inclined his head affirmatively. He had remained in the background during Wilhelm's period of helping me, but now he came forward more prominently, letting himself be channeled by several persons who were in hypnosis or meditation, always as a wise counselor. I felt that he was a Chinese doctor.

I myself did not "see" him, nor did he signal as Wilhelm had, yet occasionally I felt his presence as a gentle warmth of the heart, almost a physical sense of pervading warmth, and once as a fragrance somewhat like jasmine but lighter. He, too, had a sense of humor, as we discovered during the months following. Yet he maintained the quiet dignity that Lili commented upon: "Whenever I am channeling and you speak to him, Louise, he turns toward you, puts his hands into his sleeves, calls you 'Dear Lady,' and gives a little bow."

Almost a dozen friends have seen him in channeling sessions, many of these not knowing each other; but their descriptions of him have tallied remarkably in the visual sense: "He has a rather small round face. . . ."

This description made me think of an old Chinese sketch of a huge tiger drowsing with its chin on its crossed paws, its eyes closed, while the figure of a man was draped over the tiger's great body, his head resting on the tiger's head, his eyes closed, drowsing—both faces comically similar and both expressing uttermost, blissful contentment. The caption in Chinese characters was translated as, "Two Philosophers Harmonizing Their Minds." I had enjoyed that picture for years and had tried to draw it. The more I came to know Master Ching, the more I felt that he was like one of those philosophers in the picture.

Long after finding the first sketch I came across another with a similar mirthful message and wondered if the same artist had created it. This one was of a Chinese monk walking briskly along, his face lit by a smile, his eyes alert and sparkling—and on his shoulder, firmly balanced, rode an enormous frog, its mouth in a wide grin, its big eyes sparkling—its face a counterpart of that of its human companion. I do not remember that there was a caption for this sketch, but surely it might have been, "Two Philosophers Progressing into Future." As I came to know Master Ching better, I even wondered if he himself had been the artist who had created those sketches!

He accepted the playful name, "Master Ching," which Francie, one of the ladies in our meditation group, gave him because his gentle wisdom reminded her of the quotations from the *I Ching* that Kung Fu, a character in the television series of that name, often repeated.

In the higher sense the descriptions of Master Ching given by friends also tallied: "He is very beautiful—all shining and golden. He is very high," said Lili. I felt profoundly honored that he had accepted me as one of his students, and was enormously pleased when several of my own students reported that "Master Ching came to us during our group session and gave us messages." He came the first time spontaneously to each group or individual. I felt that he was offering his blessing to each and I felt sure he meant that they might call upon him from now on.

When I asked him if I should mention him in my previous book about death, he asked in return, "Will people believe?" Probably most people will not believe, but in these years of widening spiritual awareness I feel that enough people will be open-minded so that I may speak freely about Master Ching, Wilhelm, and other discarnate beings whom we have come to know and consider friends and guides. Many people are already acquainted with the discarnate friends of Ruth Montgomery, Jean Dixon, Jane Roberts, and others who have published books telling of the wisdom received from such friends.

As for the third master, it was Nan, our ESP instructor, who saw him. She said she told him, "You look like Father Time"; and he answered, "Sometimes she (Louise) makes me feel like Father Time." (Now what did he mean by that?!) I have not yet become well-acquainted with him. Maybe he is waiting for me to grow up? Or to lose the trying-not-to-worry, too-much-to-do, time-tired symptoms? Okay, Father Time, I'll keep working at it. I remember that Moses, very reluctantly, began his greatest work when he was eighty years old. . . . I guess if he did, we can, too, we octogenarians.

# We Ask "High, Wise Spiritual Beings" to Assist

People have given various names to these Bright Beings, these spiritual helpers. There are several classes into which they may be grouped, but they are all motivated toward the spiritual guidance and protection of human beings and can be called upon to assist us when we need them.

Many of these are Great Souls who have been human and have garnered much experience in the hard school of the earth-plane. Great historical religious figures head this list: entities like Zarathushtra, Buddha, Moses, Mary, Jesus, Mohammed, Baha'u'llah—to name a few in more-or-less chronological order. There are also the saints and many other wise and saintly ones who have chosen to remain close to the earth-plane after death, sometimes at considerable sacrifice, in order to help the living who are still struggling in the physical life.

Besides these there are many other human souls—healers, scholars, educators, and "millions who, humble and nameless, the straight, hard pathway trod—" (Carruth, 1929) who remain after death close to incarnate human beings, volunteering to stay "down here" this "low" although most no longer need to do so. They teach and instruct and protect.

Among these discarnate helpers are some who have agreed to stay near the earth-plane in order to work out part of their own remaining karma as they assist humanity. Some are less highly evolved than others; sometimes they even disagree among themselves as to how best to help in a certain situation—and they are not infallible. Even so, their vision is frequently clearer than ours and we do well to listen respectfully to their channeled messages, although we need to retain our own wisdom and common sense. Each of them individually is growing, evolving, progressing, as each continues to serve the Light by serving humanity.

These groups of helpers we call guides, teachers, and masters; some people say in ascending order. I often speak of them collectively as "Spiritual Advisors." My own present Spiritual Advisor, Master Ching, is one of those on a high plane. Wilhelm was not so high. These high beings are not mere concepts or names; they are living and real, full of love and wisdom. And we can feel their love and joy when we manage to do good work "for the Light."

All of these spiritual helpers wait for an invitation, which implies openness on the part of the would-be recipient. *They do not push in or invade* the personal privacy or the body or aura of their pupils, disciples, or students, though they *may offer thoughts for consideration.* They themselves—all of these in all these groups—remind us that *they do not command*—that each of us has his or her own conscience and free will. When I invite one of these Bright Beings—for instance, when I call upon Mother Mary to come and help a lost soul who is burdened by guilt; or when I ask Mohammed, the Muslim "Prophet of the Lord," to speak to an arrogant unrepentant Muslim sheik—I see, or hear, or simply feel the responding presence of the High Being. (Examples of these contacts follow.)

It is profitless to debate and question all this and dissect with the analytical part of the mind. This is work that needs to be done from the heart, through the right brain, with humility and faith. It is in this childlike spirit that we meet these Beings of Light and benefit from their wisdom and assistance for ourselves and for the people we wish to help.

Perhaps, when in hypnosis my client sees Mother Mary or Mohammed or Zarathushtra, it is actually a thought-form of the Bright Being that had been sent to them; but even if so, that thoughtform is ensouled by the living wisdom and power of its original, the Great Being, and converses with us. The appearance of the vision to the client, however, may be colored by the client's own ideas about the historical person. Thus, an American may see the vision of Mary or Jesus with brown hair and blue eyes; an Italian might see the vision of Jesus as emaciated and on a cross; and so on.

# Manuel

From my own records I select a few examples of visits by Bright Beings to offer here. The first is from a workshop that my coworker, Mary, and I gave in 1992. We wanted to call and release any earthbound entities that had died in the vicinity of the large hotel in which the workshop was given. The last to be found was a twenty-year-old Spanish soldier who, in a rage at discovering that another soldier had been stealing his girlfriend, had killed the man. To kill a fellow soldier, however, was a military crime punishable by death; and so, after a brief trial, this young soldier was hanged. Knowing his own guilt, knowing that his punishment was justified, knowing that he could not forgive the man who had wronged him nor cease his rage, he felt unworthy of seeking a way to any higher sort of existence, and therefore remained in the primitive, forested area of the death scene.

I asked him the year in which he was condemned and then told him, "Well, Manuel, it is now 1992. For almost three hundred years you have been hanging around—" My own words exploded in my brain! *How could I have said that?!*

Keeping my voice as casual as possible, I went on as if the words had not been said and covered them up with an overlay: "You have been staying around that place—"

But a burst of laughter stopped me. Manuel was laughing—literally laughing "fit to kill" himself! And with enormous relief, I began to laugh with him—as did the audience! When the laughter had moderated somewhat I apologized, but the seriousness of the event had been broken and Manuel could begin to accept my understanding of his anger, his impulsive rage, even the madness leading to the murder. But after he had punished himself, in addition to the inflicted hanging, by "hanging around for three hundred years" in this place, I told him it was time for the situation to change. He needed to ask forgiveness.

"Were you a Catholic, Manuel?" I asked.

"I still am," he replied.

"Then I am asking Mother Mary to please come and speak to you. Tell me when you see her."

The channel said afterward that Mary appeared almost at once, and Manuel knelt down at her feet. We did not hear what he said to her, or whether he said anything at all; but when I asked him to look into her eyes and see what her expression told him, he whispered, with tears, "She loves me."

And so we committed him to the care of Mother Mary and thanked her for coming

## "Z"

This next case is from a session in 1985 in which I was having a friend channel to attempt a remote releasement or depossession of "Z," a young woman whose early education in a far-off culture included the techniques of what we call black magic. She had been friendly with one of my young cousins, and I felt that it was a very unhealthy relationship, that she was trying to control him. She had tried, I felt, to control and manipulate me as well. The Bright Being who came and spoke with us was a human soul staying near the earth-plane by his own volition, to fulfill a "sacred vow."

With my coworker Lili in hypnosis I started out by saying, "I am calling the strongest entity attached to Z. Please come out and speak to me, and tell your name."

A voice answered, "A. A. A.," speaking three Arabic-sounding names distinctly. He said there were four entities in Z, and he said that his function in Z was to protect Z from herself: "She hides from who she is; she keeps not truly to what she is. She is a shadow—she takes on the form of whatever is around. I am here to protect her."

He sounded all right, yet I wanted to check further. "Who is your superior?" I asked him.

"All those whom you call Great—Mohammed, Buddha, the man you call Christ."

"Then, A, I am glad you are in her. What of the other four?"

"She is an inferior product of them. No, they are not always good."

"I was taught that *good* entities do not enter a person. What of you, A?"

"Correct. I am *close*; but you said the *strongest*."

"Yes. And I only said 'attached', not 'in'. My intent is to release these four and free her. But if this is done without her knowledge and consent, is it right for me to do so?"

"You may do so if you want them to come to *you*. Contact *her*. She's a kaleidoscope. It is all right upon her permission."

"Can you tell me more about these four?" I asked

"I could but I am not at liberty."

A called them "banshees." He said it would be all right to contact them through Lili—that there would be no danger to her, since she had given her permission to be the channel—but that there might possibly be danger to me, "because you are connected to the soul of the man she fiddles with." He stated firmly that the only way to protect myself was "*not to call them*—not till there is permission." He said the only right way to reduce the power of these four in Z was "binding chains, send back to her the pain she gives to others; it becomes her own."

A admitted that the gifts Z had given to me tied me to her: "You are the sole link to the man she toys with." He could think of no way to destroy that link but to return her gifts—rose sachet, rose water, etc.—adding, "She looked you in the eyes and touched your hand, and thus bound herself to you. You may give her back that."

"Shall I send back her gifts with a letter? Or call her by phone?"

"Invite her to your house. Put her on your 'turf,' as you Americans say. Leave it an open invitation, and she will come—mainly out of curiosity—with a plea for you to *help her*—and what a surprise she will have." He chuckled mirthlessly "I promise," he went on, "that *if* she comes, I will protect you, although I am attached and bound to her by karmic ties, for gifts received in the past. I am living out my vow."

"All these four do need to be sent away from her: true?"

"She's not ready—she likes them. They make mockery of people. When she comes to you, she'll be ready. That's why an *open* invitation. It will be a constant reminder."

"I do hope to keep the commandment given to me, 'Touch *everyone* you meet with love.' How can I help her and still protect my cousin? I feel sad for her, A."

With sudden intensity A said, "I feel *tired* of her. She desecrates *who* she is and *what* she is and *where* she's from; and if I were not bound by a sacred vow, I would not stay with her." He said that Z "binds everyone she meets to her.

She's a *banshee*—she gathers together, like an octopus [his arms grasped his chest] and snake-like coils around, while she is laughing hysterically."

"How can my cousin be released? At present he doesn't want to be."

"True—but I must go. She is getting into a situation that needs my presence. Good-bye!"

Lili commented afterward, "I felt that the karmic ties had something to do with her grandfather, who had helped A at one time, and in gratitude A made the vow, maybe to help the family. He said he was 'living out his vow.' But he didn't want you to ask more about that! And he left in a great hurry—he was feeling it really urgent to get back to her."

At present, several years later, Z is following a different path and my cousin, no longer so young, seems to be free.

## "S"

A few years after the above session, my coworker Mary, and I decided to see if we could do anything about a prominent military figure whose activities were destabilizing the status of several small countries. My friends and I felt despair at the thought of one more war in this century of conflicts. We had been told to "send love" to the warring factions. It was easier to say than to do. Mary volunteered to channel any obsessing entities who might be in the military man whose arrogance and aggressiveness were so conspicuous.

With Mary in hypnosis I asked first if it was all right for us to work for the man "S" today. Mary's finger said yes. The "yes" finger also rose when I asked if it was all right for us to talk to any obsessing entities in S. Then I requested the presence of S's own High Self, to supervise the session, and asked that Jesus, the Prophet Mohammed, and other

Bright Beings also be with us. With this protection and strong backup, we began.

The first to come when I asked for the strongest entity in S was Sheik "M." He said he found S when S was only five, and entered him at twelve. "I used his own instincts to seek vengeance on those who have hurt mine and me for centuries. He thinks we get vengeance only while we *live*. That is a misconception! We'll go on until all eyes and teeth are restored for all my brothers in the name of Islam, the Holy One. The fire burns just as hot when we pass over.

"There are many opportunities," he continued, "from any who are oppressed, beaten, harmed, as was S. Their hatred opens them to us easily, but only when the body is mature enough to be used. Of course if the children were not so harmed by those around, by those adults in power, we could not use them. If people would learn to take better care of their children so that they become better adults, the world would improve.

"Now you think that I'm 'evil'? A 'dark entity'? No," he went on, "I am a very highly developed, intelligent, proud man, like my brothers; but we cannot allow the score to be broken. Karma will be fulfilled to us."

Mary, the channel, was thinking, as she reported after the session, "Oh, this may go on all day!"

And I, the facilitator, was thinking, "As strong and stubborn an ego as M will not respect or listen to any 'infidel' not of his religion, or especially to any woman. But he would listen to the Prophet, a Bright Being who was once a human, a man of his own religion."

So I said, "I ask the Prophet to speak. Sheik M speaks of oppressions and hate, and I know that there have been many such things suffered by his people. Centuries before you, Prophet of the Lord, there was a master who said, 'Hatred ceases not by hatred at any time. Hatred ceases by love.'

Another master said, 'Love your enemy.' But if there is revenge for 'all eyes and teeth,' will there ever be an end to vengeance? Will the Prophet speak to us?"

With only the briefest pause a voice spoke: "We feel much sorrow for this poor soul and all the others. They are just babes. Our love for them is great. Yes, I believe—I *know*—I *know*—the day is coming when love will overcome hatred. . . . There is always some hatred; the world is a Babel. Babes grow into adults with some harms. The harms will grow less as time goes on.

"Some, like you, Louise, have overcome hatred. As each one overcomes hatred there is a pull to love. The same for this one (Sheik M), who is very close to the *earth*-plane. That love will overcome this one.

"You people on earth need to develop your *own* love and step in when you see no love—not passively! Love is strong! It expresses itself in many, many ways. The motivation must be love. Search the self constantly for the motivation. Love is the *opposite* of hate and the negatives of fear and anxiety. Love is *more than the absence* of negatives like fear and hate. When you have love, you *know* it where your heart is—and there will be peace.

"Now," he finished, "I place my hands on this one's head" (Sheik M's) "and pour into him the love he was denied in his lifetime. I see S as a small child—so hurt—and I pour my love into him. And I ask M in the name of Allah to leave S, and I command him to enter the Light, and from now on to do good, and to bring his brothers with him—for they do love me."

"We also, Mary and I, send our love," I murmured. "Thank you, Prophet of the Lord."

Three children, two brothers and their sister, remained in S. The older lad said his name was Fahid, his age about twelve. They had chosen to go into S when S was eighteen;

"He was *fun, exciting,* boisterous, adventuresome, strong! It's not so exciting now. But the war is exciting. He has things planned."

Fahid said that other entities came and went in S. "This is all, right now [he and his siblings]. When his anger is very bright others are attracted. I'll miss M and his people—they are so beautiful, so proud and sure! They knew what they had to do!"

The children had heard what the Prophet said but didn't understand it. I explained in simpler words that children sometimes get harmed by what the elders teach them, and so on. Fahid seemed less than interested.

"I'd like to go where M went. Soon this will be an empty shell, anyway."

"You mean that S's body may soon die?"

"I feel that it will."

"He is willing to die for Allah," I reminded him.

"He is willing to die for *self,*" corrected the boy. "He doesn't allow *any* force outside of self to dictate to him, not even Allah. M gave strength to what is already there. S has much hatred."

"The Prophet said he was pouring out his love into S."

"Yes, I see it—it's there, but to change him it's too late. He has set his course and must go the distance." He sighed. "Too bad the fun is over."

"Oh, no, you'll be starting a whole new type of life! This is just the beginning," I assured him.

"We'll be happy to go. . . . We are very dirty," he ended.

I suggested that the children "pretend" that all the dirt was on the outside of their garment: "fear, hate, selfishness, lust for power, the excitement of harming others. When all three of you have done this, signify by Mary's 'yes' finger." After a brief pause, Mary's finger rose.

"Wonderful!" I congratulated them. "Now shuck off that

filthy garment and stand clean and clear, strong and beautiful."

"Can we go play in the river?" asked Fahid.

With my permission they joyfully rushed off, to return a few moments later. "We need something to wear." At my suggestion each one thought of the type of garment and the color desired, and found that they were clothed.

"Your thoughts are very strong. Whatever you need you can simply think about, and it will be there for you. Now I ask for a guide to come for these children. Fahid, do you see someone?"

"Yes—someone very pleasant." (smiling) "This is fun! Exciting!"

"Remember, it was not fair of you to go into S's body, nor for M to go into it, either. S's body belongs only to him, as every person's body does. Do you understand?"

The children murmured that they did, and we said goodbye. But the channel said afterward that they were rather flippant, not really understanding what I was saying but wanting to go with M, whom they admired.

I had invited S's Higher Self to be present at this session, and I now addressed it: "Higher Mind of S, I know that you are glad that this obstruction to your work is removed. Do you have a message for S or for us?"

"Continue to pray for him. He has much pain to face. Pray that he will *turn his face to Allah*. His ego is strong; hate from childhood has filled him and has made *so much strength* that when he is turned to Allah—how do your Scriptures say it?—'The last shall be first.' He has a great destiny before him. His spirit, his soul, will learn much (on the earth). None of it is wasted. We must remember, we are all teachers for one another. So just pray for him to put himself in the arms of Allah."

"You say he has much pain to face. Can we mitigate the pain for him?" I asked.

"Oh, the pain is necessary; it is the pain of growth. He will cry many tears for a long, long time—but it is necessary, it is good. He hasn't cried tears for so long that the pain will be welcomed. It will be like taking the plug off a geyser: what relief!"

I asked if there was anything else we could do for S today and the Higher Mind said, "Nothing today. You have done well."

I thanked him for his presence and his message and for his instructions to us, then asked Mary what else she saw.

She sighed deeply. "I just see him in the background. He will cave in upon himself from that vacuum. The strength of M filled him up halfway. Now that M is gone, he has no choice—but to turn—to Allah."

"The pain is the pain of the vacuum?"

"Yes . . . If you and I are brave enough, we will not castigate him but will speak of him as another child of God."

The Bright Beings in this case are the Prophet Mohammed and the Higher Mind of S, the military official. Both are concerned—not with the safety of S's body nor with the "success" of his military schemes, not even with shielding him from the pains of his karma and his growing—but only with his *spiritual* experience and maturation.

## Our Higher Minds

Another class of high beings is that of our own human Higher Selves. The Higher Self or Higher Mind of almost all persons, when contacted in hypnosis, is found to be a worthy inhabitant of the Higher Dimension—the dimension of wisdom, insight, power, beauty, love, and peace. (An example has just been given in the previous case.) I have called this Higher Self the Higher Mind or Superconscious Mind. Others have called it the Spirit, the Inner Self Helper (the ISH), the Divine Spark, the Inner Mind, the Self or Soul (capitalized), or "That of God within," as the Quakers say.

It is not ordinarily tangible on the conscious level. Most of us have had conscious awareness of the Soul only in rare moments of ecstasy, in deep prayer, or in meditation. Yet in each person, no matter how soiled and spoiled the earthly self may appear, there is this center of purity, wisdom, and light. Like all things, it is in the process of evolving, growing, progressing; but it is the shining high reality of each lower self—that is, of each person's conscious personality. In meditation or through the state of hypnosis we can call the Higher Mind of a person and talk with it, receiving its input regrading the deep psychospiritual state of the lower self and enlisting its cooperation in helping to strengthen, cleanse, and protect the lower self as it struggles in the mud and dust of earth-plane experiences.

A person's Higher Self can see down into the present the problems and weaknesses, as well as the unrecognized strengths and beauties of the person, and can also see back into the childhood and infancy of the present life and into the events and relationships of past lives, and even into the future a certain distance. Much wisdom and strength comes from a person's Higher Self. For this reason it has been called one of the person's Spiritual Advisors, different from a guardian angel or a guide but with the person's spiritual welfare equally at heart.

I have found a very few exceptional cases of a Higher Mind that seemed to be not much higher than the client's conscious level. It might have been that the usual techniques of my hypnotic methods did not manage to contact the true

Higher Self of these few clients, or it may be that the Higher Mind or Soul was noticeably less evolved than normal in these several persons. The Spiritual Advisors who came when I asked for them also seemed to be more earthy than truly spiritual. At present I am still uncertain as to the causes in these cases. Past lives of these clients were abnormal, a few bordering on the psychopathic, with little or no moral sense or conscience, as if the Soul were spiritually incomplete.

## Contacting our Higher Self

Carroll, a psychic lady from Washington state, gave a workshop on the extrasensory abilities, and as an experiential exercise at the end of the workshop she told us how to access our own Higher Minds.

"Go into meditation first," she told us, "and when you have centered yourself, tell yourself that you wish to ascend into the superconscious level and communicate with your Higher Self. Ask your Higher Self for a message, and then wait and listen. If you do not receive a message during your period of meditation in the High Realm, the message will come to you as you come back toward ordinary awareness or even later. It will come as one or two or three words—not more than one sentence."

Carroll led us into meditation, invited our Higher Minds to contact our lower minds on the conscious level, and then directed us to wait and listen in silence.

I received nothing at all—and really was not surprised, for my own talents do not run to the psychic. But I still waited.

On the gentle descent back to normal consciousness, however, I got a clear perception of a few words, "Keep a-pluggin', keep a-pluggin'."

Was *that* my message?! Did my Higher Self have to tell me to do *that?* What else had I been doing for the last fifty years and more? Emotionally I really went down for two or three days afterward.

Then I decided at home to try again. Maybe the second attempt would give a clearer, better message. I repeated the meditative preparation, "inviting my soul," as Walt Whitman would say. I asked for a message. And again I waited. This time the words came, "Keep on working. Keep on working." Hm. Well, at least that didn't make me feel like an old broken-down horse, an old "plug" that was just plugging along, one foot after another. Sometimes I *had* felt like that.

After a few more days I began to think, childishly, "Well, they say the third time is the charm. I'll try it once more." So again I ascended to the Higher level in hypnomeditation, asked for a message (I wanted a nicer one), and waited. Again nothing until I was ready to return to normal consciousness, and then—with a clear tincture of amusement, a chuckle from my Higher Self, came the words, "Keep a-chuggin'; keep a-chuggin'." And this time there was an aura of gentle kidding, of kindly teasing that reminded me that the chuggin' didn't have to be heavy and plodding—it could be cheerful and light-hearted.

So I accepted *that,* realizing that I had been given definite instructions to keep on for a good while without thought of retirement until more work had been accomplished.

A symbolic message in hypnosis had been given to me in 1980 that I would continue working for twenty years more until I am eighty-eight. At that age, in that dreamlike symbolic journey, I would come out on the crest of a long sunbathed hill among juniper and pinion trees, with sagebrush and wildflowers. Standing and looking west over a magnificent view of wild canyons and deserts to the far mountains, I would tell myself, "I'll stop here. Some of the others will go on, but my life work is done." And there was a feeling of quiet completion and peace.

I did not have to accept that progression into the future as a pattern of the next twenty years, but I chose to do so. The future is not fixed; it depends on our decisions and actions in the present. I accept the instruction given me in the first contact with my Higher Mind and I keep a-chuggin' more or less faithfully, and plan to continue for a few more years. Then I can retire at eighty-eight—unless I change my mind first, and leave this plane; or re-evaluate then and stay around to work or play still longer. I believe that I have freedom of choice.

Another contact with my Higher Self in meditation resulted in the poem on the next page.

## Nonhuman Servants of the Light

A whole kingdom of invisible beings, sometimes called the Angelic Kingdom, is composed of those that have been called angels, archangels, cherubim, seraphim, and so on.

In the Hindu religion the angels would be called devas, "Shining Ones." These spiritual beings are genderless, neither male nor female, although for convenience we may say "he" or "she," "god" or "goddess," according to the quality of the attributes each manifests.

I like the story of the young Hindu disciple who asked his master how many gods there were. "Thirty-three thousand, three hundred and thirty-three," replied the old man promptly.

"Oh, yes, I know; but how many Great Gods are there?"

"Thirty-three," said the master.

"Yes, the Thirty-three. But how many *really great?*"

## A WORD OF WISDOM

A Word of Wisdom
came to me once
with the whisper of a chuckle
that I did not understand.

I waited for that Word
but I thought in puzzlement
a Word of Wisdom ought to be
a Word of sober weight
a serious Word, a solemn Word
Wouldn't you agree?

And yet, there was a chuckle
yes, an unmistakable small grin
about the feeling that it brought
and it drew near to me
and nearer, nearer yet . . .
Then it was here!
And the Word of Wisdom was,
"Some do,
and some don't."

"Do what?" I asked.
"Oh, anything," the Answer smiled,
"just anything."

And do you know—
the Word was right!

(L.I.F. 11-16-71)

"Three—the three greatest."

"Yes—the Trinity. But which of these?"

"One and a half," said the sage. [I believe the "half" is what we human beings feel as "evil"; it is less than *one*.]

The disciple paused, then persisted, "Master, I need to know how many gods there are in the deepest, final sense."

And the old man said softly, "Son, there is One, only One."

"Then what are these thirty-three thousand, three hundred and thirty-three?"

"They are all God's attributes and qualities," said the master. "Each represents a part of God."

The more we learn about the invisible realms, the more we learn that there is still much more to be learned about their invisible populations. Instead of the over-simple concept of the Invisible World as merely God, angels, and demons, we who are in the work of Releasement and Rescue begin to encounter discarnate beings of various other types. And we begin to listen to the discarnates with whom we converse during these sessions, for *they often instruct us.*

## Dan

An example came during the first session with a young man, "Dan," who was alcoholic and who had been on drugs previously. He called his spiritual guide "Lucy," short for "Lucy in the Sky with Diamonds" (the title of a Beatle's song, referring to LSD). I was not sure at first that Lucy was really a true type of spiritual advisor but she convinced me by her answers to my questions (which I tried to make as tactful as possible).

After releasing several undesirable entities from Dan I contacted one more entity in his head. This entity told me that he was there to help Dan—a story that many entities tell. This one said that he was not human, was genderless, and had come into Dan's brain temporarily to try to restore the damaged parts to healthy condition, the places harmed by alcohol. He said that Dan knew of his presence and had nicknamed him "Blackie Carbon," referring to the advertisements about a certain product used to eliminate the carbon buildup in car cylinders. Lucy agreed that Blackie was really a help to Dan, not a hindrance as is usual with entities inside. Therefore I let Blackie remain. Categorizing himself, he said he was a "technician."

Just before I counted Dan back up to normal awareness, Lucy told me, "Louise, now that you have met Blackie, he is acquainted with you and is willing for you to call him to help with other people that you feel may need his assistance." It touched me to have Blackie volunteer to be a coworker with me. I gladly accepted his offer and have called upon him a good many times (after explaining about him to my human clients and asking their permission). I have also asked Blackie to help me (myself) at times. I have felt that his work is mostly with repairing the physical aspects of the body rather than with the psychospiritual aspects. A feeling of rapport, of warm friendliness, has grown up between Blackie and me, an understanding that both of us (along with innumerable other beings both incarnate and discarnate) are servants of the Light.

## Formless High Spiritual Powers

For a description of a very high nonhuman spiritual being I might quote from the writings of any of the mystics of the centuries past and present, but the one I choose to include here is selected for its very simplicity and for the fact that this Presence came when the therapist's own wisdom failed to suffice and she called for assistance. The author of *The Presence of the Light* (1994), Annabel Chaplin, writes of a session in which she was trying to think of a way to comfort and heal a deep childhood trauma that was corroding her adult client:

"Inwardly I asked for help. In a flash the answer came: Heal the past. . . . The thoughts, the impressions, were coming quickly, and at the same moment I became aware of a pink glow enveloping a beautiful, overpowering female Presence. . . . I knew that the Presence was going to help us. . . . [I felt] at that moment the universality of all mothers. . . . I spoke with great difficulty as the power of the mother-image overwhelmed me. . . . I realized that the important thing to remember was the almost untranslatable feeling of love that came from the Archetypal Mother—a love that filled the whole room with the power of its beauty; a love for this little boy . . . and for all children in emotional distress. And, yes, forgiveness. We must remember to include the real mother. Even on the other side of life, she yearns for forgiveness. . . .

"The unexpected appearance of the angelic being of Mother Love had a profound effect on me. . . . In that extraordinary session she had shown us how to repair the damage done by unknowing, and often cruel, mothers. . . . "On a personal level, I felt that I had had a transfusion of the Mother Love, which nurtured and healed my old feelings of childhood neglect and rejection. More strangely, from that time on, I felt connected with others needing the power of Mother Love to heal the sorrow of abuse by their mothers.

"But most importantly, a sense of the presence of the Angelic Being of Love never left me, a connectedness that seems to be strengthened as time goes on."

Religious persons would probably identify the Angelic Being of Love with a figure in their religion, such as the Virgin Mary or Kwan Yin, but those would be limiting concepts. The great "Goddess of Universal Compassion," as one author calls it, includes the mother-instinct of birds, reptiles, and other creatures as well.

When paleontologists discovered a nest of dinosaur eggs over which the skeleton of the mother dinosaur was crouched, her legs embracing the circle of eggs beneath her dead body, they were astonished at this sign of mother-concern and protectiveness in an animal considered so primitive. Poets have written of mother-instincts in birds and four-legged animals, but many biologists have spoken of the signs of parental protectiveness of the young as "only instincts"—not true emotions such as human beings have. (There goes human arrogance again.)

When biologists or bio-psychologists begin to study the evolution of the psychospiritual aspect of animals, a new science will emerge, one which may prove to be the cradle for a still higher science—that of studying the formless archetypical powers and presences, which at present are spoken of only in terms such as Chaplin uses above, or by names of goddesses (if the presence "feels" feminine) or of gods (if the power or presence seems masculine).

## Visible/Invisible; Dark/Bright

I studied zoology and botany for a good many years in colleges, have been interested in geology and astronomy informally for a long time, and have found all these fields multifaceted and incredibly complex. I have been wondering if the invisible worlds are not just as complex and wonderful—wonder-filled—as the visible physical worlds are. Nature is immense and often surprises us. The Intelligence that created Nature must be far greater than our limited human intelligence can grasp. And as this enormous complexity applies to the form-aspects, so it may also apply to the invisible and psychospiritual aspects of creation.

We need to remember clearly that the negative aspects of the psychospiritual worlds are never as strong as the positive aspects, the dark forces never ultimately as strong as the bright powers; and that even though there may be a delay, the bright forces, *when called upon,* will overcome the dark forces. Therefore, even if one cannot at present "believe in" the bright forces or their power, it is wise for one to accept this axiom as a temporary belief and go ahead and *call* upon the Bright Beings for assistance when assaulted or tempted by dark forces.

Bright Beings are too high to feel humiliated by anyone's disbelief in them, and they are too high to "punish" a person for feeling uncomfortable about asking for their help. Their attitude is one of understanding and sympathy toward human beings who are so arrogant while yet so unaware and relatively powerless. Much of the power we utilize is not our human power; it comes from either dark or bright forces; the choice is ours.

*chapter 7*

# NONHUMAN ENTITIES

Not infrequently—perhaps once in every ten or twelve clients—as I check on the nature of the parasitic entities within them, I discover that I am contacting one that claims never to have been human. The question, "Have you ever had a human physical body of your very own?" is the test that Baldwin suggests we use to differentiate. When the answer is a simple "no" (usually a finger answer), I accept that answer. If the answer is something like, "Yes, this one," more questioning may bring out that the entity is not an alter personality or a splinter of the client, but a nonhuman spirit trying to pretend that it owns the client's body.

Of the various types of nonhuman entities listed by Baldwin in his comprehensive work (see Bibliography) I list here only the ones that I have personally encountered in one or more clients. Remember that during a releasement session neither the client nor I know what is going to be found nor what type of entity may be contacted, and the classification of the entity is up to me to decide, after considering the information. The entities do not come conveniently labeled already! Therefore it is possible that I have mislabeled some of the following cases.

## Types of Nonhuman Obsessing Entities

These seem to fall into two main categories: those that are individual beings, and those that are created by humans. The latter would seem not to be "entities," perhaps, but the techniques useful in dealing with them are almost identical to those used with *bona fide* living entities. Therefore I list some of them here, although a few I shall leave for a later chapter. The first four types here are created by human beings.

1. *Thought-forms,* created on the mental plane by the thoughts of people. When strong, they come to have a life of their own, but have no "personality" or "soul" except from the original thought. They can think and speak, within limitations; they have no concept of right or wrong and their only goal is to follow the instructions of the person(s) who created them. More will be said about them below.

2. *Emotion-forms* or "feeling-forms" (a suggested term), similar to thought-forms but based on emotions, similar to personified splinter-portions of a person's own character or that of another person. They give their names as "Fear," "Anger," "Pain," or even "Death." Nearly all are undesirable negative elements, although a hypnotist could probably also call out elements such as "Honesty," "Courage," or "Wisdom." Only the negative ones cause trouble. I talk to all these as simply as if each were a living being with understanding.

3. *Vows,* and spells sworn or invoked in the past. Some may be ancient, from past lives of long ago. These come to have an enduring life of their own, like thought-forms, whether positive or negative—although even the "positive" ones have negative aspects, such as a desire to control, to possess, or to overprotect. Perhaps understandable, even appropriate at one time, such loving or protective vows come to be prisons deep in the subconsciousness as lifetimes pass.

4. Animal-like *"false protectors"* (Baldwin's term), snarling, growling, threatening. Some (or all?) of these may be thought-forms. Such entities present themselves as protectors of the host. I have not encountered animal guides of the shamanic types as invading, obsessing entities. Helpful beings do not invade.

5. In a very few instances I have encountered an *animal soul* as an obsessing entity—a wolf in one case, a lamb in another, the latter the cause of a terrible fear of wolves in the client.

6. *Nature spirits,* including those described by various religions: spirits of trees, of rocks, of clouds, and so on. I have not found many of these as yet, but they appear to include the "little people" described over the centuries by many persons who have astral vision as elves, fairies, gnomes, trolls, etc.

7. *"Spiritual viruses"* or "concordant elements" which seem to be the same as what Baldwin calls "group mind" or "group family influence." Such entities we have encountered several times. A passive infectious agent on the psychospiritual level, such an entity can spread throughout a family down the generations, like a curse, or spread

outward to other persons, infecting them. These tell us that they can be rendered dormant but not killed.

8. *"Elementals"* and *"legions."* Invisible, nonphysical beings that are intellectually rather dull. They may or may not have names. Not intrinsically evil, still they are usually on the dark side and need to be treated like recalcitrant children, kindly but very firmly. There seems to be some overlap between these entities and minor demonic ones, at least in my attempts to classify.

9. *Demonic beings,* definitely on the dark side. Some claim to be followers of a more powerful dark force such as Satan. The minor ones may say they have no name. These are relatively weak although they may try to present at first a bombastic threatening façade. Strong dark entities, however, are vicious, intelligent, and sly with a profound hatred and contempt for human beings. They may cause the client to convulse or become violent as they try to push the obsessive stage into complete possession. (Discussion of these is in the next chapter.)

10. *Extraterrestrial beings.* To date I have encountered only a moderate number of these entities who claim to have come from some other planetary system; but other therapists have contacted more. Some are entities which—*not* invading human beings—offer counsel and advice to the human race. The ones we have dealt with are the lower types, the invaders, the manipulators, or else the merely curious.

The following report of a brief releasement for a young man will serve as an introduction to nonhuman entities.

## Cody

This young man, "Cody," said he had had a drinking problem and had had rages and irrational behavior starting at the age of twelve. His finger movements said there was an entity obsessing him. When called out, the entity, expressing itself through the client, began to snarl and hiss, showing its teeth. It said its name was "Casterlai," hissing the name through its teeth and making the client's body quiver tensely all over.

I placed my hand on the client's chest and said, "Be calm . . . that's good," as the body gradually relaxed somewhat.

Casterlai said he had entered the client when Cody was six but became more "interested" in him when the boy was twelve.

"Have you ever been human?"

"No."

"Are you of the dark side?"

"What do you think?!" he said sarcastically.

"I ask the Bright Beings to place a net of light around you—the warmth is all around you. Can you feel it? Yes? And you can feel my hand as I place it on Cody's arm, and you know that I care about you. Isn't having someone care about you better than your being lonely?" "Yes," he murmured.

"I think you don't want to be lonely." "No," he said, his bombast gone.

He said he had not been "created" by anyone; that he was not "an individual being"; and that he was not "a spirit of darkness." When told to look deep inside himself into the core of himself he found *cold*; told to look into the midst of the cold, he lay with eyes open, passive, not answering.

I went on, "There is *warmth* in the very core of you. Turn away from the darkness and the cold. Feel the warmth—feel the warmth of the Bright Ones. Open your heart to their light and warmth. Do you feel it? Look into the eyes of the Bright Beings; see the expression in their eyes. Do you see anger? Do you see hate?"

"No," he said.

"Do you see kindness, gentleness?"

"Yes."

"Do you think they would turn you away if you went to them?"

"No."

"Bright Ones," I addressed them, "take this tired being to his own appropriate place where he can rest and change silently, miraculously, into a new being through your energy and light. Casterlai, hold out your hand to the Shining Ones. You have made a decision to turn to the light and to gentleness. . . . Cody, what do you see?"

There was a pause. When I asked if Casterlai and the Bright Beings had gone, Cody said "Yes."

I think of these nonhuman entities usually as more or less male, although they are actually genderless; and from old habit I tend to think of them as being more or less humanoid in form, although clients describing them, or the entities describing themselves, often use terms like "shapeless," "like a gray blob," and so on. I speak of their "heart" and their "hand" and occasionally an entity may correct me: "I have no heart; I don't have hands." So I change my wording to "in the very core of yourself," "reach out," and then I wait until after the client returns to full consciousness and listen to what the client has seen: "The entity was like an amoeba and stretched out a prong of itself. . . ."

I suppose Casterlai is to be classified with emotion-forms, not "created" as a thought-form, not "an individual being," and not a spirit of darkness, a demonic type, but more like a personification of the helpless rage of a child covering that child's deep feeling of *coldness,* of being unloved.

A second entity, a human female, was also found in Cody. After assisting her into the Light, I began to count Cody back to normal consciousness. He was humming softly. He thought it was himself singing, but I wondered if it were not also Casterlai or poor "Betty" singing at last. As we see, both human and nonhuman entities can be present, obsessing the same client.

## Thought-forms, Including Emotion-forms

*Thought* is extremely strong. "Thoughts are *things,*" agree many sources, and repeated *thinking* can produce reality—swiftly in the invisible realms, more gradually and slowly but nonetheless surely on this side of death.

The combined thoughts and concepts of many persons over the centuries have created many powerful thought-forms which have been represented both visually, in artistic portraits and sculptured images, and in mental/verbal stereo-types. Some are tremendously powerful because of having been accepted beliefs for ages by myriads of people and can be either noble or terrible, wicked or good. The good and noble ones may become visible at times to earnest persons as visions. The evil or terrible ones may influence human beings as nightmares, hound them as oppressive fears, angers, etc., or invade as obsessing entities.

The thoughts of individuals also create thought-forms, which are mostly evanescent, but when deliberately cre-ated by one or more persons in rituals and sent out to perform a stated purpose will contain the power of the creators' concentrated thoughts, desires, and directions. Both black and white magic exist. These thought-forms come to have a life of their own but are limited. They usually feel that they have no free will and no goal except to fulfill their instructions, with no concept of good or evil. They can think in a limited way and can speak.

## Created Thought-forms

The thought-forms I encounter when performing release-ments are usually of a negative nature. A number have turned out to be the creations of human individuals, including teenagers, using ancient rituals of magic from old books now being republished. Some of these people started out with white magic, which aims to do good; but, tempted by the feeling of power, they went on into "gray magic" (using the power for selfish purposes) and then into "black magic" (using the power to control, manipulate, and even harm other people and animals). I call and talk to these thought-forms almost exactly as I do to trapped earthbound psyches, but instead of using the idea of *love* to soften resistance, the idea of *happiness* is often the key for a nonhuman entity.

### Jock-1

"Jock-1" was a highly talented and intelligent young man, unemployed at the time. He had had a number of streaks of bad luck and felt that negative forces had been directed toward him, starting two years previously when he had been holding a child in his arms, and was meditating to cure the child's fever. The child's father had come home, struck his wife for permitting Jock to hold the child, and ordered her, "Never let him touch him!"

In hypnosis he responded quickly to my call for the strongest entity in him to emerge. The entity said his name was Mikedor; that he had never had a body of his own and had entered Jock "to destroy him."

"Are you energy 'conjured up' by a black magician?"

"I just *am*. I was created by a person to destroy this one."

"Why did this person want to destroy Jock?"

"I do not know. The source from which I came sent me; my purpose was to disrupt and destroy this one's mind and body."

"Are you happy, doing this task?"

There was a little pause. "No."

"It seems to me it was a poor bargain, for you to be controlled, to have no freedom, no pleasure."

"It was not a 'bargain'. I have no will of my own."

"Mikedor, I'll explain. There are forces of destruction and also forces of growth, positive forces. You *do* have a will of your own. You *can* be happy. I am calling some Bright entities. Now all you have to do is to turn toward them; just turn around so that their light shines on your face, that's all. You have the choice whether you go down to the darkness forever—and never bother any living creature—or turn to the Light. I'll count slowly to three while you think and make your choice: one, two, three. . . . What did you decide?"

"To go forward—toward the longings—to move into the Light."

When a moment like this comes I feel profoundly moved. There is nothing shallow nor false about such moments. I also feel profoundly relieved. Rarely has an entity made the opposite decision but the pause when things hang in the balance is a breathless one.

I suggested now to Mikedor, "Why don't you go toward the Bright Beings and incline your head before them? Now don't you feel happiness? Look up into their faces and tell me what their expressions are."

"Open and loving."

"Did you ever see anyone look at you lovingly before?"

"No one has *ever* looked at me before."

As he said this I felt the loneliness of such an existence. "Mikedor, the path is not a short one. If you are willing to go to the Place of Learning, hold out your hand to one of the Bright Beings." There was a pause. "You have never been allowed to make decisions until now? All right, are you ready to go into the Light?"

Again he answered affirmatively; and Jock saw that he went with the Bright Beings, going away "toward the longings."


## The Energy of Vows, Curses, and Spells—Nonhuman, "Nonentities"

These influences, sometimes personified and sometimes not, may continue to affect people from one generation to another, following either the physical lineage, as in one example given below, or following the karmic lineage from one life of a soul through succeeding lives. Almost always the ones we have encountered have been negative even if originally begun from "love" or "protection"—these turning out to be much more on the order of wanting to control or to possess the "loved" one than representative of clean unselfish tenderness.

Sometimes the vow affects the life course, not only of the victim of a curse, but also of the one who made the vow, as below. Sometimes the vow or curse is encased, so to speak, in a shell of strong intent and thought, and sent out away from its creator as a separated entity directed toward the person to be influenced. The vows or curses in the latter instance are more like thought-forms. There seems to be considerable overlap in the types of conditions and the kinds of obsessing or harassing influences.

## Jock-2

An example of a strong vow is that of the Persian entity Baltar whom I discovered next in "Jock." Baltar spoke of the first entity (who had told me, "I was created by a person to destroy this one,") saying, "I am different from that other one, for he never *was,* and I *have been.* My mind is upon this one. He did destroy me at one time. I have vowed to destroy him. My vow shall not be broken."

Then he recited a long tale of political intrigue. "This damned one before you (the client) was my brother. I sought to control him and make him subservient. I knew more—I had more power—yet I could not subjugate him. The more I tried, the weaker I became. He *allowed* me to waste my time and efforts, and when I was weakest, he disrupted my mind. . . . It is true, I have incarnated numerous times. I have not forgotten. I had great power!"

"Baltar, your sin was a large one. Controlling anyone is a sin of arrogance and egotism. You had chosen the Left-hand Path of evil. What of this one?"

"He was on the Right-hand Path *until* he disrupted me."

"Baltar, those who try to control others are called manipulators, deluders, or destroyers. You are a destroyer. But this is an era of change. Will you change, like Mikedor?"

"You must not speak to me this way. I have a purpose.

It is my purpose to destroy. He did to me what I told you and I have followed him to destroy him. He no longer wished to fight. He had anguish for what had occurred. He would not use his power. He mocked my power—"

"No, he didn't. He merely defended himself against your power. . . . I am going to call the Bright Beings that I called before. Which Great Being was in the world when you and your brother fought?"

"Zarathushtra."

"I ask you to come, Zarathushtra, to look upon this soul of hatred and anger. Baltar, I ask you to look at Zarathustra."

Baltar turned his head and muttered, "I cannot look. I have separated myself from whence I came."

"Not forever! You came from the holy Fire of Ahura-Mazda. If the Spark grows dim, we simply approach it to the Light again, to the Great Fire," I responded, using the terms and images of Baltar's Persian religion. The vision of Zarathushtra, the Bright Being, still held him.

"I shall go—I must go to the Light—to the area above me. . . . *My oath is upon this:* For all the wrong that I have done, I shall bring good to this one, clarity to him. I will bring clarity to him that will surround him. You are right. All you have said is right." Gone were his anger, vengefulness, and pride.

"I am so happy for you, Baltar. Just do not restrict him in your actions to do him good. Before you go, if you see anything in his body that needs to be remedied, will you do that?"

"It is not I, nor my actions nor will, that cause the lung problem. It is the presence of my being that brings great sadness to him."

"But great happiness for your freedom now. You are free, and he is free. I send you with our blessings."

Afterward I found myself smiling: Baltar could not help making *another vow!*

## Jock-3

At the same session for Jock, after neutralizing Baltar's old vow and releasing that formerly embittered human soul, I found a third entity. It said, "I have no name and no form. I never had a human body of my own. I come from the thoughts, actions, and will of others."

"Are you a thought-form?" I asked.

"I do not know this. I *am*. I am here because I am drawn here. It is my destination."

"Who draws you?"

"Many individuals; by their will they draw me together. My purpose is to draw away the will of this one, to minimize his efforts, and return his will to those who sent me."

"Do you have any sense of right and wrong?"

"No, it is but to fulfill. I am the link between him and them. I have no desire; I wish him no harm; I am but a conveyer. My 'personality' is that from whence I came."

"I think I understand. If those from whence you came are dark, you are dark, too."

"I am not dark nor light. I do not feel either good or bad. When I shall have fulfilled my orders—when the will of this one dissolves—I return to them to be replenished."

"This is a time for changes: changes of purpose, of instructions. You sound something like a robot. . . . I call the technician Blackie: Blackie, will you come, please? As a technician you know how to clear away obstructions so that the 'points' are clean, the 'circuits' open. What words do I need to use to deal with this entity?"

Blackie answered, through Jock's voice, "Return to your masters."

I hesitated. "Wouldn't that be returning their force to them?"

"They are weakened already. They receive a weakened form. They are free to 'conjure' again—nothing can stop that. 'Return to sender,' like a letter that is refused. This impulse is very weakened and dissipated. To return it will not strengthen or weaken them."

I thanked Blackie the technician for his suggestions and insight, feeling glad that I had thought to call him. I sent the "impulse" back to its creators, without its having "dissolved the will" of Jock, and was glad to know that Jock was free from such an invader, weakened though it was.

## Lili

The next example is similar in some respects to the previous one. "Lili," one of my students and also a friend and coworker, had been feeling exhausted. She had a suspicion that dark forces had been directed at her, oppressing her. In fifteen or twenty minutes, this was part of what was received in hypnosis:

Lili said, "I see a man—a male form—right there. Right *here*. He's hovering closer."

When I asked the form's name, Lili's head moved negatively.

"What do you want us to call you?" No answer. "Why are you here?" Lili's arms jerked and her face grimaced.

Finally the entity spoke. "I came to do what I was told to do."

There was considerably more conversation, much resistance and stubbornness on the part of the entity, who was strong, convulsing parts of Lili's body and making her features twist and grimace.

Finally I used a technique I had heard about in an ESP workshop. I clapped my hands loudly right by Lili's ears and shouted, "COME OUT OF HER! COME OUT RIGHT NOW!" Her twitchings and grimaces grew somewhat less.

"I will not go," stated the entity.

"I ask the Christ Spirit and the Enlightened One to please come."

"I will not go."

"Entity, I think you were told you have no free will. That is not true; you do have free will. I can prove it to you. . . . Tell me, have you ever been happy?"

The features twisted sarcastically. "Happiness is only a delusion. There is no such thing."

"Oh, haven't you ever seen little children or young animals just running and jumping and playing for the sheer joy of it? Innocent joyfulness—that's happiness."

He sneered.

"Wouldn't you like to find out what it feels like, a little bit? I can tell you how."

He made a face, but his grunt seemed to be only a pretended refusal.

"It is easy. All you have to do is to turn around. Simply turn around from the darkness and face the Bright Beings and feel the warmth in your face. That's all. It's so easy."

He hesitated. His face changed; a tiny smile tried to come but was quickly suppressed. (The influence of the Bright Beings was reaching him, softening him.)

"See? Didn't you feel a little sparkle of happiness?"

"Mmmm . . ." He seemed to be trying to remain hard and obstinate.

"Would you like to feel a little bit more happiness? I can tell you how. . . ."

He thought for a moment. "We-ell, . . ." plainly wavering.

"What you do is to take a step toward the Beings of Light, one little step. You are already turned toward them. Now if you take one little step . . ."

He tried to control the smile that was growing larger. "M'hm." (The influence of the Christ Spirit and the Buddha were softening him still more.)

"See, you did choose to turn around. And you did choose to step toward the Lights. Do you want still more happiness?"

He was beginning to succumb more willingly, though still trying to maintain his obdurate stance. At my suggestion he took one more step—then another—then he bowed his head to the Bright Ones, a genuine little smile on his lips now.

"Now look up into their eyes. What do you see in them?"

There was a very short hesitation—then a soft, incredulous smile. "Love," he whispered.

"Yes. And—if you want to—you may go with them and they will take you to your own appropriate place where you can begin a new existence! You do have a choice—"

Almost interrupting, he said, "I will go."

I reminded him that he had the old negative instructions to unlearn, to undo; "but your face will be in the light and you will find increasing happiness as you learn the new ways."

He nodded, his face luminous.

I really did not know what to do with him from this point, so I told him good-bye and committed him to the Beings of Light.

As after a good many other sessions of this nature, there was a sense of awe and reverence remaining in the room afterward. I could not help thinking of the verse, "There is more rejoicing in heaven over one sinner who repenteth—" Later another quotation came to my mind, this one from Buddha: "Never in the world does hatred cease by hatred; hatred ceases by love."

## False Protector

Another example of a negative thought-form is that of an entity which was channeled through Lili with the permission of a young woman whose mother believed the daughter had an entity within her. Although the young lady herself was more than doubtful, she gave her permission for us to release any that we might find. Here is a condensation of part of the session.

"I am calling the strongest entity in 'Winnie F.' She has given permission for you to come, and Lili has given permission for you to speak through her mouth and vocal cords. Won't you tell us your name?"

While I was speaking Lili's face began to change into an expression of a snarl, with lips drawn back over her teeth. A snarl was the only answer to the request for a name. I chuckled.

"That's not a very nice name."

A sort of growl was the only reply. I laughed.

"Is that your real name?" I teased. "How about if I call you 'Snorp'?"

The entity replied, "Growl—growl—growl!" These sounds were a sort of cross between a dog's growl and a cat's hiss: a vocalized hiss, loud and harsh.

"Now Snorp, why don't you calm down and talk to me properly. Were you ever human?"

More growls and snarls.

"You can talk English if you want to. I bet you were never human, were you, Snorp? Put your thoughts into Lili's mind . . . she will speak them for you. . . ." (No answer except more growls.)

"Why don't you talk to me? Come on—you *can* speak English. You know you can." (The reason I felt so certain is that thoughts in any language, or none at all, are received by the mind of the channel, translated into English, and the channel speaks them aloud. Snorp could *think* if he could *growl*.)

Louder roars were the only reply.

"I think you were created by someone, weren't you? Is that right?"

A softer growl seemed to agree with my statement. From then on I asked Lili to use finger movements, and through the fingers we got that Snorp had not been created by a man. There was a hesitation when asked if he had been created by a woman, with his head sideways as if thinking. He had not been created by a child. But yes, he had been created by "a person in a woman's body but whose soul is a child-soul." (I had in mind a certain woman when I posed the question in these words.)

When the fingers said "yes," Snorp gave a weird, high-pitched little cry that startled me. I do not know what it signified.

"Thank you for answering, Snorp." With a few more questions I tied down that the creator of Snorp was indeed that woman I had suspected.

"Why did she create you, Snorp? Tell me, WHY did she create you?"

In a tight, strained voice the entity said, "For protection."

"Protection? For whom?"

"Winnie."

"Protection from what?"

"I never knew."

"Is that all you are to do?"

"M'hm."

There followed a conversation in which Snorp revealed very little knowledge and even less logic. Occasionally he relapsed into growls again. At last, gently but emphatically I said, "Snorp, it seems to me your characteristics are dark ones like anger, jealousy, malice, and hostility. Don't you agree?"

This time he really roared! I laughed aloud at him.

"WHY did the woman create you and *say* it was for 'protection'? What is she trying to achieve?"

The answer held no logic. "Snorp, do you represent

things that are in that woman, characteristics like malice and anger, jealousy and hostility?"

Snorp ignored the question. "She let me *become.*"

"Did she use rituals or magic practices to create you?"

"*Thought.*"

"What was that thought, the main thought in her mind when she created you?"

Snorp paused as if thinking or trying to express: " . . . to *come* . . . to be *in between* . . . to *come.*"

"When you were in Winnie, what influence did you have on her thoughts and behavior?"

"On *others,* who came to her . . . Roar . . . ROAR . . . ROAR!"

"That would make others afraid of her, wouldn't it?"

He snarled and nodded.

"Why do you want to make people afraid of her?"

"To protect her."

"From what?"

"For *her.*"

What does she want from Winnie?"

"I—don't—know." He gave a snort.

"Snorp, I imagine she told you that you *had* to do exactly as she told you, didn't she?" He nodded. "But if you *have* to do just what you are *told*, that means you are a slave, doesn't it? Snorp, you do have free will. She should have explained that to you. . . . Before you came I invited some Bright Beings here. They are in this room. You do have a choice. If you want to feel brightness and happiness, you only have to turn and look at their brightness and feel the warmth. It's very simple. . . . Did you turn to the Bright Beings?" There was a nod. "I am so glad for you! Now look at their faces." He nodded again. "Look at their eyes. What do you see in their eyes?"

There was a moment's pause; then he murmured, "Peace."

"Yes. And would you like to feel peace forever?" His murmur was affirmative. "Then just go to the Bright Ones and give your strength to them. You are strong; I asked for the strongest entity to come, and you came. Just turn your strength over to them to become part of their light to use as they see fit. . . ."

There was a quietness on Lili's face that indicated that all was well. I wish I had given Snorp a new name before he left. Usually I do, or have the entity choose one. This time I forgot.

For a similar entity that I encountered some months later, I offered a choice between giving his strength to the Bright Beings to become part of their strength (this brought a head-shake) or holding out a hand to the Bright Ones and letting them lead him to his own place in the Gardens of Learning. This was accepted at once. I had the feeling that the entity had refused the first alternative mostly from long habit of contrariness rather than from true aversion. It did give me something to consider, however: Even these created thought-forms value their beingness: "She *let me become.*"

As for Snorp, when Lili came back to full consciousness she turned to me and said, "Weren't you frightened? He would have *clawed* you! And you laughed!" She said he wanted to take her arm and reach out and claw my face with her fingernails. She, however, was in control of her body and would not permit him to do more than make faces and cause jerking of her limbs.

"No, I wasn't frightened. I knew I had a powerful backup in the presence of our teachers and Christ and the Enlightened One. With those four on our side, I knew there was no danger. We asked once before if you needed more protection in this work and were told no. The same for me. We are protected."

"Yes, but if I didn't trust them and you, it would be a little frightening to me to be just lying in the middle of it all, having given partial control to the entity and not knowing what it is going to do. But you laughed!"

"Well, I had meditated beforehand that I would somehow know what to do and what to say. Maybe it was the right thing to laugh at him."

Lili had incurred the anger of a man who practices black magic in the area. She would not tell me his name, but she knows where he lives and calls him "the man by the river." She had had nightmares about him in the past, and in hypnosis we discovered that he had been attempting to influence her. It was he who had previously sent his stooge to enter and obsess her. When we expelled that strong thought-form and it chose to go into the light, the man by the river looked for other ways to harass Lili.

As she was leaving after one of our work sessions, she mentioned that for the past two weeks she had been having strange unpleasant happenings in her home, poltergeist-type and very crude and unclean: human excrement, for instance, inside a pair of trousers on top of her pile of clean laundry.

"Nobody else was there"; she insisted, "not even the dog could have gotten in. Another time one of the beds was wet and no one was there."

Although the hour showed that it was nearly time for her to go, I decided to see if we could find out in a few minutes what this was all about. Lili agreed willingly. She went into self-hypnosis; I deepened the state very briefly and then called the entity. It came at once.

When I asked its name, however, the lips compressed and then it sneered, "I don't have a name and if I did I wouldn't tell *you!*" It turned its head away and folded its lips still more tightly.

To myself I wondered if the man by the river had created this thought-form and had told it not to talk to me. Finger movements confirmed this suspicion. Lili told me afterward that although she and I had given the entity control of her mouth and vocal cords, she still controlled her fingers and could give answers through them herself, knowing the entity's thoughts.

I gave the entity a scolding for doing "crude, unclean, gross things" in Lili's home. Then I found myself telling it, in third person, about a different entity who, also stubborn, had resisted my suggestion that he turn around toward the Light but grumpily admitted that he felt the Light "on my behind."

"Then you know that the Light and warmth are real," I had reminded that entity. "Now how about turning sideways so it can warm your face a little?" and so on.

The entity in Lili was quiet during the whole of this story. For awhile it covered its eyes, and to my questioning why, said it was because the Light was too bright. I assured it that although the Light was brilliant, it was never the kind that would hurt the eyes. The fact it was aware of the Light was a good sign.

To my amazement the entity was remarkably quick to make the decision to go into the Light. When I suggested that it select a name for itself, it paused only an instant and then said, "Sunshine."

It had been a very short—about ten or twelve minutes and touching transformation. We bade Sunshine goodbye and both of us felt his happiness and freedom.

I do not doubt that the man by the river is still more angry with Lili and me. We have been told by our teachers that he is permitted to live and be active but only in his own area. Several persons have been drowned swimming or canoeing in the river at certain places; I imagine that one of those places may be where he lives. He is apparently able to send out thought-forms even though confined to his home grounds. Lili and I were told not to bother him; that he is too strong for us at present; that he is allowed to be there for a while, for "it is not yet his time"; but that we are protected from him.

## Emotion-forms

Another brief example of a "feeling-form" or "emotion-form" is one that came initially as a rumble from the throat of a young woman in hypnosis, a nameless force that described itself as "fear and resentment toward this one [the client] which lingered in her and allowed me to *become*. I have great resentment, sometimes going into pity and then anger. She was open and allowed this to happen. *Her fear* of J. (a male acquaintance) allowed him to *deposit his feelings* in her. There are some other latent things—nameless, formless—joined with me. She has not strength to protect herself."

These "latent, nameless" elements were described as "fragments—collections." About itself the emotion-form said, "I do not understand why I am here. I don't have a form. I am confused." It willingly turned toward the Light at my suggestion and gladly went with a female guide whose name had been known to the client as a discarnate friend and helper.

Asked to take with it the "fragments and collections," the emotion-form saw them as tendrils clutching tightly at the client, like a vine: "I do not know how to express it. They *grow,* like a plant . . . they must be cut. I cannot sever them. They only obey—no, *grow*—and have their own life. I can't take them all; I can pull out some that came with me. They have no mind. . . ." I thanked the emotion-form for its cooperation and suggested that maybe now it would like to have a name, a name it could select for itself—perhaps the name of a beautiful flower or butterfly or bird—

"Periwinkle!" it decided, with almost no pause for thought.

I thanked Periwinkle again, but it replied, "Thank *you!* If that's what 'death' is like, it's beautiful."

A psychic friend present, in meditation at the time of this hypnotic session, saw Periwinkle as a cloud-like shape that stretched out an arm-like extension of itself when I requested it to take the "fragments" with it. The extension grasped and pulled out of the client a string of bead-like shapes and drew the string after it as it departed. "I never saw anything like that before," she declared.

As for the tendrils that could not be severed, I offered the client the image of a sword of light, and in guided imagery I attempted to help her see the tendrils falling apart when touched by the sword. She felt that some were deeply hidden. Clinically, I felt that at least some of those tendrils of fear were cut.

## Elementals

Elementals are individual beings of rather low intelligence. (This is the name given by Theosophy to these rather unevolved discarnates.) They may be trapped in a living human body as obsessing entities or they may be free-roaming and merely attach themselves at times to the aura of a living person, as do other types of attached entities.

My friend Joseph L. was a therapist doing fine work in a city where he was the only one using hypnosis to treat

alcoholism. During my visit there we discussed releasements and he suggested that we find and release any
entities that might be in him. Because of his long experience with hypnosis, the induction and deepening were
very swift and easy. His fingers said that three entities
were in him.

When I called "the strongest attached entity" and asked
its name, a slow, dull, drawling voice answered, "Sna-a-g."

"Were you ever human, Snag?" The name did not sound
human.

"I . . . don't . . . know."

"What kind of creature are you?"

"I . . . don't . . . know." Every word was slow and
drawn out, a dull monotone.

'Are you under the supervision of a greater force?"

"No . . . I don't think so."

"Do you have free will?"

"No . . . I don't think so."

"When did you enter Joe?"

"A lo-o-ng time ago."

"In a past life?"

"No . . . this life."

"When he was just a boy?"

"Yes . . . probably five, or six."

"Why did you enter him?"

"He went to a funeral."

"Were you the soul of the dead person?"

"Part of it . . . Dotty Carr . . . I was the bad part."

"How do you mean 'bad'?"

"Mean . . . ugly . . . evil."

"Why did you choose Joe to enter?"

"He was the same age as Dotty. . . . He lived across the
street . . . and he had a mama and a daddy."

"Didn't you?"

"Dotty didn't have a daddy . . . just a mama."

"Did Dotty do bad things?"

"She didn't want me around. She was too good. She didn't want any bad in her."

"You aren't a true part of her, are you?"

"That's where I left from."

"Where were you before you were in Dotty?"

". . . I don't know."

"Were you in somebody else before you were in her?"

"I don't know . . . I must have been."

"Why do you call yourself 'Snag'?"

". . . I think that's my name."

"Is there anyone who gives you orders?"

". . . No . . ."

"When Dotty died, why were you left behind?"

"I'm ugly. . . . She didn't want me at all. . . . She didn't want anything bad. . . . I was looking for a place to go to."

"Where is Dotty's soul now, the rest of her?"

"I've lost track of her. She went off and left me and I don't care where she is. I'm kinda resting here in old Joseph."

"Would you like to be happier? I don't think you've been very happy."

"I'd lo-o-ove to be happier."

"Then start by pushing out all the mean, ugly, bad things; just shove them right out of you. Make a pile of 'em there in the ground. Do you want to do that?"

"Yeah . . ."

"Fine. Just put all those dark things right out of you, the things that made you mad or cross—and if you begin to feel 'full of holes,' as one entity said, it's all right."

"There's nothing left for me to *do*."

"Oh, yes! There's lots to do—new things! Now how do you feel?"

"We-el-l . . . I'm tired. Lot of work putting all that junk out there."

"Snag, I'm proud of you. It took a lot of courage and strength to do that. Got a big pile now?"

"*Gr-r-eat* big!"

"Fine. Now you are ready to look around for a light. Do you see a light?"

"It's all around me. Yep."

"Now go to the brightest part of the light and get a new name. A Bright Being will come and take care of the junk and will lead you to your own proper place."

"I can just see 'em coming . . . kinda dim. . . . Light's so bright I can hardly make 'em out."

"Good! Now ask them what your new name is."

". . . Ansel . . . Funny name."

"Okay, now you'll have a lot of fun as Ansel! Go with them into your new life in the white light. . . . Joe, tell me when they are gone."

Joe's arm had been rising stiffly. "Yes, they're all gone."

Afterward he said that he raised his arm to point over the horizon where they were disappearing.

I did not get to check, for my visit in that town was brief, but I wondered if Joe's speech, which had always been very slow, had become speeded up a bit since Snag's departure!

Elementals like this are treated kindly and directively, with firm correction when necessary—not punishment, but correction of mistaken attitudes or "logic." They are quite susceptible to suggestion and can be led by judicious praise as well as controlled by judicious reproof.

A somewhat more intelligent entity that I believe might be called an elemental was a nameless one that I called Gorf. A young woman told me that she had felt a foreign, undesirable element in herself and had meditated repeatedly until she felt free of it. Although her meditations had pushed the entity outside, we discovered that it still clung to her aura and affected her moods at times.

When I called "any entity in 'Corie's' body or attached to her aura," the entity came at once. It was playful, teasing, uncooperative. When I informed it that it did have a choice between going to the darkness forever or else going into the Light, it said scornfully, "*That's* no choice!"

"Yes, it is," I insisted.

"I'll go back to her parents," decided Gorf.

"Oh, no, that's not an option. Neither is staying in her aura. Which do you choose to do?"

Reluctantly Gorf finally allowed the Bright Helpers to pull him away from Corie into the Light; but she told me afterward that she was not sure he wanted to stay there. This session took place before I had learned better how to handle resistant entities and before I had learned of "intermediate" places.

Corie also told me that her parents had had years of arguments and disagreements but that lately they had been getting along much more amicably with each other. She felt that Gorf could well have been part of their trouble in the past and that, as he had implied, he had indeed left them to go to her.

# Legions, Group Entities
# Similar in Nature to Elementals

In three or four cases an entity obsessing a client has said its name was "Legion."

The first time I encountered such an answer I asked for a spokesman to come out and talk with me, and Legion said,

"We are many but we always stay together as one. Think of a natural sponge: It is one thing, yet it is composed of many individuals." From my background in biology I understood this analogy at once. And so I talked with Legion as with one being—and found it a sarcastic, taunting sort of being.

"Are you going to send us into the pigs?" it asked, apparently referring to the tale of Christ's sending "Legion" out of an insane man and into a herd of swine. I was surprised by the reference.

"Well, you *asked* to be sent into them," I reminded it, "so you got what you asked for."

"Hm," said Legion, as if remembering, "I guess we did."

"And the pigs all drowned, so you didn't get to stay in them very long," I added.

I continued with the usual persuasions and Legion was finally willing to change its goals and aspirations and go to the Light. But I found myself wondering if Legion had been able to distract even the Carpenter of Galilee and trick him into sending it into the swine—with the resultant freedom for Legion after the swine had drowned.

Another interesting example of a Legion's nature is revealed by the releasement I performed at the request of a Persian (Iranian) woman for her young son. This request was relayed to me through an American man who knew the little boy. The actual work was done with the assistance of a coworker of mine who channeled; that is, it was a "remote releasement." All that I knew of the child's situation was what the American man had told me, that the child had little or no self-confidence, probably because the mother had so little for herself. "Persians as a group have a tremendous martyr complex," he had added. "They think the whole world is against them and that nothing good can ever happen to them."

I called "the strongest entity or soul in young 'Abu'. Please come and talk with us, but stay outside our bodies.

Put your thoughts into Mary's mind and she will speak them for you. I would like to know your name. Mary, just say whatever comes into your mind first."

"Legion—in the Bible we are called 'Legion'."

I was surprised to hear this Legion also mention the Bible.

"How old was Abu when you entered him?"

"He was in the womb."

"Why did you enter him so early?"

"Well, the negatives in his mother *drew* us. She was a miserable, unhappy person. *She* drew us, and he was a good place to go. We stay together. Now we are in him. She may feel some residue."

"Why did you leave her to go into him?"

"We had no choice. These women with child should know this! *Their* weakness goes into the child. The child had no defenses."

"But *you* forced your way into him, and yet you say you 'had no choice'?"

"We just follow the path of least resistance. There is no resistance in the unborn child; sometimes even the soul isn't there (yet). Sometimes the soul won't come in, and the body dies. Young children [after birth] are vulnerable, too, but the *most* vulnerable are in the womb."

"What negatives were in the mother?"

"She was just *miserable*. . . . *Why* are people miserable?"

"Oh, some are unhealthy, some are hungry, some lack money for necessities. There are lots of reasons. . . . Are you what are called 'demonic beings'?"

"Well, we certainly are not angels." (I chuckled.) "We're not positive forces. Some call us demons or devils. . . . Sometimes when we are in negative personalities, terrible things happen when they become adult: murders, cruelties. . . . This child just *happens* to be a *victim,* so negatives like drowning kittens, etc., haven't happened, AS YET—but they could. You are wondering how to get rid of this? Well, this is not our favorite abode, but we will stay here."

"No, you have other options but you will not stay here."

"Will you transform us into pigs?" This Legion, too, seemed to be referring to the Biblical account of Christ's casting out the unclean spirit called Legion into a herd of swine, at Legion's suggestion.

"That was not transforming—that was merely *transporting* you. And you asked for that."

"Hm. I guess we did ask to go into them. *You* think you can transform us?"

"I don't do it. Higher Powers do it, and only when you choose to be transformed. You have free will."

"Hm . . . I thought we were *necessary*,"

"You were told that. You were told that negativity had to exist to be a block against which people could push, like the starting block for a runner. But there doesn't have to be any block; there can be a rope for people to *pull* on to get a good start forward. You were told lies by the Father of Lies, your boss. There is negative energy, and there is positive energy, and one can be transformed into the other.

"I think," I went on, "that you have been unhappy, miserable, lonely, cold—haven't you?"

"No . . . hm, no, we feel none of those. We just go where we are called. No problem at all for us. Those are human things, not ours."

"So you think you are exceptions to the Laws of Life, that you are exempted from that Basic Law which states that what one sows, that is what one also reaps? If you don't believe me, ask the Shining Ones. They are here. I invited them before we began this session."

There was a short pause. Then Legion said, thoughtfully, "Hm-m . . . they say that *we are* reaping what we've sown, in this hell that we create. But it's so dark. We don't know any better. We don't know what to do."

"Yes, you've forgotten—it was so long ago that you knew better. Look into your own heart. What do you see there? Look deep under the black, in the very core of yourself, each one of you. What do you see or feel there?"

". . . a tiny little pinpoint . . . it's very pink, pulsating . . . very pretty . . . it's *interesting*. But I think I should explain to you: we are like a sponge, one thing, one being, made up of many individuals but only one."

I wondered if Legion was trying to turn the conversation. "Yes; but keep on looking. What is happening to the pinpoint?"

"Well, it's shining out—it's shining out through everything, through everywhere!"

"Yes! And now that you can see that, you *are* becoming transformed! I ask you to invite others like yourself, your peers and subordinates, who may want to follow you and go to the Shining Ones, too."

"I don't think you can change all of them, dear Louise." (Was Legion truly transformed entirely already, or did I detect some sarcasm in this comment?)

"Oh, no. But some may hear our voices and choose to go with you."

"Some of them will come. Some need to be cleaned up. . . . Before we go, be sure to tell this woman that *she* is still responsible for this boy and should get help for herself. She is still miserable. She influences this boy."

Legion was trying now to give helpful advice for those whom it had previously harassed.

"Yes, I'll tell her; I'll get your message to her. Good-bye, Legion. Go with the Bright Ones. You belong to them now."

I ended by visualizing, with Mary, that we were contacting Universal Mind and asking that a capsule of protection be placed around young Abu and his mother and that light shine into them to dispel the darkness and unhappiness, transforming these into gratitude for the good things they do have. (I was thinking, as I talked, of a time when one of my own little sons urged me, "Be happy, Mama. Make me happy." That is a parent's duty along with protection and physical nurturing, so far as is humanly possible.)

In this case, the success of the releasement all too clearly depended on whether the lad's mother could change her own attitudes. If the person's attitudes or circumstances continue to "open" or "perforate" the normally protective aura, other negative entities may take the place of the ones that were released. For this reason the mother's unhappiness and discontent needed to be dispelled or diminished by treatment for *her,* psychologically and perhaps physically.


## Alien (Extraterrestrial) Entities


A few years ago I had not found any "E.T.'s" among the parasitic entities that I had contacted during the years of my Releasement work. Since then I have contacted more than one that seems to be definitely an off-planet type, an extra-terrestrial type. There have been several different kinds among these.

During a small class on Releasement that I was teaching, one of the men, Harry, found himself channeling for a lost, confused, apprehensive spirit that had ventured away from its home environment and had begun to realize that earth and its inhabitants were so different from itself that it was lonely. The picture developing seemed similar to that of a lost teenaged earthling who had fled home for adventure but found confusion and disappointment instead.

I did not know how to locate "home" for this entity, but knowing that the universe held all answers and that the energy of thought reaches easily to the farthest star, I simply asked that one of its own kind please come at our call and take this spirit back to its proper place. I asked for "a wise counselor" to come. The lost entity was glad to be helped but admitted that it was fearful that it might be punished or at least severely reprimanded by its escort. It was afraid it could not live up to the expectations its own kind had held for it.

When the counselor came at our invitation, Harry breathed hard a moment and then whispered, "He is so heavy—he feels like he's crushing me."

All this was totally new to me. I had to "wing it" but followed what seemed most direct and simple.

I explained to the counselor that his presence was felt as a crushing weight by Harry's sensitive human body and asked that he lighten his presence. He did so—by some means or other (perhaps just by desiring to or thinking of lightness).

Harry told us afterward that the counselor did not seem to understand the little lost entity's fears; that the counselor seemed to take it all very matter-of-factly, with a tinge of irritation that the little entity had caused this inconvenience. (Could there be a sort of generation gap in communication on other planets as well as in our human race?) At any rate, the lost entity is back with its own kind again and, we hope, happy.

Baldwin encounters extraterrestrials occasionally and follows the format of the television series "Star Trek" in his conversations with the E.T.'s. This approach seems to work very well. The basis for communication is telepathic, or what Monroe calls nonverbal communication (NVC), requiring only thoughts, not words in any language at all, although Baldwin expresses his thoughts in English and receives the aliens' thoughts as if worded in English. (This applies to deaf-mute humans and to animal souls as well.)

In 1994 I offered to give a one-day workshop on Releasement to a group of therapists, and in the proposal said that I would ask for four volunteers, and that from among them I would release any entrapped entities that might be in them, including at least one nonhuman entity. (I knew how that promise would sound to anyone reading it. It meant that I was really "sticking my neck out" and risking my reputation! So in parentheses I explained that I would ask my Spiritual Advisor to select and send an entity suitable for the class situation, adding that I had used this method several times before and had never been disappointed, although sometimes surprised at the choice—which nevertheless had always proved the wisdom of the Spiritual Advisor.)

Somewhat to my amazement, my proposal for the workshop was accepted, just as I had offered it. The acceptance showed not only the committee's trust in me and in my Spiritual Advisor but also their own open-mindedness and experiential background.

Now here I was at the conference, with the fourth volunteer. Three volunteers had had multiple entities including a rather remarkable assortment of human discarnates (from a domineering female to a timid teenaged boy to a very young infant); and by that time I was so involved with the drama of these that I had really forgotten that we were still waiting to discover a nonhuman entity.

It came almost as a surprise when the volunteer began to describe the entity "Gota" who came out. She called its appearance like a "monster." Pressed to be more specific, she toyed with several attempts and then came down to the word, "*gargoyle*—those monsters on the outside of cathedrals. That's what he looks like." My Spiritual Advisor, knowing of my trust that he would select one that would not frighten anyone in the audience (although all were therapists and so were probably inured to sudden and worrisome events), had chosen a nonhuman that another therapist might have tabbed as being an extraterrestrial and would have questioned it along that line. Somehow that possibility did not occur to me right then and I continued the original plan of questioning, as if the nonhuman were an elemental or minor demonic type. It seemed to be intelligent and quite innocuous and, in fact, the young lady did not think she wanted to lose it. She felt that it had given some valuable things like increased insight, artistic sense, and so on. "What will I be without him?" she asked, dubiously. The entity itself did not really wish to leave but was willing to go, since I assured it that its leaving would benefit the young woman.

When the volunteer remained doubtful at the end of the workshop about letting this entity go, I reminded the audience that each client does have free will; and therefore I only added some extra hypnotic suggestion for her wisdom and protection before bringing the volunteer back to normal awareness, leaving the entity within her. I felt somewhat restless that evening, however, wondering if I could have used a different approach. . . .

Yet the next morning when I met the volunteer fortuitously in the hallway, she greeted me with a big smile, telling me that she had decided to send on her discarnate alien friend and was now free to be only her own self. I admit that I was relieved. In hindsight I realized that it had been an interesting little lesson for the audience, to see how one might deal with a client who refuses to let an obsessing entity go. Perhaps my Spiritual Advisor had prodded this volunteer in order to show the audience that very lesson? She said that all the hours before the workshop she had been debating whether to volunteer or not, undecided to the very last, raising her hand only when I asked for "four."

In this case it appeared that Gota knew who he was and where he belonged. I had merely asked that a guide suitable for him come to escort him to his "appropriate place." (I had no idea where that might be.)

One other similar case comes to mind at the moment, this one involving one of my sons. I had noticed that some of his actions had been out of character during the past several years and had suggested to him—as tactfully as possible—that a releasement might be in order. (How does a mother tactfully suggest to a grown son that he may be "obsessed"?!)

To my surprise and relief he was open to the idea and was willing to be his own channel. In the little session that followed we found a being that he described as being lizard-like, with intelligence but apparently no real understanding of human sensitivities in some respects. I called the being "Lizard," a name that it accepted; and in the course of the short session it agreed to leave and go to its "appropriate place." I do not feel that Lizard was one of the animal spirits that help human beings, as in the shamanic teachings. This entity seemed to be like most other invaders that we have dealt with, "not part of this person, not belonging to this person."

## Nature Spirits

Many teachers and mystics down the ages have taken for granted that the forms of nature are indwelt by nature spirits of one type or another, and names have been given to these types: fairies, trolls, elves, leprechauns, salamanders, and so on. The Buddhist scriptures speak of the gods of the trees; the Native Americans speak of the Thunder Beings. Lili, one of my coworkers, has seen (with her astral vision) what seem to have been Thunder Beings. The anonymous British author of *The Boy Who Saw True (1953)* once saw "a big fairy sticking to [a person's] aura," and once saw "a little man" like a gnome in a garden. If we accept that some people have astral vision that the rest of us do not have, we shall respect what these special persons tell us, even if we can not directly confirm what they say. If they are, for example, able to see certain "colors" and the rest of us are color blind to these "colors," who are we to say that those "colors" do not exist?

I have met very few entities that I might call nature spirits, but therapists and other people who have met some agree that they do not have the same sense of ethics and morals that human beings subscribe to. That explains the "pot of gold at the foot of the rainbow" idea: Catch a leprechaun, hold him fast until he promises to show you where to find the pot of gold, then turn him loose to lead you—and he disappears, and the rainbow forever recedes from you: no pot of gold!

## Concordant Elements (Spiritual Viruses)

I asked Harry, a member of our meditation group, to write down what he had perceived as a nonhuman, nonentity presence during one of our releasement sessions. He did so and with minor editing I share it here.

"When one of our channelers was asked to explore whether or not a member of the family had an entity

in her that might account for her difficulty with relationships both in and outside of the family, the channeler was informed that there was no entity present.
Further exploration revealed that there was a presence, but the channeler's guides knew of no way to
deal with it and were not sure there was any way it
could be dealt with.

"At a later date with Louise Ireland-Frey as facilitator I approached the presence. We approached it as
if it were really an entity just trying to evade detection.
We were clearly informed that this was not the case,
and were we to find a way to cause it to leave, it would
leave the individual in a very vulnerable position,
without effective protection from a worse presence
coming in to take its place.

"In trying to understand the nature of the presence
we explored what it did in a person. It seems to
function at the psychological level much as a virus
does at the physical level—for which reason we called
it at first a 'psycho-virus'. More correctly, it functions
at the mind/spirit level and enters the person's complex when there is a great deal of emotional content,
such as repressed anger, which may be a product of
both this incarnation and other past lives and resulting
in karma that is unresolved, hence can infect an entire
family. This seemed to be the case in this family, where
there is a lot of thinly masked hostility.

"Since I am not a passive channeler I interact with
whatever it is that I channel and hence come away
with a lot of *feelings* about the presence I am channeling that sometimes takes me a considerable time to
process. I use the term *presence* in the most general way
to include anything that is present in a person that is
not part of the person. I have had several months now

to process what I felt during the channeling and would like to share those impressions now.

"*Like a virus,* the presence affects an organism when the organism is in a weakened state and is unable to fight it off. A normal person, healthy at all levels, remains unaffected even though a virus enters the system, dealing with the virus easily via the immune system. The 'psycho-virus' acts in the same way except that it is unable to enter an individual unless the system is already out of balance in some way, and then when it does, it aggravates *that particular imbalance.* However, even when the person's system is back in balance the psycho-virus does not leave but merely becomes dormant and will become active again any time the system becomes unbalanced again. This is the state with a person who responds to therapy, gets better, seems to be cured, and then regresses within a few weeks or even days, this cycle occurring time after time.

"The 'psycho-virus' is also like a physical virus in that there are many different forms it can take. I did not realize this at the time, but gradually it became clear from the presence I channeled that there were many more like it, *each responding to a particular imbalance.* This one responded to *repressed anger* that seems in this case to have been carried through several incarnations.

"The presence is *unlike a physical virus* in that it can not invade any system unless that system is out of balance, and then not if some other entity is already there. It seems to be attracted to a system only when that system has been out of balance for a sufficient length of time. The 'system' can be one individual or can include several individuals, hence an entire family. It seems to function as a presence that causes the under-lying imbalance to be made manifest (if you will, to cause it to be so uncomfortable that hopefully it will be dealt with).

"Now how does one deal with this?

"The first way is to restore the system to a state of balance, at which point the 'virus' will become inac-tive—i.e., dormant. If I understand correctly, as soon as the particular imbalance begins to reappear, it will become active again, reminding the individual(s) that the system is out of balance in this particular way again.

"The second way, of course, is to get the 'virus' to leave. As yet, that does not seem too likely. It does not yield itself to the usual persuasion (effective with entities) and cannot be simply ordered out. It has made clear that *it must stay to prevent a worse presence from entering*: as long as it is there, others will not come.

"My deepest sense of this presence is that it is in no way malicious. The best way I can phrase it, is that it just comes if there is persistent imbalance involving anger, particularly if the anger is repressed and being acted out in hurtful ways; and it will continue to remain active until the balance needed is restored. It does just this and has no other purpose. A positive that comes with this is that no other presence can come into the system while the 'virus' is there. The excep-tion, as I am given to understand it, would be another presence of the same type which would be there be-cause of a different imbalance, hence would be func-tioning in the same way.

"Better than the term 'psycho-virus,' which tends to imply that it is some kind of mental disorder (which it is not, even though its manifestation seems to be mental), I would like to associate this type of presence with the idea of an *elemental* because it is *cellular* in its nature—i.e., has a single purpose. Further, I sense it as being *concordant* in the sense of being harmonious with the particular imbalance involved, this harmonious quality *able to amplify the condition.* This may seem on the surface as a very negative quality. However, much as a fever indicates an infection and causes a person to pay attention to a problem and not ignore it, or pain makes one aware of an injury, so this *concordant element* causes the individual, or system, to pay attention to a problem that has its roots in the spirit(s) involved.

"Thus, to get this concordant element to leave, it must be dealt with at the spiritual level—i.e., the injury to the spirit must be dealt with at its source—either in this incarnation (e.g., as in hurtful family patterns, which would be easiest to deal with) or in a past life, or during a non-incarnate period. *The injury that led to the imbalance originally* must be located and resolved in order for the concordant element to leave.

"In summary:

"1. The concordant element being there means that the emotional imbalance caused by the injury was not readily resolved and went on for a sufficient time for the element to be attracted to the person(s). Since the injury was not resolved then or at any time until now, the element remains active.

"2. The element remains because its purpose is to amplify the imbalance so that it can be dealt with. 'The squeaky wheel' may get some grease, so to speak. Furthermore, it protects the individual(s) until something is done, even though it may take several lifetimes and cause the person(s) to be miserable the entire time—much like chronic pain that will not go away until a person finally does something to resolve the cause of the pain.

"Once the injury is healed and the imbalance is *resolved at its source* the concordant element will leave of its own accord, because its reason for staying will have been eliminated. My sense is that the (hypnotic) regression must be focused on the spirit, and that any particular incarnation, though not unimportant, is of minor importance, because *the injury to the spirit* and the resultant imbalance are timeless and are what need to be resolved or healed. I can't say that I have done this yet, but at least I now have a place to start, a way to approach the situation."

From the perspective of facilitator, three questions arose in my mind as we discussed these concordant elements. Harry felt that the "purpose" of such an element is to amplify an imbalance so that its abnormal presence will be noted by the victim and stimulate something to be done about a remedy. I wondered if the word *purpose* was almost too "animate." The concordant element sounded more like a chemical which interacts at certain temperatures and pressures with another, and a term like "effect" might seem more appropriate.

Another thought of mine was that when a system responds to an infection with fever, the fever is not necessarily a beneficial response but can be either a warning of an imbalance in the body or just another expression of illness, the impairment of the body's centers for temperature control. Might not the presence of a concordant element be like a fever, warning of imbalance but itself a sign of illness and imbalance and needing to be eliminated? The case history following, however, says no.

The other thought I had was that in certain types, when the person is angry, he or she may not want to be relieved of either the anger or its cause but may perversely hold and nurture, even seem to cherish it. Amplification of a negative emotion may in such persons have a harmful effect.

These are my own thoughts and I am the first to agree that we need to do more work to ascertain the facts about concordant elements. I have a great deal yet to learn, and I take seriously Harry's first-person experiences and his careful attempts to describe those experiences in words.

## Concordant Element
## or Psychovirus in a Family

In the family involved, not only the client herself but her mother, a daughter, a brother, and the brother's children are suspected of being shadowed or harassed by a negative type of influence. At a previous session we had been informed that it was not a dark entity except in one female member of the family. When I asked at this present session with Harry channeling, if the cause of the family dysfunction was "a malevolent virus," Harry's "yes" finger rose. Not knowing how else to approach it, I spoke to it directly:

"Virus, I am speaking to you through Harry. I think you are able to put your thoughts into his mind so he can speak them for you, aren't you?" It answered "Yes." "When did you enter this family?" I asked.

"A very long time ago, a *long* time."

"Are you a servant of the Light?"

"I don't know how to answer."

"You have been causing much trouble in this family by anger, harmful attitudes and habits, resentment—all those are aspects of the dark side of existence. I don't think you are contented, troubling people. What permits you to infect people?"

"Their anger, their negative attitudes. If they hate life and don't want to live, I can infect them. It's *easy* if there is resentment in them. Then they teach their young, so I can infect them, too."

"So you are a servant of the dark side. I asked before this session that a net of light be placed around you. Did I detect a note of pride in your statement that you find it *easy* to infect people?"

"Yes. Being *able* to do it gives me pleasure. In the beginning it was hard [to infect a person], but now it is easy!"

"In the beginning, ages ago, Virus, was there just one of you? No? Are you complex, made of many parts?"

"I don't understand. I just do what I do. I'm *drawn* to anger and negatives. I can *smell* it."

"When you come into a person, don't you make those things worse?"

"I don't know—I just do it."

(Since the daughter's church seems to be helping "Sally" to overcome some of her negativity, I asked if Virus infected church people.)

"I can reach only a few; it's light [in church people]. I can reach them only when the people are negative, only when there's something there [anger, resentment, hating life]—then I can be in all [who have those things]."

"When you do infect, what can stop you?"

"When there's light."

"What can kill you?"

"Nothing can kill me."

This client had asked me for help. I didn't know what to do, so I asked the Bright Ones to calm the anger, despair, resentment . . . and leave only a restfulness, a great white calmness instead. I asked the Bright Ones to draw the net of light tighter and tighter around Virus and each member of the family, asking also that the nets restrict the selfishness, greed, self-hatred, the feeling of rejection and the need to reject—habits that hurt or take advantage of young ones, causing helplessness and hate. Then I addressed Virus again:

"Virus, these are all aspects of darkness. When you infect people, you hinder and obstruct them. Let Light shine on the Virus."

"Don't shine the Light on me! No! I don't have anything else to do!" insisted Virus.

"You may survive only as a seed [of light]. Jesus, Buddha, great physicians, you both healed psychologically as well as physically. Light will shine on the human beings in this family. Light is shining on you, Virus. I am asking spiritual helpers to take you where you need to go."

I addressed the Bright Beings, "Please take Virus out of all the members of this family. Leave calmness and quiet that will heal this family. Virus, as I place my hand on Harry's heart, feel gentleness and power of that Light through my hand."

"You must let me stay."

"I don't accept orders from any but the Bright Beings."

"If you send me away, someone else worse—a dark one—will come."

"Bright Beings, is this true? Or is it our responsibility—within our power—is it permissible—to remove Virus from this family?" The answer was a simple "yes" to my confusing question.

"Permissible; is it *possible* to remove Virus permanently?" This time the answer was "no." "Then can we reduce the power of Virus?" I asked; and the answer was "yes."

What occurred next in my mind I am not sure, but I went right ahead with wording to send Virus clear away, as if I had not heard those answers about being unable to remove Virus permanently:

"As I remove my hand from Harry's heart," I said, "I *draw* Virus out of the family and CLAP it [loud hand-clap] into oblivion. Breathe *in* strength for yourself, Harry, and breathe *out* the Virus from this family. And you, Virus, encased in your cocoon of light by the Bright Ones, will be taken to your appropriate place. . . . Harry, is Virus still in the family?"

Harry found that none remained.

"Is there more that we can do for the family?" I inquired. The answer was no . . . then a pause . . .

Then Harry went on, "There are thoughts in my mind: Virus is not totally of the dark side; it has been placed there as a way to *warn* people. I have an image—it is hard to find words. . . . If Virus were taken away totally, there would be no warning to people who are drifting away [from Light]."

"Yes, I understand that; but a *neutrality* can be attained."

"I understand," he agreed, "and yet I am confused."

I spoke to Virus again. "Virus, I want to remind you: There's *plenty* of warning! *You* don't have to feed on them, the people of this family. Let the Light reduce the power and pride you have."

"I have no power of my own," said Virus. "I gain it through *them*. They *call* me by their anger."

"I understand. Nevertheless, I ask the Bright Beings to shine light on *everyone*."

"If the light is in them I am powerless. I am the *lesser* of the dark ones. If I go, a stronger one, a dark entity, will come."

"I appreciate your telling me that. You are more honest

than dark ones. Light, please shine in to cleanse the pain and yearning and replace them with quietness and trust. "

"I feel the whole family needs light," said the channel.

I began to mention the members of the family, name by name, asking that light shine on each, shining into the bitterness, the unforgiveness, the guilt and sorrow, "a great sunburst of light with a beam shining into each member of this family and the three of us here. . . . When two or three are gathered together in the name of Love, there is Love, and Power, and Light shining into *all* members of the family . . . healing old hurts, resentments, angers. And Great Light, we thank you! . . . Is there anything else we need to do today?"

Harry saw that "every day every day" we needed to meditate and surround the whole family with Light and Love. "Gradually they will heal. The Light will keep the dark ones away. If Light is there, Virus can't come. If the aura is open, Virus will come."

"Is Virus a protection? Is it wrong to put Virus in a cocoon?"

"It seems to be. Sally has sought the church; she is safe."

"Has it been a hindrance to the family to place the net around Virus?"

"Yes, because Virus becomes totally dormant. Virus *seems* dark and yet is not, really. It is confusing—part of a mystery. All we need to know is that if the negativity goes, the Virus is dormant. The Light flows in. While Virus is there, dark ones are content because Virus *seems* to be one of them."

I was still not entirely convinced and wanted to recheck: "Master Ching, dark ones can be sly. They try to trick us. It sounds to me as if Virus is trying to say it is all right to stay active in these people. Master Ching, are these words from Harry's lips *right?* Please answer through the fingers."

"Yes," said Harry's fingers.

"All right. But we have to be careful that we don't say yes to a dark one."

Master Ching's calm voice spoke: "It is a mystery hard to explain. Harry has done the best he can [to explain]. In days to come, we will try to bring clarity. But I can say to you as a physician that Virus is around all the time. Virus can only have an effect when the body is out of balance. When Virus warns early, the body can be brought back into balance." (Apparently he includes the auric body as well.) "Virus won't affect this family if there is *Light*. The pain will vanish."

I thanked Master Ching and the other Bright Beings who had protected and assisted at the session. Harry had some last comments about one of the causes of present guilt and sorrow in one family member, causes that came from a past-life event; and after returning to normal consciousness he added, "It was confusing. Virus wasn't really of the dark, yet it wasn't light. It was more—more like a warning that something needed to be changed."

"Maybe like gravity," I suggested, "it just *is*: good if you walk gently, bad if you walk off a cliff." And we laughed together.

As for the client herself, she has passed through several stages of fatigue, distress, and other emotions as she has dealt with the tensions between herself and her siblings, the prolonged illness and eventual death of her mother, and so on; yet she has weathered all of these and has become more calm, more self-confident, and in various ways appears to have become more mature and assured. Her friends are supportive, and she is meditating daily with her husband. All seems to be going more smoothly with her now.

*chapter 8*

# MINOR DARK ENTITIES

It is all too easy for a writer to lean defensively toward apologies to the academic world and the secular leaders of literature when the writer begins to speak of "nonhuman entities," most especially of "dark nonhuman entities." And the tendency toward apology increases if one uses the word "demonic." F. Scott Peck, in his book *People of the Lie* (1983), was very courageous to include, without apology—although with explanations—the chapter on his contacts with demonic possession.

I should like to quote a few paragraphs from Peck's book.

". . . For the past three hundred years there has been a state of profound separation between religion and science. This divorce . . . has decreed that the problem of evil should remain the custody of religious thinkers. . . .

"Science has also steered clear of the problem of evil because of the mystery involved. It is not [so much] that scientists have no taste for mystery as that their attitude and methodology in approaching it is generally reductionistic. . . . Their standard procedure is to bite off tiny little pieces at a time and then to examine such pieces in relative isolation. They prefer little mysteries to big ones.

"Theologians suffer under no such compunction. Their appetite is as large as God. The fact that God is invariably larger than their digestion does not deter them in the least. To the contrary, while some seek in religion an escape from mystery, for others religion is a way to approach mystery. The latter are not loath to employ the reductionistic methods of science, but they are also not reluctant to use more integrative 'right brain' means of exploration, meditation, intuition, feeling, faith, and revelation. For them, the bigger the mystery, the better.

"The problem of evil is a very big mystery indeed." (pp. 40, 41)

When I first began to write about unusual information that I had received during hypnotic work (my first writing of this type was in 1955–1957, the records of my own prenatal sessions), I did not find it necessary to mention mystical and paranormal words and attitudes, except to insist on the reality of several levels of conscious awareness during the state of hypnosis and in embryonic life. With the next book, on death and the conditions after death, I still managed to avoid much of the mystical and alien aspects that might have been included.

Now, however, I feel that it is time to cast aside the old hesitations and write simply from my experiences with my patients and clients. So, with that same attitude of accepting just what the contacted entities tell me during a hypnotic session with a client, I write of the entities that admit or even boast of their being dark ones, servants of the darkness.

When Dr. William Baldwin began doing Releasement work early in the 1980s, he followed the general teachings that he had received from Dr. Morris Netherton and patterned his personal approach to the contacted entities on the writings of the psychiatrist Carl Wickland, whose book, *Thirty Years Among the Dead,* was first published in 1924. Baldwin called his approach "Clinical Depossession" (as opposed to religious exorcism), having accepted the term "depossession" from Dr. Edith Fiore, through whose recommendation he had become acquainted with Annabel Chaplin's modern book, *The Bright Light of Death* (1977). Later Baldwin began to use the word "Releasement" instead of "Depossession." Both of these terms are still in use among the therapists who perform this work; and even the old word, "exorcism," is still favored by several (e.g., Naegeli-Osjord and Eugene Maurey).

It used to be my intention to save the word "exorcism" to describe the releasement of any strong dark entity specifically, until I began to realize that the religious rituals for performing exorcisms are focused only on freeing the client from the intruding dark entity, not following up by freeing the dark entity from its captivity to the darkness. Rather than to perpetuate this attitude I have chosen to use the term "releasement" for all types of entities. It also refers to the release of clients, of course.

It has helped me to overcome my own hesitation about speaking of "demons" and "dark entities" and "the darkness" when I recall that Buddha, The Enlightened One, and Christ, The Anointed One—towering intellectual and spiritual giants in their respective centuries—took rather casually for granted that "unclean spirits" and "evil spirits" exist and may confront and tempt a human being who is striving toward spiritual goals. Both the Prince of the Gautama family and the Carpenter of Galilee were faced by such a powerful dark force in moments of their greatest hunger and physical weakness.

If we take either literally or figuratively the accounts of these confrontations we begin to realize that similar lesser confrontations with lesser dark forces may occur to any of us lesser human beings. And it is into some of these that we enter as therapists when we contact a dark entity obsessing a client.

Rather than to discuss theoretically such cases, I prefer to offer sketches of several actual records of releasements in which I was the therapist. As with the other types of releasements, some of these were channeled directly by the client; others were channeled by a third person in hypnosis as a surrogate for the client; some were channeled remotely for an absent client, the geographical distance varying from a few miles to many thousands of miles. The friends and coworkers who served as channels varied from homemakers to nurses to artists.

In brief, what the dark entities themselves say is that they never had a physical body of their own—that is, they do not belong to the human kingdom but are members of the so-called angelic kingdom, being the negative aspect, composed of the "fallen angels" and their slaves. This is not drawn from any religious source; both Baldwin and I have been told these things by the dark entities encountered. A number of them have told us that they are delighted to get us to believe that they exist *only* when we think of them, speak of them, and "believe in" them—it makes their work of invading easier! On the other hand, thinking fearfully of them, brooding compulsively, talking often of them certainly does predispose a person to attracting their focused attention.

In general, the dark entities fall into two categories, minor ones and the very strong ones, although there is a gradation, many levels. The minor ones may at first contact seem to be strong, but they try to present that appearance in order to frighten and impress the persons contacting them. Actually rather weak, often not important enough to have a name, they are unhappy with their existence and with persuasion become willing to change their nature and leave the darkness with its slavery, its rule-by-fear, and go to the Light.

The strong dark ones, however, are sly, tricky, intelligent, and most are not amenable to persuasion. They are full of hatred for human beings and contemptuous of efforts to dislodge them. Theirs is the mocking laughter we have heard described as "demoniac laughter." The first time I heard such laughter directed at me, it made the hair on my neck literally stand on end.

Does all this sound frightening? That is exactly what the dark ones want it to sound like. Master Ching told us, "Fear is of Satan; fear *is* Satan." And on top of the fear is often *anger* or rage, to cover up the fear; and under the fear is often *pain* (as also with human souls). So when I speak to a dark entity, I keep this in mind. The dark ones become vulnerable when we direct their thought to their own pain, their own loneliness, their own unhappiness. They do not know how to meet our compassion.

In any case, we have asked the Bright Beings, the spiritual helpers, to be with us even before we contact the dark entities, so we know that we are protected and guided with wisdom and power higher than any of our own—and greater than any that the dark ones can claim. If we have deliberately called on the presence and assistance of the Source of all Light and Power, there is no need to fear.

## Releasement of Entities Haunting a House

"Millie's" house in Montrose, Colorado, had been haunted. A dark shape had been seen, night noises heard, and so on. It had become so unpleasant that the family did not want to live there. Referred by a friend, Millie came to me with her grown son, and although unacquainted with hypnosis, was willing to channel.

After the routine clearing (e.g., with a whisk broom in guided visualization), I asked her subconscious mind to respond with a finger movement as to whether any entities dwelling in her house were present with us. Her "yes" finger lifted and her whole body jerked.

"Stay at a distance," I commanded the entity, "but put your thoughts into Millie's mind and she will tell them to me. What is your name?"

"Beardsley," came the answer in a loud voice totally unlike Millie's soft voice. In answer to other questions he said, "I'm eighty. It is 1986. I'm not in good health—depression is hanging onto me. . . ." He began crying hard. "My wife divorced me—I was seventy-five, I think. I was moody, mean, and depressed, depressed. I killed my body—I shot myself, I shot myself. I was lonely, I was sick. I was manic depressive, not mean because I wanted to be. She didn't understand me!"

He was rolling in misery in the cot, although I had told him to stay out of Millie's body. Not knowing whether his wife was dead, I called her anyway, "Ruby, your husband is crying. He says he wasn't mean because he *wanted* to be. Let part of your mind come here. Can you be patient with your former husband and forgive him and the old memories?"

When I received affirmatives, I asked Beardsley if he had forgiven his wife, too.

"Yes, I did. Ruby, forgive me. I didn't mean to shoot myself. I'm sorry. Forgive me."

"I understand now," responded Ruby.

I asked that someone who cared for Beardsley come, and

asked him to look for a Light, but his amazed exclamation interrupted:

"*My God,* my dog is with me! And Ruby's been here with me all the time!"

"I've been here *sometimes,*" amended Ruby. "The dog, Blackie, has been there. All of us have been in that house a long time. That lady [Millie] is *nice!* . . . There's a light—a pretty light," she suddenly commented. "And there's my grandma—so bright. She looks so nice. . . ."

Millie in hypnosis watched while the grandmother led the others into the Light, and then I led a guided meditation in which we asked angelic forces to cleanse Millie's house, the therapy room here, and to protect each one of us. Millie's last message to her former ghosts was, "Go in peace."

After all this, however, Millie still saw something dark. I called it: "I am calling you, Dark. Stay outside of Millie but put your thoughts into her mind for her to tell me. What is your name?"

"Don't have a name."

"Is it okay if I call you 'No-Name'?"

"I don't care. . . . My age? I don't know. No, never had a physical body of my own."

"I can help you, too."

"*I don't want to leave!*" No-name was shouting. "I want to stay in this room! I don't hurt anybody."

"You made Millie feel scared."

"I just made that house dank. And yes, I made Beardsley shoot himself. He *wanted* to! Stupid bastard . . ." He continued to shout, thrashing Millie's body around on the cot.

"Be quiet!" I ordered. "Look inside yourself. What do you find?"

"Nothing! . . . Filth—filth—nothing."

"In the very core of yourself—in the very center?"

"Ah—I don't know . . . used to be love. . ."

"You're getting close." (He shivered; I put a blanket over Millie.) "I think you are tired and cold and unhappy. You say there 'used to be love' in the core of you. That core is still alive; it is still a spark of love. It was created by the Great Light." (Millie's finger said "yes.") "It proves that you are a Child of Light, not a child of darkness."

"I've been dark a *long* time."

"Too long," I reminded him.

"It *used* to be a nice house. Now still it's a nice house, with the Light here now."

I asked him to turn toward the Shining Beings and open his heart to their light and their love. He began to cry.

"It *hurts* to love!" he wept.

I allowed him to weep a minute or so, reminding him, "Yes, it sometimes hurts to love, but it is a good hurting, cleansing away a lot of old darkness and pains. . . . And now I can't call you Dark One any longer, and you need a name. What new name do you want for yourself?"

After a moment he chose the name "Bethany," the name of one of the villages in which the Carpenter of Galilee found friends and peace. "Bethany" then went on to his appropriate place of peace to complete his transformation out of darkness.

I had expected this session to accomplish everything that Millie needed to free her house of unwelcome invisible inhabitants, but the very next day she phoned to tell me that the clearing had been only temporary and that now the problem was worse than ever. A psychic from Denver recommended candles, holy water sprinkled in each room, and so on. Millie asked if anyone could come to Montrose to exorcize the house in person.

I thought I would try a *remote releasement* with a friend to channel here; but in the end I had to compromise and do the releasement *over the telephone:* from Cedaredge to my nurse colleague in Delta, for Millie's house in Montrose! A rather strong dark was finally released. The session, condensed, follows:

First of all I invited Beings of Light for protection, wisdom, and guidance of my coworker and me, as well as for Millie, and asked that a net of light be placed around the entity in Millie's house.

"I am calling the strong entity in the house at . . ." (I gave the address in Montrose.) "Please come and tell me your name. Speak through Charlene's voice; she gives you permission."

"ICE. Cold—*Ice*."

"Yes, I imagine you are cold—and lonely, too."

"Yes, lonely."

"I doubt if you are happy, either."

"I don't know what you are talking about."

"I know you don't—nor when I speak of love or peace, or compassion, or friendship. All of these belong to a universe you have no idea of."

"I have friends."

"You have lots of companions. I doubt if they are friends. Look inside yourself. What do you find?"

"Cold . . . hate . . . nothing . . . hate . . ."

"Look deeper, beneath all those, in your very core."

"Heat . . . HEAT! It's melting me! It's hot!"

"No, it's not hot, it's only warm. Who told you it was hot?"

"My friends told me—heat is bad; it is dangerous; it will destroy me."

"Your friends told you lies. Feel my hand—I am imagining that I place it on Charlene's hand. It is warm. *You can feel* that I am telling you the truth."

There was much more arguing, objection, suspicion, and fearfulness. This is characteristic of almost all minor demonic entities, who have been told that "Light" is bad, a form of fire that will destroy them, and they fear it. My Spiritual Advisor advised us to tell each dark entity two things: first, that there *is* such a thing as the Light; and second, that each entity has free will. I add a third that in the center of each entity can be found a spark of the Light. The Quakers for centuries have held this to be true, and in clinical situations Dr. Bill Baldwin uses this powerful concept to convince dark entities of their own *intrinsic original purity and worth.*

"I think you have courage. I *dare* you to go close to the Bright Beings. Let their warmth draw you."

"I don't see them . . . I *feel* warmth."

"Bright Ones, will you laser some of your Light through to Ice, so he can see you?"

There was a pause and then a voice said, "No. It is to develop his faith *not to see until later. . . .*"

"Then just *feel the warmth,* Ice, and go in that direction."

"What is 'faith'?" asked Ice.

"It is believing something we can't see. It is trusting. You know I am telling you the truth, so you are beginning to have faith in what I say. Go to the warmth."

"They will grab me and force me to go with them."

"No, they never grab and force; they let you have your own free will. Free will is a wonderful gift from the Father of Light—a dangerous gift, for it can be misused. You chose to take in coldness and hate and nothingness. But if you choose now to go to the warmth, you won't be Ice any more. You'll need a new name. What name would you like—something warm and bright?"

"Not 'Sun'—that's too hot."

"Yes, the sun is too large and bright. How about Moon, or Star, or Lamp, or Candle? Or Glowworm, or Firefly?"

"Mmm . . . Firefly!"

And so I committed Firefly to the care of the Bright Beings to be taken to that intermediate place, which has been defined by them as being "*of* the Light, but not *in* the Light," to complete his transformation from heavy cold Ice to swift, joyous, sparkling Firefly.

Various therapists have described this intermediate "place" as being garden-like, quiet, peaceful. Some formerly dark entities have been so happy about their change that they feel no need to change more, and want to begin working eagerly on the earth-level to undo former troubles that they had caused human beings and do other good works. I believe that most of these still need more "unlearning of the old habits and learning of new ones," and need to go first to the Places of Learning in the intermediate level, but the change in attitude and goals is remarkable.

Most minor demonic entities have been enslaved by stronger dark beings and have been fed lies to keep them in line by fear of punishment. This is told to us by the entities themselves, little by little. Then in later releasements of such entities we can ask as leading questions, "Who told you that the Light is hot and dangerous? Was it your commander, your 'boss'?"

You can see how the various categories of Releasement work overlap. Here is an example of the rescue of a group of ghosts (Beardsley, his dog, and also his wife, who was a part-time occupant of the haunted house), followed by the discovery and releasement of two nonhuman dark entities, first the little No-name who chose to become Bethany; and later the stronger Ice, who had been hiding from us but who, in the end, chose to become Firefly.

# Molestation of Child Due to Dark Force

One of my friends, "Dora," phoned in distress to ask for an appointment to discuss the letter she had just received from her daughter "Molly"—a letter accusing the mother of failing to listen when Molly was a child and had tried to tell how the grandfather had hurt her; of failing to protect the child from later molestations by the grandfather and two neighbors; and accusing the mother of throwing the daughter out of the house. Almost in tears, Dora sketched this much of the story over the telephone.

In hypnosis at my home Dora was still so upset that I used finger answers for the first part of the questioning and was told that Molly's accusations about grandfather and the neighbors were "basically true"; that Molly was not obsessed by another spirit; and that these accusations were not flashbacks to previous lives. Dora's fingers (her own subconscious mind in contact now with that of her daughter, at my suggestion) also told us that Molly was now in an interlude, and that as the old memories were recalled she would be healing later, assisted by her therapist.

Asked to regress to the time when Molly was three years old and to contact Molly's feelings, Dora said, "She's frightened, confused, shocked . . . I don't know. . . . She *wants* to tell someone, to get protection, but she's thinking, 'If I tell, granddad might hurt me again. I'm too scared to tell.' She didn't communicate to a point so that her mother knew—unless by whining and crying. I don't even remember her whining and crying when she said I threw her out of the house."

Dora, in regression, heard herself saying to the chid, "Go on outside and play, because I'm busy. Don't you see I'm waxing the floor? I've got lots to do."

"What is in *her* mind when you say that?"

"She hears, 'Get out. Don't bother me.' She thinks, 'My mother doesn't want to be bothered with me, *ever.*' She thinks that I want her to leave."

"Higher Mind, go forward to a time when the mother says something that cancels the former impression."

"A hug—a kiss—'I love you, Molly. You're my little sweetheart.'"

I asked Dora to repeat that twice more and then contact Molly's inner response.

"'Mommy doesn't want me to leave. She does love me. But she doesn't believe what I try to tell her . . .' She doesn't know that I couldn't understand. She feels I don't *listen.*"

Then I had Dora contact Molly's three-year-old mind again and asked Molly what she was trying to tell her mother.

"That Granddad had molested me."

"How did you try to tell her?" There was no answer. "Sometimes big folks don't hear or are too busy, or they don't listen, or they don't understand. How did you try to tell her?"

". . . I *cried* . . . I wanted her to put her arms around me and protect me and tell me she understands, *without my telling her!*"

"She couldn't understand without your telling her. Do you understand that, honey? Go into your mama's mind, Molly. What is she thinking as her little girl is crying?"

"She *wishes* she could help me. . . . She doesn't know what happened. . . . She tries to comfort me by hugging me, telling me she loves me. She says, 'Everything will be all right.' But that's not true!"

"When it turned out to be not true, what did little Molly think or feel?"

"She thought she couldn't trust her mother again."

"Yes; but that would be so only if the mother *had* known what happened and didn't protect her little girl even when she knew. But she didn't know. Molly, let your mind go to the High Place where you can see the past, the present, and the future. Higher Mind of Molly, please tell us *why* Molly had these experiences, if it is permissible for us to know."

After saying "No," the molestations were not karmic balancing nor had they been planned by the soul, the Higher Mind said "Yes," they were due to a dark force that affected Molly. I shifted at once into releasement questions, calling for the strongest dark force and asking it to reply through Dora's voice as a channel. It said its name was "Joe" (the name of Dora's husband and Molly's father).

"I think you are trying to trick me, Dark One. Maybe you are *in* Joe?" It said "Yes." "In Molly, too?" It said "Yes." "Did you come from her grandfather?" It said "Yes." "And when you caused pain, helplessness, fear, anger in this little girl, how did you feel?"

"Powerful!" said the dark one.

In answer to further questions the dark one admitted that it got satisfaction from that feeling of power; that it had been in Granddad all of Granddad's life. After this, however, the dark one listened to my explanations and instructions without objections as I spoke of the warmth of the Light, of the shining helpers, and suggested that the dark one "Open your heart and let the Light shine in and melt away the lust for power, the satisfaction in causing trouble—and feel lighter, freer. Are you doing this?"

The dark one said it was. It admitted that in its heart it found a lightness. . . . "Getting lighter and lighter—till I'm gone. I want the dark to be gone." As its new name it chose "Just *Happy*."

Before Happy left it told us that there were other entities in Molly; but Dora, speaking as herself, said quickly (still in hypnosis), "Just positives—no more darks!"—not wanting to channel any more dark energies.

So I began the usual formula for undesirable entities that are to be released at a later time; but as an afterthought I added, "Or, there is another option: Would you rather follow Happy into the Light now?" When this got a quick "Yes" answer, I, too, was happy, as I know Dora was.

"Good! Then all of you go with Happy; let the light melt away the darkness in you and start a new type of existence."

The releasement had emptied Molly of the dark forces and now it was the stage of filling those empty "spaces" with positives, healing the old mistrust, pain, fear, and suspicion. This was done at some length both by verbal suggestion and visualizations.

Dora felt much relieved after the session. She realized that the change in her daughter might be more gradual. She also understood that part of her own responsibility was to *continue* to "send light" to Molly in her prayers and meditations.

# Remote Releasement
# of Dark Being from "Butch"

"Butch" is a middle-aged man who has had an abnormal life since conception. He told me that his grandfather is his father; that incestuous relationships were common in the family; he has been in and out of prison several times and at present is sentenced to four years for sexual relations with his teenaged stepdaughter (with her consent, it seems). In spite of all this, Butch has an inclination to the spiritual, and after taking half of a workshop on Releasement, he asked that we do this session for his own releasement. The channel was "Kay," an artist friend and coworker of mine.

I asked Kay (who had placed herself in hypnosis) to "stand back and see the situation clearly and describe it."

"I see a dark maelstrom, a whirlpool of dark swirling energy . . . I do not see the source. It seems to be within him."

"Is it a part of his own being?"

"I fear so."

"Now I am speaking to the maelstrom of dark energy," I said. "Come out of Butch and be visible to Kay. Tell me your source."

"You well know my source!" loudly answered the maelstrom.

"Stay back. Yes, I know your source. I ask Master Ching to talk with you, for Butch *asked* us to do this work, to separate him from any dark forces trying to obstruct him; and 'ask and you shall receive.' Master Ching, will you speak?"

"Butch should be liberated. All so possessed should be liberated."

"Are we to do that now, Master Ching?"

"You must try," he said, implying that perhaps the attempt might not be easy, that this dark one might be strong.

I started right in with, "Are you happy, dark one? I don't think you are."

"I take satisfaction from those who let me in."

"That is not real happiness. Do you know what happiness is?"

"Should I?"

I mentioned other words, like "compassion," to Maelstrom (whom now I thought of as 'he'). I told him about Light, and asked him to look into the center of himself. He found a black spot there.

"Look in the middle of the black spot," I directed.

With emotion he suddenly asked, "Why do you wish to hurt me?"

"I don't wish to hurt you, Dark One," I said gently. "You need to be brave. What do you see or feel in the very center?"

"Pain! There is where hurt lives . . . under the hurt? Evil! Under the evil? . . ." Then the words bursting out, "Why cannot I be like the others?!"

In the middle of his center, under the pain and blackness, he finally saw "a very little child."

"And inside the little child?" I prompted, softly.

"You know."

"Tell me."

"That word you call love."

"How do you feel when you say that word, 'love'?"

"The little child—love is healing the little child."

"Look inside the little child. What do you find there?"

"What you call gold . . . a golden light. . . . I feel—dif ferent. . . . The whirling darkness is still around. . . . I really don't want to do this."

I did not know whether this was Maelstrom or Kay speaking. Assuming it was Maelstrom, I continued, "You've been dark a long time."

"I'm good at it!" he said grandly.

"Yes, you have been; but you've covered over the little child and the light with all the darkness for so long that you forgot that the child and the light were there."

"I liked it that I forgot. I don't like the hurt!"

There was more of this back and forth conversation. When I told Maelstrom that I was going to place my hand on Kay's, she flinched from the reaction of the dark energy. Maelstrom told me that he whirled because "if you whirl, nothing can get you."

"Who told you *that?* That only means you become a big

self-centered whirl not caring about anything or anyone else."

"You bet!" agreed Maelstrom.

"You cover up the pain and the little child with darkness."

"I don't think about that."

"You have been walking in the darkness of your own shadow. This is your moment of opportunity, Dark One. All you need to do is to turn to the Beings of Light that I invited here."

"They keep shooting that white light at me."

I told him that he had free will. I asked if he didn't feel the warmth of the light. I told him about another dark one that admitted he felt the light "on my behind," and then turned sideways to feel the warmth on his cheek, then on his face.

"You're quite a salesman," said Maelstrom. I laughed. "Is it enough to say I'll try?" he asked.

"It doesn't have to be *your* power. Just turn to the Light. . . ."

"I see Light . . . but if I leave, there are many others to take my place. . . . I am willing to leave; but it's a long way to go—it's very steep. . . ."

"The helpers will help you to get up; you are not alone. They will take you to a place where you can rest as long as you need to, and unlearn the old things and learn wonderful new things. A whole new life is ahead for you."

"Where's that little one?" he interrupted.

"Safe in your heart."

"It's not hurting now, but it will always be remembered."

"Yes, it's no longer hurting. But you are no longer dark. You need a new name." He thought that just "*trying*" would do, but I suggested that he make it stronger, something beautiful, something he wanted to become.

"This is so hard," he objected.

I suggested a name like "Courage," or "Strength," or "Trust."

"I have no courage."

"You have trust in the Light and trust in the helping hand. How about *Trust?*"

He said that was okay, but would not speak the word. "I think '*Climber*' is better."

"That's a good name. And the Helping Hand will help you up, and the Everlasting Arms are always underneath you. Are you happier now?"

"Well, it's different."

"And remember, you are your own boss."

"I thought you were my boss."

I chuckled. "Oh, no, you have free will—you are your own boss. And you were brave—you had more courage than you thought. . . ." (Climber was trembling.) "What's the matter, Climber?" I asked very gently.

"No problem."

I spoke to the Bright Beings. "Bright Ones, help him to rest now. This period will be like pupation. You know, Climber, how a caterpillar spins a cocoon around itself, then splits its skin and is not a caterpillar any more but a pupa almost in suspended animation. But then the pupa splits its skin, and—what comes out?"

"Butterfly," he murmured.

"Yes, no longer a ground-crawling caterpillar or a dormant pupa but a creature of beauty that flies in the sunshine and sips sweetness from bright flowers. . . . Now I am speaking to the *new you,* Climber: Do you have a message for Butch before you leave him permanently?"

Climber, the former dark Maelstrom, said, "He must *fight* the dark. He makes it so easy for the dark to come. *He* must work as hard as *I* am—he must work *every moment*. He must turn to spiritual things. . . . I see the Light. It will be a hard trip—but it is *my* trip and *I* must do it."

"Yes, but 'Ask and you shall receive.' You can ask the Shining Helpers."

"Hey, you guys," called Climber loudly, "give me a hand!"

"Good-bye, Climber. Happy journey." And Kay said she saw them floating up, climbing.

Then we turned our attention once more to Butch. Kay's Spiritual Advisor, in contact with Butch's Higher Self, told us, "This is quite enough for one day, but *he must work for his own salvation*. It is up to him. He will get answers. He gets answers but doesn't hear them. . . . He needs help."

We ended the session with a visualized white protective capsule around Butch.

(Butch is now out of prison and is living with friends. "Things are better than I was afraid they'd be," he wrote to me.)

## Psychic Attack by a Discarnate

"Vera," a young woman in my family, was near term in her pregnancy when she had a horrible dream of being tortured to death, and, in spirit looking down at her mutilated body, was fearing that her husband might be the next to be killed. In fright she awoke, and waked her husband to receive his comfort. Later that morning she told me of the dream. I was visiting there and did not want her to sleep again until I had at least contacted what I felt was an attacking dark entity and had made it promise to remain quiescent until I could later talk with it. This I did, with the young lady's eager consent, the entity saying "Yes," it would remain passive until then.

A week or so afterward, with Charlene as channel in

hypnosis, I prepared to call the entity when Charlene suddenly said, "Dark water . . ." (This is very unusual—for a person in hypnosis to volunteer verbally spoken words before being asked to do so by the facilitator, especially at the beginning of a session.)

"I see dark water—like a backwater—tree roots in the water, trees standing around on the bank—not a symbol—it exists—in Florida, maybe. . . . There's a feeling of closing in. . . . It is hot, steamy . . . rather dark. . . .

"Something is trapped in the water," she went on. "It's settled down deep in the mud—a dead body, caught on a limb of a tree with silt deposited around it. . . . It has been there a long time . . . looks human but it is not intact. It is female; I don't see any legs. There's not much left of the face. The hair is short, light-colored. . . . This was in 1832 on the Gulf Coast of Florida. She was an evil woman, killed, and her body brought here to this back bay to hide it."

"Was she really evil?" I inquired.

"Yes. She was a witch. She made sacrifices to the devil, to Satan—sometimes animals, sometimes babies. Her body was in the mud for a long time; her soul, too, for a long time. Then it sort of moved around, looking for a place to go. . . . Her name is Jenny. She is twenty-two."

"Jenny, I'm calling you. *Why* did you sell yourself to the devil?"

"Because my family made me leave home, because I loved a black man."

"Love is not evil unless it is made so. Did you have anger and hate that turned you toward the devil?"

"That was partly it. The man I went away with practiced devil worship and made me help. . . . Yes, I think I knew it was evil, but I was afraid of him. I loved him a little bit, I guess. I stayed with him quite a while back in the swamp area. . . . People came for meetings. They knew—black people knew where to find us. Then some of my family, sort of like a posse, came looking for me. They looked a long time. . . . They *didn't want me*—they didn't want me to come back home. They came—to kill me, I guess."

"Had you injured any of them, by curses, for instance?"

"M'hm."

"Then they hoped to protect themselves by coming after you. There is a basic Law of Justice, Jenny, a Law of Compensation, that says whatever you do to others comes back to you. Did you know about this law? No? Then you were ignorant of the law. But you did know it was wrong to sacrifice animals and babies, didn't you?"

"I didn't know it until I was going to have a baby of my own. . . . Four of them came in a boat for me. They tied up the others there—there weren't many others—and took me into the swamp area, tied me to a tree—one was my brother—all four of them raped me—all four shot the guns, so nobody would know who did it—shots in the head, hips, chest—and the baby died. . . ."

"What were your last thoughts and feelings? Did you feel that you deserved all this?"

"No. It was their fault in the first place for making me leave. I wasn't doing evil things then. I didn't know the black man was evil."

"You said you were afraid of what the black man might do to you if you didn't help him. You had fear and felt helpless. Now think of the babies who were sacrificed: *They* felt helplessness, fear, pain. *Now* do you feel you deserved your death?"

(Long pause) "No, I don't think so." (Such callousness is usually an indication of an obsessing dark force in the speaker.)

"Look inside yourself. Is there an entity in you, Jenny?"

Jenny paused, then said, ". . . There's something—something cold inside."

"Come out, 'Cold'," I ordered. "What is your name?"

Cold said it didn't have a name (which made me understand that it was probably a minor demonic type). It said that it entered Jenny when she was "very young, about three or four. . . . She was never too smart, but she was comfortable, a good place to live. It was easy. She wouldn't mind too much."

"What was your influence on her?" I asked.

"Well . . . What do you mean?"

"Oh, make her have temper tantrums? Make her fall in love with an evil man?"

"I might have given a little push along the way," replied the no name with a smirk.

"Is there a dark one like you, a brother of yours, in the black man?"

This time there was a grin: "Might have been."

"Cold, you sound cheerful but I think that's a pretense. You pretend to have fun; but I think you are really lonely and unhappy. Isn't that true?"

There was a long pause. "I haven't been unhappy."

"What is your definition of happiness?"

"Happiness is going about your business, doing what they tell you to do."

"*Who* tells you to?" (condensed here) "I know who your boss is. He wants you to think that instant obedience without thinking is 'happiness'. He tells you that you *have* to obey everything he tells you to do; he says light doesn't exist and warmth is dangerous and will burn you. He considers you his slave, his robot, with no free will. He is the Father of Lies. You aren't as smart as Jenny if you believe all that he told you!"

Needled, Cold answered, "I'm smart—I do what he tells me; that's why I'm smart, so he won't do anything to me!" There was more conversation and argument on both sides, and finally Cold made a cautious decision. He did not want to go back to the darkness and the cold; he didn't like the sound of the "round bare room lined with mirrors" that would force him to look at himself; he hesitated about going to the Light; but he did consent to move to one of the intermediate astral levels—one of those conditions characterized by the Bright Beings as being "*of* the Light but not *in* the Light"—where he could "rest and unlearn the old things and learn wonderful new ones."

"Before you go, tell me: What about Vera's dream? What was the reason for that?"

"We had a plan. It was a good plan. Jenny wanted to go where her baby was. She couldn't find *her* baby, so she'd go find a (pregnant) body, and I went with her. The dream—sometimes if you are frightened, upset, sad, sick, it's easier for us to get into a body."

"Was Vera ordinarily too strong to be entered?"

"Yes," admitted Cold.

"I placed a protective capsule of light around Vera and her baby, to protect her from entities like you. But now you are not 'Cold' anymore. Why don't you choose a new name for yourself?"

With sudden childish eagerness, Cold said, "That's what I was thinking about all along! That's what I want, a name!" After a moment he decided he wanted *"Homer!* I knew a guy named Homer once. He was kinda dumb, but he was all right."

"All right. Then hold out your hand to the guide, Homer, trusting the guide. Good-bye, Homer."

"Good-bye . . . thank you. . . . That's a good word, too, isn't it? I'm not very cold now—a little, but not very."

(I should perhaps have worked more on this residual chilliness and may recheck on this at a later session.)

"Now Jenny. You didn't *want* to sacrifice babies, did you?"

Slowly Jenny answered, "I never *did* do what I *wanted* to, ever—just what's *easiest* to do. . . . I don't think I ever did anything good to anybody. My parents were good to me; maybe they spoiled me. . . . Maybe I made them happy. . . ."

"You are honest about yourself, Jenny. It takes courage to look honestly at yourself and see your own selfishness and weaknesses. It takes courage to do what is good; but there's a thrill, a sort of breathless feeling like an adventure, when you are brave. So you have honesty and courage. Now what about Vera's dream? *You* wanted a baby, so you wanted to frighten her and make her open, so you could push into her body? Is that the reason for the terrible dream?"

"That's part of it. I didn't know if it would work . . . but when her baby was born I'd take its spirit away. . . ."

"To where? You'd take away the baby's spirit, let the body die, just take the spirit?"

"I haven't figured that out. . . . I was in the water a long, long time. Then I came out and looked for someone. . . . I couldn't find my baby. . . ."

"Jenny, are you sorry for the past things you did; are you sad about them?" (She said, "M'hm.") "If you 'never did anything good to anybody,' maybe it was because of the dark heavy things inside you, like selfishness, cruelty, dimness of mind." (Jenny, through Charlene, put her hand to her forehead.) "Now just put out of you those dark things, put out of your brain the dimness so that your mind is clear, calm, cool. Put out of your heart the anger and hate. And now can't you see a light? And see someone coming for you?"

She saw a light. She saw someone—"more than one person" coming. "One is kinda like my mother. One is kinda like me. Only two coming. Others are around."

"Ask your mother about your baby. It's her grandbaby."

"She says, 'Yes—yes—yes.' Her face looks like she's glad to have me back. She says, 'Come on back, now.'"

Before she left, Jenny gave advice for other pregnant women: "They need to rest and keep in good health, stay strong. They need to follow the doctor's advice. They need to be happy—to be happy and have love. Love will help. They mustn't be afraid."

"Thank you, Jenny. Now good-bye; have a happy journey."

"Good-bye . . . Thank you."

Vera had no more trouble of this nature during pregnancy. Although the delivery was difficult, the child is healthy in all ways, as is her younger brother.

A comment is in order here about human beings who at any time in any life become devil worshipers or make contracts or "bargains" with the darkness. Often such bargains are made either as a game, an adventure, by teens or older persons, or in a moment of terrific pressure, of despair, or of helplessness. After that moment of crisis has passed, the human being often thinks little of the bargain—may forget it entirely. But the dark ones do not forget, and it appears that they take such bargains as irrevocable contracts on the part of the human being, and keep hounding the soul lifetime after lifetime. This pattern has appeared in several cases that I have had. Even some persons who in the present life are worthy, respected citizens, healers, counselors, and so on, may be struggling still under the weight of ancient bondage to the darkness, in physical symptoms that modern techniques seem unable to alleviate, or in emotional or mental ways. The soul needs to be completely freed from the old ties and is eager to do so—but the darkness is by no means willing to let a former slave be freed and will obstruct in every possible way, often in sly, tempting ways.

The attainment of freedom from any former ties to the dark side needs to be a deliberate choice of the person's free will—a definite, emphatic command to the dark beings to withdraw permanently and an equally urgent call to the Beings of Light for assistance and protection. The aid of a therapist or a group of friends is of immense help as well.

## First Rules Concerning the Dark Path

### *For All Who in Ignorance Are Attracted*

1. You call to yourself and increase in yourself the dark forces and energies, such as malice, anger, hate, resentment, hostility, jealousy—and also fear.

2. What you send out to others is what you sow; and what you sow, that is what eventually you will reap for yourself: injury, misery, fear, ill fortune.

3. Strong as your own power may become, there are always still stronger white powers which can overcome yours. Therefore, no matter how mighty your power may become, it is eventually destined to fail.

4. There is always a point of decision. No matter how far you have gone on the downhill path of darkness and arrogance, you may still make a choice between going farther on the "Left-hand Path" or stopping and turning around.

5. If you decide to continue as before, you have deliberately turned from the Light; and in front of you is a dark shadow—your own. The shadow brings confusion and uncertainty; your steps are not sure. The shadow also brings delusions of grandeur. The shadow seems huge, as huge as your own picture of your powers, your own swollen ego.

6. If you decide to turn around, you forget yourself and your shadow. You think of the brightness, the change, the different and wonderful feelings of peace, openness, and love. You may have a long way to go back but the important thing is the change of direction: You are now heading up again, seeing the Light as a beacon, feeling its warmth, comfort, and protection, moving toward it.

7. If you turned around, you are no longer on the path of darkness and you are ready for the First Rules of the Path of Light, which begin, "Do no harm."

*chapter 9*

# STRONG DARK
# (DEMONIC) ENTITIES

There appear to be several different types of strong dark entities. I have not encountered any of the types described in Malachi Martin's book, *Hostage to the Devil* (1976), or any of those described in Naegeli-Osjord's book, *Possession and Exorcism* (1988). Nor to my knowledge has Baldwin or any other American Releasement therapist. As Baldwin found, however, so also I have found that the dark ones tend to specialize, some focusing on causing physical suffering, as from cancer and other diseases; some specializing in destroying relationships between human beings, alienating parent from child, sibling from sibling, man from woman; and so on.

And, surprisingly to me, the old legend or myth of Lucifer and his fall from grace because of his inordinate egotism and arrogance appears to be as near to the truth of the origin of Evil as human concepts have been able to express it. I had tossed out of my mental library this old anthropomorphic religious idea; but when Baldwin before me found that the dark ones themselves seemed to be supporting it in its spiritual sense, and my own cases also did, I have to accept it as a working basis when dealing with the dark entities.

The old books of black witchcraft contain rituals by which to invoke some of the dark ones by name. It is distressing to know that a widespread interest in such things has been growing among the youth of the land, even children in junior high school, and also among some adults, who have discovered that when they hold a seance and invoke an entity by name and give instructions, *things happen*. This gives the group a feeling of power—and that is the temptation that continues to draw the members of the group together repeatedly, playing with this dangerous power as if it were a new toy.

Two brief examples will show what I mean: The first concerns a beautiful girl in a high school near my hometown who was reported to be the female leader of a group of students involved in such activities. On the school bus she loudly accused one of the Hispanic girls of some minor thing that displeased her and "cursed" the girl, telling her that she was going to get beaten up. One of the other girls on the bus related all this to her mother and said that the next day the Hispanic girl appeared, bruised from having been beaten by her father the night before.

The other instance is far more serious. The mother, a one-time witch by her own admission (in this case using what I call "grey magic" instead of "white magic"), had apparently taught her son, now in his early twenties, how to perform the rituals or invocations to produce certain events that he desired. Angry at one of his male acquaintances, he impulsively directed a vicious thought-form or curse at the young man . . . and shortly afterward the newspaper reported the death of that young man in a terrible accident, for he fell into a vat of boiling beet sugar and died in great pain, helplessly.

It was the mother herself who told me about her son's sending the curse, that the young man should have "a slow painful death"—and of how intensely remorseful her son now felt. It is also a good example of how insidious is the lust for power and the enjoyment of power, even when its dangers may be half appreciated. Looking at this case with the knowledge that I now have, my educated guess is that the son was possessed temporarily by a very strong dark one. I well remember the cold chill with which I heard the words, "a slow painful death"—because they describe the manner in which the sender of that curse will himself sometime die, even though perhaps in a future life. He had condemned himself, unknowingly.

In the movie version of *The Ten Commandments* Pharaoh condemns the firstborn of the enslaved Jews to death. When the returned Moses hears of this, he is beside himself with helpless grief and anger, for he knows that Pharaoh has sentenced his *own* son, Pharaoh's son, to death as the firstborn—son also of the woman Moses had loved in earlier times. It truly is a law of the spiritual life that what we give, we eventually receive back; "what goes around comes around."

## Examples of Strong Dark Entities

One of the first strong evil entities that I encountered through professional activities was a living woman. This was in 1987, before I had learned that whenever a human being, living or deceased, exhibits evil tendencies, there almost always is present *within* that person a dark (nonhuman) entity, a servant of the darkness. (The evil tendencies of the human beings, alive or dead, abruptly become much less pronounced or even seem to be obliterated entirely after the dark nonhuman entity is released, removed from the human host.)

# Evil in a Brazilian Witch

When I was in college, a graduate student became one of my special friends. Coming from Eastern Europe at sixteen, knowing hardly any English, Albie managed to survive and put herself through college and then through graduate chemistry. During further graduate work at another university she agreed to marry a Brazilian widower with two young children. This meant that she would go with him to his home in Brazil and learn to speak Portuguese while caring for the two children and supporting his work. She was in her mid-thirties at this time. We have kept contact with each other all during these many years.

In 1987, when she was about eighty-six, she wrote me one of her long letters. Her husband had died some years before and she had developed a close friendship with the young man she had hired as gardener. She wrote how deeply it hurt her when this gardener and another man broke into her house and stole some articles. She had also suffered various illnesses and accidents recently. She asked me to do some channeling work with my friends and discover why these things were happening to her. She felt that the gardener's wife, jealous of the friendship, might be causing these occurrences by means of black magic. She could not believe that the gardener, "Mario," would have used her friendship so callously.

With Lili channeling, we contacted Albie's Higher Mind and questioned it. It said that Mario had originally had genuine affection but that he "has no depth. His love is like a child's, like an animal's. It can change easily, like the wind. . . . In the beginning he was not trying to *use* her; greed changed him. This is a selfish stage. He is a 'young soul'. He reminds Albie of someone she knew when she was sixteen. Her need at sixteen was unfulfilled. Mario fulfilled a need when she needed him. In reality this friendship with him was a blessing.

"Yes, it is Mario's wife who is directing black magic toward her. There is jealousy, a great deal of anger. The wife is strange. . . ."

Lili's voice fell so low that she was barely able to whisper. I could not hear what she was saying. Another member of the group spoke, "She says, 'She's here. Make her leave. Make her leave.'" Lili's body was tensing, her face twisted, her breathing changed. She began to shake. Not until I called on the Christ-light to shine down and dispel the dark power could she relax and speak.

I asked, "Master Ching, what should we do—turn this darkness back to Mario's wife?"

"Yes," he said, emphatically. So all of us present, with our masters, asked that Universal Mind send the darkness back to its creator and give protection to Lili and also to Mario; and at Master Ching's suggestion we "lifted Albie high—emotionally, mentally, spiritually, in all ways—so that her mind may be open." We also visualized her enclosed in a protective capsule of ruby-red light. "Is red the right color for her?"

"Yes, and elevated above the earth and earthly affairs. Cut the bonds between the wife and Mario and allow him to grow. She [the wife] has kept him in bondage."

I visualized a sword of light floating firmly down between Mario and the wife, and Lili's body again tensed up until the Christ-light was called upon, when she again relaxed.

"Let this sword sever the control this woman has had

upon Mario. Let all bonds between them be cut. May the wife be receptive and see the Light. . . . Is there anything else we need to do?"

"Albie and Mario are accepting the change," said Lili. "The wife never will."

After returning to full awareness, Lili amplified, "That woman was *evil!* She attacked me—not you or Albie or Mario—and I was taken by surprise—I had never had that happen before. She just suddenly came at me like *this—*" (Lili's eyes got huge and she reached claw-like hands out.) "It was like a nightmare—I couldn't move, I couldn't talk. I felt like I was shouting but no sound came out. Oh, she was much stronger than the others we have dealt with. She is evil! When you asked that she be receptive to the Light she seemed to shrink way down and be like a tiny spark, but she still said, 'NEVER!'"

Looking back at this, I feel sure that a strong dark entity was in Mario's wife, perhaps possessing her completely. At the time of this session I had not yet learned to check *every* cold or vicious human being for possible obsessing dark entities. Albie is still living, in her 90s now and no longer seems to be a target for dark beings.

## *"Pride" Chooses to Go to the Halfway Place*

Concerned about the activities and orders of a powerful American figure, we debated whether he might have an obsessing entity in him that was causing him to issue various orders that seemed to us to be arrogant and ill advised, orders which could easily involve the entire nation, even other nations, in unstable situations. I shall call him "Mr. Matthew Bartlett"—or "Bart," and I shall say that he was the president of a certain immense corporation—which is not far from the truth. Our first question, of course, needed to be that of the ethics of our desire to release any obsessing entities that might be in him.

With Charlene, R.N., as channel, we started by asking Master Ching if it was all right to ask Bart's Higher Mind about his lower self. Charlene's "yes" finger rose at once. "And if we find an obsessing entity, is it our responsibility to release it?" "Yes," was the immediate answer.

"Thank you, Master Ching. Now, Higher Mind of Bart, we know that you want the very best, spiritually, for Bart's evolving soul. I ask your supervision in this session, along with Master Ching's." Then I asked for the strongest entity to come out and tell us its name, through Charlene's voice.

"You may call me 'Pride'," came the reply after a moment.

"We may *call* you 'Pride'? Are you a part of Bart, or are you an entity in yourself?" (no answer) "Are you an individual, Pride?"

After a rather long pause, eight or ten seconds, Pride said, "I am a proud person. He is a proud person, too. We get along fine. . . . I found him when he was 15 or so. I did not enter him then—well, I did and then I left. I knew I could come back anytime I needed to. I had a plan in mind that wasn't working out at that time. I entered him again about ten years ago when he was much older."

"About the time he was only vice president of the company?"

"About that time."

"Pride, you told us that you are a proud *person*. Are you male or female? Have you ever been human, ever had a human body of your very own?"

Pride told us that he was male and female both—that he

was strong, and getting stronger—that his sustenance was fear and hate. "There's lots of it. I don't have to be hungry!"

I laughed, "Yes, there's lots of it. I think you have a boss, Pride. Who is he?" (no answer) "You have a commander, don't you, Pride? What is his name? . . . Why are you silent?"

"I don't want his name mentioned. He gets credit for too much as it is."

"You feel *you* want the credit?"

"Yes. We're working that way now. Before, it was a more general area. There were many of us; we were just going around at a quieter pace, just whispering things into people's ears to create fear, hate. Now some of us are in a position—*I'm* in a position—to *do something* about it, on our own."

"And if you are in Bart, you certainly *are* in a high position to 'do something about it.' And if you do, what happens?"

"There's a PLAN. It may work out *now;* it may not. If it does, we hope for POWER—power over the human race, power over mankind."

"Will you use your power through Bart—is that what you are looking for? Will he assume this position of power?"

Then Pride spoke the words that showed his nature most truly: "We won't need him when the time comes, either." He would say no more about when the time might come, or who would decide when the time had come. He remained silent for several minutes.

I used that pause to explain to Pride about the "Basic Law of Life," that what an individual gives is what he receives back. I pointed out that power does not make happiness—that entities focused on pride or power do not even know what happiness really is; that such entities are lonely, cold; and that I thought Pride had been lonely, "haven't you, Pride?"

Pride pursed his lips tightly. "No."

With a chuckle I asked, "Do you ever tell lies, Pride?"

Loudly he declaimed, "There's no such thing as a lie."

"Now that's an interesting statement. 'There's no such thing as the truth' would be an interesting one, too. But probably the word 'truth' isn't in your vocabulary, either. I think you have been cold, too, haven't you?"

"Not that I know of," he said, flippantly.

"And it is your pride that keeps you from being truthful now. That's understandable, because if the truth gets too close to your heart, it may make you turn inward and look into your heart. And that's what I want you to do: look into the very core of your heart. What do you see or feel there?"

Wearily he said, "Emptiness," and I knew the turning point had come.

"Look into the middle of the emptiness. Something is there."

Listless still, he felt "a pulse beating." At my suggestion he continued to "look still deeper," moving his hands slowly over his body, and finally saying, "It's like—a steel anvil."

I told him about the Light. "It exists. Your commander—whoever he is—told you it *didn't* exist, true? But that if it did exist, it was hurtful, that you should fear it. True?" He admitted this. "Well, your commander is called 'The Father of Lies'. He told you a lie. He deceived you, Pride, from the very beginning. You are intelligent; you know you can tell the difference between truth and lies, if you want to. You told me the truth just now, when you said that your commander had told you the Light didn't exist, and if it did, it would burn you, was dangerous, fearsome—you said *that* was true."

I went on, "I am to tell all the dark ones three things: That there is the Light, it does exist; second, that it is warm and welcomes all who come to it. They begin to feel happy. . . ." (Pride put his hand to his head.) "Happiness, joy, peace—all of these exist in the Light. The third thing is that every individual does have free will. That means you are not a robot, Pride. Your boss told you you *had* to obey his commands, didn't he?"

"I wanted to."

Pride admitted that if a servant of the commander didn't follow orders (he paused a long time) "they were called down . . . down to the cold, to the deep . . . for so long—many ages. . . ." He said he had always obeyed orders and had never been called down.

"Pride, you tried to be faithful to the boss; you've done what he told you to, you've followed orders, you've believed everything he said. But you didn't know that the truth is that he *is* the Father of *Lies,* and he deceived you—and that's a sad thing. I'm going to put my hand on Charlene's hand, and you can feel that what I am telling you is the truth. You can feel it!" Pride began to shrink away, his body (Charlene's body) quivering. "Don't shrink from it. You can feel the Light. I told you it was warm, welcoming. . . ." I continued to tell him about other dark ones who had resisted looking for the Light at first. "Can you feel it, Pride?"

His hands were clenched. He did not answer.

Challenging him, I reminded him that he did have free will and could make his own decisions. "You don't have to wait for a boss to tell you everything. If you make a decision here, the boss cannot send you down because you have the protection of the Bright Beings. You are intelligent. . . . What's the matter? You are restless."

"Nothing. You are bothering me."

There was much more to this back and forth conversation. Pride was now on the defensive: When I urged him to look into his heart and find something "like a diamond or a pearl," he replied, "I don't want to see it. I don't—*don't want to see.*"

I laughed softly. "That's another lie. You do want to see it. And you don't like what you are doing about the Plan but you are full of fear, aren't you, Pride?"

"No. I've worked hard to get where I am."

When I reminded him of the law that says the misery one causes others will rebound to the one who caused it, he said petulantly, "How about the misery they've given *me?* I suffer too, you know!"

I urged him again to look deep into his heart. "It's not a glowing pearl; it's more precious than a diamond. It's your *real heart.* Focus on that, Pride." Softly I added, "It's light—*in you!"*

"Yes," he whispered. But he was not yet ready to surrender. There was much more objection, resistance, even while perceiving the presence of the Bright Beings and feeling their warmth.

"Maybe I'm not ready. The job is almost done, almost ready."

"What *is* your job? I asked.

In a forlorn tone he said, "I don't know now—just don't know." He could see the light in his heart. "It's like—a glowing coal—not bright, but glowing . . . I can fan it—if I want to," he finished defiantly. "But what I've been doing—we're almost there! Almost there! I've worked so hard—"

Back and forth went his arguments and my persuasions. I pointed out that his traits included persistence, faithfulness to his commander, the ability to work hard and long—all fine characteristics, but pointed in the wrong direction, toward a wrong goal. If he would only turn around from the darkness in which he had been existing and face the Light, he would begin to lose the coldness and feel the warmth, to feel happiness, to start a whole new existence. But he hesitated.

His personality became petulant, childish, as he tried to

bargain with the Bright Ones: "Will they wait for me? Can I just stay here, just stay here till I decide?" When I suggested that he ask them, he said they answered, "No, not forever." Then, in a high childish voice he asked, "Ca-ca-can't you just leave me here and come back later and check? I wouldn't go, I'd stay right here, just on the edge."

He relayed their answer, "That wouldn't accomplish much."

He did go close enough to look into their eyes and see their expressions: "A bright, bright light—but it didn't hurt. . . . They may want to help. . . . Might—might been—might have been that they want to do away with the hurting. . . ." But he did not go close enough to hold out his hand to the Bright Beings, and I repeated that they never came to seize or grab anyone—they waited for Pride to make the first move.

The channel felt "very much confusion" in Pride: "He doesn't want to go back (to the darkness). He's not quite ready to go forward."

I described to Pride the "halfway place, a round bare room lined with mirrors where you will be alone—no one will bother you—alone with yourself, seeing only your own self. And you can think. . . ."

In a weary murmur Pride said, "I am thinking: I couldn't do—I couldn't do— Whatever's good, whatever's bad, or which is which, I don't know. But I wouldn't be doing either good or I wouldn't be doing either bad. . . ."

There was still more hesitation but finally Pride chose to "go through the door" into the round room. His voice, starting out very small but growing stronger, sounded rather sad.

"All right, Pride, and as I said, it's not forever but only until you figure out what to do. Anytime you call for the Light, one of the Bright Beings will come and free you. You do understand, Pride, that the only way out is if you yourself ask for the Light?"

He said he did.

"All right. Then good-bye. You go with my good wishes."

"Good-bye . . . Thank you." (in a barely audible murmur)

"Did you say, 'Thank you,' Pride? Is that what you said?"

Pride grimaced, paused. "Mmm—not really. No."

I had to laugh a little. "Well, Pride, I am putting my hand again on Charlene's hand and you can feel it. I thank you for your thanks—and you can feel my sincerity. I thank you for your gift. Now as I remove my hand, it just draws out of you any secret things you want to have gone—I don't need to know what they are—and I'll just shake them off and they will fragment into a harmless vapor: confusion, for one thing, and selfishness, and indecision. . . ." There was a long pause. "I'll come back and talk to you some other time. Good-bye." Then there was quietness.

I considered it a promise that I had made, and in meditation I have once or twice spoken to Pride. As for Bart, he is no longer in that high position, and he seems more relaxed.

### *"Satan" Chooses Death*

"Jill" is the adopted daughter of K, who is channeling to discover why the relationship between them is so unpleasant. Several of Jill's past lives were contacted in which she had been a member of a Satanic group. At the end of one life in which "she did a lot of damage—was wicked, malicious, romped around, spiteful, harming this one and that . . . she died unrepentant, invoking the devil, cursing God. . . ." In the next life Jill was a woman in Palestine, the mother of a child who was K. This life for both mother and daughter was uneventful, "absolutely routine," as chosen by K's soul: "I'd had such a really turbulent, wild, exciting, outside-of-law series of lives as seer and magician, as pirate, as zealot previously, that I was a little tired. I entered a life of conformity as a self-discipline to tone down the sense of being above and beyond law. . . . I had been a zealot in Palestine, was killed, crucified in 63 B.C., eventually entered Palestine again real fast in 230 A.D. I was Jewish. I wanted some beauty—a girl's normal wish for something romantic. All was dreary, drudgery. The wedding *should* have been one of magic and beauty. There was little enough even then. Never any poetry in that lifetime. I suppose I held that against my mother. . . . That 'witches' thing is still hanging on."

K placed her two index fingers together in a steeple. "It is the sign for 'protection' out of the old wisdom against demonology."

I interrupted to ask, "Do you mean that she laid a curse on you?" The answer, through finger movements, was "yes."

I invited the Beings of Light to beam their protective light on K, to wash her aura and clear it of the murky taint, and eradicate the "smell of fear" and neutralize the old curse. Then I asked if we were to send the curse back to its creator.

"The curse is washed away as if down a stream," said K. "It is neutralized; no one else is affected. It was created *long* ago by a dark entity. I myself had the wisdom to dispel the curse long ago, but I'm accepting present help. I had power by myself, but I might have been *proud*—so I had negative feelings about Jill. I'm still angry and judgmental—don't want to be. . . ."

I asked K's Higher Mind if Jill is still a member of the Satanic group, and K's voice said, "I think yes. My lips are quivering uncontrollably! . . . Boy, is she involved with a wicked spirit! Somebody is manipulating her with all its power. The Jill I know is a mask. She herself isn't there. Boy, I don't like what I'm seeing! I'm hearing a clamor, 'Get her out! Kill her!' It's not my Higher Mind!" K gave a deep sigh.

I called for my Spiritual Advisor, for the Christ Spirit, for the White Light to shine on us and asked, "Is Jill possessed? Are we to exorcise her?" I assured K that "the Great Ones are backing us up" and asked her to tell me what she saw.

"Boy, am I afraid! . . . I am assured that we are quite safe. My other children and I are indwelt by the Christ Spirit. Jill can dwell among us. We can pray for her and contain her. I see a vision of a wedge of light in which she can rest. There's a possibility of redemption at all times. We create for her a container in which she rests; we don't redeem her. We are undamaged and will go on with our lives. After I am gone, my other children will continue to pray for her."

I asked, "Is today the right time to help Jill? Is her opportunity <u>Now</u>?"

It was K who answered, "Yes, let's."

And so I called Jill's Higher Self and asked that it begin to re-evaluate mentally Jill's past lives and present activities.

K murmured, "I think she is possessed; I see a spirit within her. I see strongly a cradle of light—she *will* be healed, even if not in this lifetime. Jill herself—hm?—it's like this other had made something to indwell. My Jill is to be saved from them—there are two there—one is sleeping."

"Is it our responsibility to call this entity in Jill and talk?" ("Yes.") "Jesus, Buddha, other Beings of Light, please come."

"I sure hope you know what you are doing," wavered K.

"You are protected. We have the backup of these Great Ones. I am calling the entity who is in Jill. What is your name?"

Without argument came the name, "Marie." Asked how old she was, she said, "Ages, ages." Asked what country was hers, she said, "In Ethiopia, Egypt, Chaldea, Samothrace—"

She said that her name "Marie" came from a life in France when she had been killed as a witch.

"Were you a real witch?"

"Yes. I didn't do any bad—but was boiled. I only did bad to bad people."

"Were you judging who was bad?"

"If they hurt me, I hurt them."

"A Master once taught, 'Hatred never ceases by hatred.' You can't kill hatred by hating."

"People were always being mean to me. I got them good."

"Hurting for hurting continues down through the ages!"

"It seems you're trying to trick me."

"No, I'm not, Marie. Retaliation continues forever."

"The only way to get by is to *hurt first before they hurt you.*"

"Oh, no. The Silver Rule says, 'Don't do anything to others that you don't want others to do to you.' Because what you give is what you get back eventually: You don't get figs from thistle seeds that you've planted. If you plant seeds of love, you get love."

"I love Billie. [Jill named one of her sisters.] I don't want to hurt her." (It was not Marie speaking now.)

"Billie loves you first, so you love her. If you love others *first,* then they love you."

"I try to love my mom, but she's always criticizing."

"There's another type of life, helping others to be happy."

"I liked doing bad things." (Marie seemed to be speaking again.)

"Is there an entity in *you,* Marie?"

"Satan is in there," responded Marie without hesitation.

And now follows one of the rare sequences that sometimes take a therapist by surprise. Thank goodness I had read of something like this when I was in my teens, the very rare case of *true death.*

"I am calling you, 'Satan'." (I accepted the name, though believing that the entity had chosen it only to try to frighten me, pretending to be strong and evil.) "You have made Jill your house; you are ruining her life. As a witch, Marie was killed and in her pain she felt betrayed and turned to evil."

"She invited me long since. She enjoyed being important! It was far back in the mountains of Greece."

"She is about to change her mind. Satan, look deep inside your self. What do you see?"

"Emptiness, hollowness . . ."

"That's not very rich, is it? Look deeper. What else is there?"

"Loss . . . loss of my God, of my place, of joy . . . I see death . . ."

"That need not be. Look still deeper. Don't you find a pearl, something that glows?" (I used the leading question.)

There was a long pause, then, *"There's no hope. . . ."*

"Oh, yes, there is always another opportunity! The Bright Beings, the Shining Ones, are here to help. Turn your face sideways, feel their warmth, feel their light! Now see how it feels on your front, full on your face. And it is never too bright, never too late. The Bright Ones protect."

I continued to talk to "Satan," reminding him of the Silver Rule: "Don't do to others what you don't want done to yourself." "I suppose you enjoy controlling Marie and Jill, but that is not happiness. Turn to the Bright Beings. *You do have free will;* it is your choice. Can you feel their warmth?"

There was no answer, only a deep sigh. I continued, "There was another dark one who cried out to Jesus, 'Jesus, it isn't time! There is still too much to do!' and a voice answered, 'Yes, it *is* time; it is time to rest, to cast off the burdens.' Satan, have you turned toward the Bright Ones?"

Both hands were covering the face. This was a moment when challenges or scolding might be inappropriate. Gently I asked, "What's the matter? What's the matter?"

"I would cease to exist."

"Ask the Bright Beings if it is not true that you can let the Light wash you clean and let you start fresh. What do they tell you?"

"My existence is to be grief and burdens."

"Those are the seeds you sowed."

"I could never face that. I could cease to exist—and melt, as darkness melts in light."

"You do have free will. Is this your choice?"

"Yes! That would be a blessing, just to cease to exist. I'd be glad just to dissolve."

I hesitated. Vaguely I was remembering what I had read many years before, that in certain instances an entity might accept total death of its individuality instead of working out endless negative karma. But was this such a case?

"Do you *choose* to do it, now?" I asked, stalling for time.

"Yes, I will."

Still uncertain, I spoke to the helpers: "This entity has chosen death of his own free will and he says he is glad to go. I ask the Bright Ones to help perform this ritual. Is there certain wording that needs to be spoken?"

The answer was clear: "LET THERE BE LIGHT."

I repeated the words, adding the words of the entity himself, "As darkness melts in light, let the darkness of this one be dispelled by the Light. LET THERE BE LIGHT."

The entity murmured, with a little smile, "It is happening. . . . It is peace. . . ."

(K told me afterward that the melting took a little while, that I should have waited a little longer before going on. I recalled her advice at another such session a few years later.)

After "Satan" had gone I called Marie again. "Marie, your ruler has made his choice. Now you can turn around to the Light or go to the dungeon. You, too, have free will. If you put out all the negative aspects of yourself, the revengeful, hateful, jealous, angry parts of you, you will go to the Gardens of Learning in the astral world."

"I feel anxiety: Will I be hurt, punished?"

"No, the Keepers of the Gardens are firm but kindly and understanding. They will not force you. What is your decision?"

"Yes, I want to do that."

"See, you are smiling. Now is your opportunity to get rid of all the darkness in you."

"I see the Light. I see a place to go. Someone's hands are reaching, several of them, to lift me up. . . ."

We were told on rechecking Jill that there were still several small entities in her, that she herself was asleep but would eventually "come to life from being lifeless" when wakened gently. These others were described as being little playful spirits, "but she can be happy" even with their presence still in her.

### *"Power" Is Held Fast until Changed into a Star*

At a previous session a strong dark entity had been released from a young man, son of one of our group members; but a few days afterward he told his mother that the dark entity had returned. She requested that his case be the subject of a demonstration for a workshop on Releasement that was being held at the time and volunteered to be the channel. When Harry, another member of the group and an experienced meditator, offered to channel, however, she accepted with gratitude. He fulfilled the important qualifications of having no fear and of being somewhat detached from the emotional situation.

With Harry in his self-induced hypnosis, I spoke: "I am calling the dark entity that is in 'Thorvald'. Please come. Remain outside of Harry's body but put your thoughts into his mind and he will speak them for you. Please come and talk with me."

A heavy, coarse voice, unlike Harry's, said, *"What do you want?"*

"Why did you come back to Thorvald?"

"Because I wanted to come back! No, he didn't invite me back—it was more what he *did*. He was *proud*. He thought he was so great because he got rid of me. Of course when he's proud it's easy to get back in . . . I *help* him. I have lots of power. I will teach him all he needs to know about power!"

"You like power and I think you get a thrill out of controlling people but I doubt if you are happy. I don't think you know what 'peace' and 'love' are, either. I doubt if those words are in your vocabulary."

"Why have you had me channel through this man?"

I was taken by surprise. "Why do you ask?"

"He is uncomfortable."

"Harry, are you uncomfortable?"

"No," said the dark entity, *"I* am uncomfortable in him. It's like talking to you about peace and love. The only thing that makes me happy is POWER."

There was a good deal more conversation back and forth—not to say arguing!

At last he exclaimed, "How do I get out of here? I hate this place. I would like to go, but I am held by this man."

"You have three options."

"Go away. *This* is the best place for me."

"First is to go back to the darkness and stay there forever and *never* bother any living being, either human or nonhuman. Second is the one I'm urging you to choose for your own sake, to go now to the Light. Third is to choose to go to the round bare room lined with a million mirrors. You can see yourself, admire yourself, talk to yourself as long as you desire. It may get boring. Only when you *ask,* of your own free will, for the Light to come can you be free. Oh, there is a fourth option, to accept annihilation and be blotted out of existence as an individuality. This is very rare, but one dark one did choose it, of his own free will. He said, 'It would be peace.' Now I am going to count slowly from one to ten, to help you decide."

I began to count slowly, reviewing the options between numbers. The dark entity muttered, "I don't want the darkness . . . I don't want the mirrors. . . . If I go to the Light I'll die. The darkness is the only life I have."

"Who told you *that?*" I asked. "The Master of Lies? Look inside yourself, Dark One. There is something there that belongs to you but you have forgotten it. What is there, in the very middle of the darkness? The very center of yourself?"

"You keep trying to get me to see the little tiny star that is there, the tiny pure white star."

"Yes, that's what I mean. Watch it. What happens?"

"I'm trying not to watch it."

I laughed. "Watch it anyway."

"It wants to expand. I don't want it to expand. . . . It feels like I am dying. . . . It feels like I am dying. . . . The star is hot. It will burn me!"

"Who told you *that?* It is not hot, just warm. Some dark ones have found that under the darkness in them is pain, but under the pain is light and its gentle growth."

"My memory knows nothing but darkness."

"But now there is a star—your star, and it proves that you were created as a Child of Light. You know I am telling you the truth."

"You trapped me. Why don't you let me go? You could make this man let me go. This man makes me stay and listen to you. My strength is disappearing. . . . My strength is going. . . . Is it Harry's serenity? . . . It's going—it's waning—" (He was fearful.) "There is so little left of me. . . ." (voice feeble)

"One dark one said he was so small after all his darkness had gone that his name should be 'Infinitesimal,' but he was happy. Use your little strength to go into the Brightness."

"They will dissolve what's left of me."

"They cannot dissolve what is light—only the darkness. *Become* the star. *Desire* to be in the star. . . . Look, feel . . . how peaceful, how quiet." (I was speaking very softly.) "You feel you can *grow* and *expand*. You don't feel powerless. . . .

"I am proud of you," I continued. "I can't call you 'Dark One' any more. I'll call you 'Star'."

"I still feel darkness. It's hard to let go. He (Harry) won't let me lie to you. There are corners and traces of darkness I kept for *me*. It's all I've ever known."

"Star, let them go, and all your memories of darkness. Turn your mind to the other memories. You forgot your life as a star. Recall *those* memories. Ask the Bright Ones to give you the memories of your star. . . . Turn toward the Bright Ones, [etc.]. . . Turn toward the Bright Ones, Star. Do you see them?"

"There are two—kind of spheres of light that are coming for me. They are drawing me. Can I trust them?"

"Of course you can trust them. You could not trust anyone when you were dark. And you have free will as to whether you go with them or not. Yes, you can trust them."

"Why was I thrown so far into the blackness?" asked Star plaintively. "There was nothing to *be* but to be black."

Mentally I rejected his word "thrown." "Star, I don't know why you were so far in the blackness. Some entities seem to start out as little mischievous ones who find it 'fun' to trick and annoy others, and then little by little they become more malicious and darker, and then a strong dark one captures them."

"Who's watching over Thorvald?" he asked suddenly. And from here on his thoughts were for his former host and slave.

"I entered through his right side. . . . You must find a way to close and heal the open place. . . . I am being drawn away from all that was dark, and this place is fading Will you take care of Thorvald?"

I assured him that not only Thorvald's mother but also Thorvald's own Higher Self were taking care of him. "Do you want to say anything to him?" I ended.

There was a pause, then, "I am sorry . . . I am so sorry. . . . I meant no harm." He continued in a whisper, with tears coming, "I am so sorry, I'm so sorry. . . . Please take care of him."

He was weeping softly. "It hurts. It hurts."

"Yes, birth often hurts." I placed my hand on Harry's forehead, "Let the pain ease, let the pain ease, let the pain come into my hand and then go out of this room harmlessly." (Harry said after the session that the pain and weeping were catharsis and needed to be allowed to continue longer, for perhaps five minutes or more.)

As the Lights drew Star away, he was still quietly but deeply weeping.

"And let the pain ease," I repeated. "Tell us what you see, Harry."

"He's going, but he's in great pain. This pain is *enormous*."

I asked my Spiritual Advisor: "Master Ching, is there something we should do for Star's pain?"

He answered, "The Light will heal him . . ." There was a pause. . . . "I had to calm Harry first. He felt the pain of the dark one. . . . Focus hard on Thorvald. Bring him into the center of this group [in meditation] and fill him with light. He is unnerved right now. Surround and fill him with that light and send him peace. Do that now."

We did so as I led a guided meditation, asking also that Harry's body be renewed with all the strength he needed and sending our blessings after Star. Harry brought himself back to normal consciousness.

Then we sat around discussing some of the points of the session.

Very strong dark beings are usually difficult to persuade. They may escape—they simply leave and break the contact established with the facilitator. Harry as channel was able to "confine the dark one within certain vibratory limits" and prevent the dark one from moving freely and making an escape.

Harry was also able to prevent the dark one from telling lies and saying that *all* its darkness had been dispelled.

"Its shape was something like an object with corners, and it was keeping bits of darkness hidden away in the corners. It wanted to retain those bits as seeds for its very life. It truly felt it would *die* if *all* its darkness was dispelled."

Harry felt that the dark one was genderless, neither male nor female. This dark one was focused on power and the control of Thorvald. Others are focused on other things, such as their "assignment": e.g., to confuse a victim's mind; to cause the victim suffering, as from cancer; to stir up discord in a family; to produce despair and suicidal thoughts, etc. Most say they were able to enter during a moment when the victim was in great fear, anger, or pain.

Before this demonstration Harry had asked me, "Do you

believe that there is a spark of light in *every* creature, in *every* dark one?"

I had answered seriously, "From all my experience with releasing dark ones and other beings, I can say that I truly believe that there is. I have come to be convinced that there is a light in *every* creature, human and nonhuman, like sparks of the One Original Light."

After this experience as a channel Harry said, "You told me that you believed that there is a light in every dark one. I don't *believe*—I *know*."

"Yes, and I consider the dark ones as just Prodigal Sons not yet returned home."

"That's what they are—Prodigal Sons," agreed Harry.

(This case was first printed in *The Journal of Regression Therapies,* Vol. VIII, No. 1)


## Jack Has Rage, Bicki Has Both, and the Boss Comes

"Bicki" sat quietly, describing her problem:"I'm not consciously suicidal, but I have had a serious drug problem—began to drink when I was five—had an alcoholic mother—once considered suicide; slashed my wrists when I was twelve; overdosed on drugs lots of times. . . . But for this past twelve years or more I've worked *hard* to unravel this dark thing—have been completely off drugs all this time, but sabotage is right behind me. . . . Since I was a baby I've wanted to die. . . . I have memories of being molested—and other traumas. . . ."

I explained about invasive entities to her and suggested that we find out first of all whether any of her problems were not really her own. Although the idea was unfamiliar to her, she was willing to try this approach.

Her "yes" finger said there was an entity in her. There was a slight hesitation before the second answer, "No," however. Sometimes this is significant of one "nested" in the first.

The entity I called out said his name was Jack; that he was 24; that he had been attracted to Bicki when she was only two because she was "sexual, and so beautiful." He tried to hold her, but did not enter her until she was about six.

I asked, "Did you cause the dreams she had, or the feelings she had as a child that she had been molested?" He did not reply.

When he went back to the last time he was in his own body, he told about being with a "very beautiful dark-haired woman. She's a stranger in the distance that I admired. She knew how I felt. She rejected me by being *aware* of my attraction. . . . I got *really angry*—in a *rage*. I strangled her, took all of her life out of her. Then I kept the rage, the impulse to take more life. I felt *bigger, stronger!*"

Expecting to find a dark one inside Jack, I asked him what he saw when he looked into himself.

"A really scared, lonely man," he said.

"Focus on the rage, the impulse to kill," I directed. "What else do you see inside?"

There was no answer until I asked again, when he said, in a flippant tone, "I'm seeing my cock, Ma'am." This was not Jack's voice.

"Rage, I'm calling you out. How old was Jack when you entered him?" His answer, along with the murderous rage when sexually frustrated, had convinced me that a dark one was here.

Rage said that he had entered Jack when the boy was ten and had been caught masturbating. The lad had been shamed by members of his family and had felt great shame of his own. It was this feeling, not the masturbation itself, that had opened the lad to invasion. The dark one said yes, its own sexual characteristics were similar to those in Jack. He would not say whether he had a "boss."

Ignoring his silence, I asked, "What if you disobey your boss? What happens then?"

"He won't love me any more. He rejects me—he walls off."

Yes, he had been "assigned" to Jack, and, no, he was not happy. And, yes, he nodded, he would like to be happy. But in the center of his heart he saw a black hand. Only after more discussion did he perceive, in the very core of his heart, a little round ball of light. Now he was willing to accept that once he had been a Child of Light.

"How do you feel now?" I asked.

"Overwhelming! Joy!" was the answer.

With Rage transformed and gone, I turned my attention back to Jack and asked what he saw now in his heart.

A heavy voice proclaimed, "THE BOSS HAS COME NOW." (And after the session, the client said that his thought was, "and don't you f— with me!" but she refused to relay those words.)

I wasted no time in trying to persuade this strong dark one. Instead, I asked for "great sheets of light to pour down all around this dark one, forming a net, a capsule of light around him, and light to protect the rest of us from him." I called for the Christ Spirit and the Father of Light to "draw away this one and remove him far away from us. Light is always stronger than darkness!"

Then I asked Jack's Higher Self if there was a message for Jack's lower self.

The Higher Self replied, "He needs to forgive himself."

"Yes. And Jack, you need to ask forgiveness of the lady you killed." He nodded. "What do you want to say to her, Jack?"

Almost mumbling he answered, "How sorry . . . I really loved her."

"Did you ask her to forgive you?"

"She loves me, too," he said. There had been a past-life connection between them.

I suggested to Jack that he use a whisk broom to clean himself up and he was sent on to the Light in the company of the woman he had killed. (Afterward Bicki admitted that the woman had "teased" Jack; and that she herself had sometimes teased men. This is a common, but not universal, game that certain young women like to play—and a dangerous game.)

Bicki also commented afterward on the boss, "He was *powerful,* but he was helpless in the net of light and was suddenly shot clear away when you asked that he be 'removed far away.'" She was happy and smiling at the end of the session.

In this case, Jack himself was obsessed by Rage, so that both were in Bicki, obstructing her personal efforts to control her life. Now she is free of their influence and in a later session will deal with her own remaining problems.

## *"Johnnie" of Jerusalem*

Several times I have said that I accept just what the entities contacted during hypnotic sessions tell me. That is not strictly true, for I do use common sense and test the information with my rational mind, so far as I can. The following case will illustrate.

This entity was found in 1985 when I had not long been in professional Releasement work. It was in a middle-aged, birth-injured, unemployable man with dyslexia and severe emotional retardation though with good but patchy intelligence and a phenomenal memory. Several unsavory entities had already been released from him.

Checking to see if any more remained, I said, after inducing "Sam" into hypnosis, "If there is any other entity in this body besides Sam himself, please come out and tell me your name."

"Johnnie. I'm a little boy seven years old, and I want to be in his body, 'cause he's a nice guy. I don't want to go."

(This much talking is unusual, for entities ordinarily answer direct questions briefly and then cease.)

Johnnie said he had been hiding while the other obsessing entities were being discovered and released. He insisted that they were the ones who had been making Sam do things that he would not do himself, acting foolish so that Sam got ridiculed. Johnnie said he didn't do "much of anything."

Then I made my first mistake, saying, "Johnnie, you had a body of your own once. What happened to it?" (Could I really have made that flat statement? That is worse than asking leading questions!)

Johnnie with gusto began to tell a story filled with discrepancies. "I was eaten by a lion. I was a Christian boy in the time of Christ. I was a little boy in Jerusalem and Christ cured me of being a cripple. A Roman soldier took me to Rome and then they threw me to the lions."

("Johnnie" is hardly a Hebrew name; the term "Christ" is of Greek origin; and the term "Christian" was not used in the lifetime of Jesus in Palestine. And what boy of seven calls himself repeatedly a *little* boy? The fingers said that there was no other entity remaining in Sam, so I continued questioning.)

"Now, Johnnie, go back to the moment just *before* they threw you to the lions. How were you dressed?"

Johnnie hedged by talking about the clothing a Jewish boy wore in Jerusalem, "Sort of toga-style, with a shawl over my head." He did not know what the shawl was called. Returned to the moment before being cast to the lions he said he was "in a cell-type of deal with bars on the door. They'll club me over the head first before the lions start to eat." He said a Roman soldier had told him that. He seemed to vacillate freely between Jerusalem and Rome.

"Are you confused, Johnnie? You said you were in Rome, then you said you were in Jerusalem."

Not missing a beat, Johnnie agreed, "Yes, it's a very confusing thing for a boy of seven." Asked what his father's name was, he said he'd have to think about that. Then, "I think his friends called him Samuel." He said he was "born of a handmaiden, so I don't think my mother had a name." Pressed on this point he said, "Seems like it was 'Rebek-kah'." He did not know his last name. "Just Johnnie. I had a Hebrew name but I am unable to pronounce it." (At seven he could not pronounce his own name?)

All these discrepancies should have warned me that a sly dark one was here, but I kept on as if Johnnie were really a difficult child.

"Go to the moment when your spirit leaves your body, Johnnie; just tell me what happens." Usually this wording brings out the feeling of relief and freedom of the soul that has escaped from the body. Not with Johnnie!

"I see lions eating my body. It's a gory sight." He added more details. "Seven lions, all of them chewing on me at once," he finished with relish.

Again I tried, "Then after your spirit was out of your body, what did you do?"

"I cried spiritually. I didn't want to die that way. I thought I'd find another body and live in it so I could die naturally. I wandered for centuries till I found Sam's body. He was five years old—I don't want to leave him." I continued to lecture him gently and finally asked if he saw a light. He said he saw it; and he said he remembered seeing his father and mother go into the Light—"But I wandered for centuries," he repeated, "until I found an adult body I could go into."

I pointed out that he had said he had entered Sam when Sam was only five. I asked if he ever told lies.

Without hesitation he admitted, "It's a possibility."

When I pointed out other discrepancies he only said, "I'm too small to know."

"Oh, no, you're not. You know perfectly well what's right and what's wrong. *You* caused Sam to get confused yesterday about his past life and it was you who made him get confused about a lot of other things so people would think that *he* tells lies."

Johnnie said he was sorry about that—about not being able to occupy Sam's body along with Sam; he was sorry he could not push Sam clear out of the body and take it himself. There was no hint of remorse or understanding of ethics. I asked again if he could see any light. He could see "a tiny speck, like it's a billion miles away."

"You pushed it there, Johnnie."

He would not come out of Sam by himself so I asked the spiritual helpers to pull him out. Sam saw the helpers dragging him out, but added, ". . . The pressure is too great . . . I have an awful headache."

After a few minutes of easing Sam with suggestions of comfort I spoke again to Johnnie, who said he could see a larger light. He said he could see the spiritual helpers with "blond hair, blue eyes . . . smiling, friendly."

I suggested that they might also have a very firm look, as if they might look stern if he didn't behave well, but emphasized that they did want to help him. I committed him to the helpers to take to "the *right* place for you" and told him good-bye.

"They are pulling him," said Sam.

"He has much to learn. I am glad he is out of you," I remarked.

"Me, too," laughed Sam. "He is the one who made me lie and get confused and say things that made me sound silly."

To myself I wondered if Sam "doth protest too much." I wondered what Sam himself was like, what in him was similar enough to these entities to attract them to him. Because Sam lived in another city we had only one more session, during which I discovered that Johnnie had returned—he was a mocking dark one pleased with having fooled us, although with the assistance of the Bright Beings we did get him out of Sam again. . . .

I did not get to check up on how Sam got along afterward except that there did not appear to be any great change. It made me wonder if indeed other dark entities had moved into him, now that this first bunch had been expelled. This does occur when the client does not continue to keep the aura clear and bright by daily prayers or meditations. A Biblical reference speaks of expelling a group of unwanted entities and leaving the human soul like a house newly cleaned and garnished, which may be found and occupied by other dark entities worse than the first ones if the owner of the house does not take care to prevent this.

Entities who have to be pulled or dragged out are being evacuated against their will; and they do have free will to stay out or to try to return. Even the Mirror Room does not always keep them contained, we have found. As Master Ching has reminded us numerous times, "There is no such thing as '*make*'," in the sense of, "We'll *make* the dark ones leave him alone," or, "We'll *make* her invulnerable." The person or discarnate still has free will, with the responsibility of making their own choices. The living person has to be consciously and emphatically desirous of having the invading entity leave, and the invader has to be willing to leave—even though perhaps after much persuasion. The time spent in the process of persuading such an invader to leave is very well spent, however.

# Caution and Common Sense
# for Would-be Exorcists

I speak now to those few readers who may become overenthusiastic about expelling dark beings from persons suspected of harboring such. An attitude of caution is far more becoming than one of arrogant assumption of your power. An attitude of true humility is far better than over-confidence. Even if you are already a therapist, you still need to learn about dealing with dark entities specifically before you are qualified to strike out on your own and face these dark beings. Baldwin's book and his workshops are a good start.

### The Strong Darks Are Tricksters

One of my coworkers, "Lola" was persuaded by the mother of a young girl to attempt to expel the dark energy in the girl. Lola refused repeatedly, referring the mother and the girl to me; but I was a stranger to the mother, and she, knowing Lola, insisted that Lola hypnotize her daughter and do the releasement. The releasement was successful, but Lola felt ill at ease and phoned me at once, saying that she had made the mother promise to bring the girl to me in addition.

"The entity told me to send him into the outer darkness; he said that was what I wanted anyway. So I did," she told me on the phone. I froze. She had said "yes" to a dark one!

The trio of them came to my office, and while the girl lay quietly in hypnosis and I was sending on a harmless minor dark entity that seemed to be surprised to find itself in her (it turned out to be a decoy), Lola suddenly shouted in a coarse voice, "You can't go! You can't go!" The shout was directed to the minor dark one.

I whirled around to see Lola's eyes staring in rage.

Recalling from the ESP course what one could do, I clapped my hands loudly right by her ears and shouted, "Get out of her! Get out of her *right now!*"

And *that* was successful—the entity left, and Lola's body slumped down out of the chair to the floor, unconscious. But now I could not converse with the entity. So, telling it to remain outside of Lola's body, I allowed it to use her vocal apparatus to speak. It obeyed partially—that is, it tried to take over her body again, thrashing it around on the floor as I knelt on Lola's legs and tried to control one arm, motioning the mother to come and hold down the other arm. It was in this comical position that I held the conversation with the dark one. I reassured the mother that her daughter, still in hypnosis, was all right, in no danger, for I had asked for protection for her at the beginning of the session—forgetting to ask protection for Lola!

The dark one was quite strong, yelling out his name and taunting me, "You weak one—you weak one!"

"Oh, I know I'm weak but I have strong backup in these Bright Beings here in this room," I replied.

He began to laugh, the loud mocking mirthless laughter that I heard then for the first time. "You have nothing! You have nothing!"

I was murmuring over and over, "Jesu—Jesu—Jesu—" and it seemed a long time (though probably only two minutes or so) before I felt that we—the Bright Ones, Lola, the mother, and I—had the situation under control. The thought that occurred to me was sent in answer to my prayer, I feel sure. It consisted of a simple truth: "You are laughing to cover up your fear. You feel your power is less than that of the Bright Beings; you are shouting because you feel yourself weakening. . . . Don't fight it so hard, just be easy, come out, and look at the Bright Beings, turn to them, and think how compassionate they are. . . ."

Suddenly the entity was gone and Lola was back. She looked up at me, startled to find herself on the floor, and asked, "Louise, what are you *doing* to me? What happened?"

The dark being had stayed close to her until now, watching for an opportunity to get revenge for her having expelled him from his young girl victim. Lola had no memory of the interval during which she was possessed. She had a sore neck, for she said that the dark being had "grabbed me by the throat and just threw me away." She said she no longer wanted to channel, being frightened by this experience. And I promised never to allow her to be the channel for a dark one again, realizing that she was vulnerable.

But the dark one came back one other time a week or so later, just to laugh and mock us again as Lola was channeling a lost human entity for another client. He remained only a minute or so, but I was angry that he had made me break my promise to Lola. My own anger doubtless made the dark one feel smug. Even so, I felt that the dark one was thinking about some new ideas—about the *possibility* of his leaving the cold and the loneliness of the dark existence.

The dark ones are truly like the Prodigal Sons of the parable. They are still in the dirt and slime of the pigsty.

Eventually all are to return to their original Home. Some of them can be helped right now and are glad to leave the old existence. Others we find are not amenable to persuasion at all and only laugh.

## Dotty Had Convulsions Every Time

After a sixteen-hour course in self-hypnosis, one of the young women felt that she was capable of "doing what you do," and went right home and in her enthusiasm hypnotized her grown son. It is not difficult to hypnotize others; the trick is knowing the power of spoken suggestions to a person who is in the hypnotic state, and to be extremely careful of the words one speaks to a hypnotized person. But other factors may also be important. If I took a two-week course in anthropology, does that make me qualified to teach such a course?

Well, the son of this young lady, in *his* enthusiasm, had a hypnosis session with his girlfriend, a freshman in college—and she immediately went into a convulsion that frightened him. He had to hold her arms and restrain her. His mother phoned to tell me of this. "He was really spooked," she said. So was I, but not for the same reason! I was amazed that first she, my student, and then her son, would play around so casually with what was stressed as being *self*-hypnosis, for *self*-improvement.

We set up a time, and the young man brought his girlfriend to me for an appointment. He explained that he would sit close, to be ready to hold her down when she would convulse. (Apparently there had been more than one experiment of hypnotizing her.) But I, in my turn, explained to him that he was to sit at a slight distance and not to touch her unless I signaled that he do so.

Sure enough, as she went into the altered state, her body began to tense up and then to shake. The young man rose, ready, but I motioned him back, saying to what I was sure was an obsessing entity, "Don't worry, we are here to help you. Don't be afraid. Just relax, relax." And I placed my hand softly on the girl's shoulder and kept it there with a quiet pressure. Her tension began to decrease.

It turned out that there were several minor dark entities in her, but the strongest entity was her grandmother, who said she had entered the girl when the child was very small, right after the grandmother's death, "because she could see and hear things, just as I could, and after I went she had no one to talk to. So I went in to protect her; she was vulnerable. But then she issued invitations! Why did she do that?" She admitted that her plan of protecting the girl had not worked out as she had hoped.

The grandmother was perfectly willing to go to the Light, but was concerned about what would happen with her granddaughter. It was not hard to persuade the minor dark beings to follow the grandmother to the Light, where they would be taken to a different "place" from the human soul but would be cared for.

After the girl returned to full consciousness she told us the beginning of her story: that as a child of about nine or ten, with her younger sister she prayed that "demons would come and dance for us." The children were disappointed that they saw no demons dancing . . . but evidently this is what the grandmother meant by her "issuing invitations." The demons did come, entered the girl(s), and "danced" inwardly, with emotional mood swings and so on, and—when she went into an altered state—they could "dance" physically by causing her muscles to convulse. At least this is the way I theorized.

The main point of this story is that when dark beings are

encountered, Releasement work is best performed by therapists who have had training in the techniques as well as self-training by meditation and dedication to the pathways of the Light. The dark beings know our fears and weaknesses and use that knowledge to their own advantage. I am thinking of an example in Martin's book, *Hostage to the Devil,* in which a demonic entity called the priest-exorcist by a name that only the priest and one other human being knew—a name that the other human being had called him at a long-ago time, one which embarrassed the present-day priest. Clearing up one's own guilts and fears is a good way to begin preparing to do Releasement work with dark beings.

And the other important thing is trust in the Bright Beings and their power, wisdom, guidance, and protection. If you have never been in the habit of thinking of guardian angels or guides, then when you decide to do Spirit Releasement Therapy you should begin to include the Bright Beings in your mental scenery and get acquainted with some of them. At first you begin to think about them. Next you might begin to think about speaking to them; and next, actually begin to speak to them. Then in meditation, *listen* for them to send thoughts back to you. Ask them questions, and listen for answers. People vary in their sensitivity, so don't be discouraged if you do not "hear" or "see" any Bright Beings. Neither did the little girls "see" demons dancing! If you issue invitations, it will be the guests who are invited who will come.

You will eventually begin to feel friendly toward the Bright Beings (whoever they are—a saint, a religious figure, or an admired human mentor who is deceased). Maybe it is God himself, either as a human figure or as Source of All-That-Is. And after friendliness, next you begin to realize that there is true friendship between you; and trust builds a firm temple of protection, confidence, and openness to wisdom from that higher level. Then when you need the help of your friends, you know that it is already there and you need only ask for it. *It is important to ask;* and they respond to your call.

So, just as the power of the Bright Beings is greater than any power of the dark ones, so as we end this chapter we remind you that in you, too, the Light is always greater than the darkness, and you know that you are a Child of the Bright Universe and *are not alone* and need not fear. (Just call on the Bright Ones, and use common sense!)

*chapter 10*

# OTHERS DO
# RELEASEMENTS.
# YOU CAN, TOO

Each therapist has been at one time a student, and each of us has had a first-time client and performed a releasement for the first time. It has been a benefit if we have had a releasement ourselves, even if of only one entity. Such an experience gives us the ability to understand better the feelings of our clients, especially if we were unaware of the entity and felt that "no one else is in *me.*"

Even if the entity is a harmless little one—a child accidently killed, for instance—the experience of hearing the child's words coming from our own mouth and feeling the child's emotions, knowing its thoughts, realizing that they are not our own—these experiences help a therapist to empathize with the client and to facilitate the session with more authority—not of plain authoritarianism, but with the knowledge of personal experience. It helps the therapist to become what Melikowski calls a "participatory scientist."

This chapter is intended to repeat and sum up portions of the preceding chapters and to sketch the various methods of releasement, the different types of approach, that modern therapists are utilizing, emphasizing as they do that you, also, can learn to perform releasements. This field is not an elitist one; but we do stress that each would-be helper first learn from other books and train himself or herself with humility.

# How You Can Do Releasements

Several books have included suggestions for lay persons who wish to help earthbound or obsessing entities to be released. In chronological order their suggestions, condensed, are offered here. All persons who are serious about this work need to consult the chapters as written, full length, in these valuable books.

In 1977 Annabel Chaplin *(The Bright Light of Death)* wrote of souls earthbound by their fear of death:

> "The bereaved . . . can render a great service to these hapless sufferers. Conversing with them daily for a few weeks after the death is one way of helping them. . . . [T]he so-called dead seem to get the message . . . If there have been any disagreements and misunderstandings, talk about it. . . . Forgive! Ask to be forgiven! . . . All the while constantly reassure the lost ones and tell them to follow the Light. The Light is always there—they must be told that it is there. . . . The dead need our words of comfort not our overwhelming grief. . . . The time for working out problems in an active relationship with the deceased is over. The time for severing the tie has come . . . to put into practice *the Act of Severance.*

". . . If for some personal reason you are reluctant to engage in this effort, then ask someone whom you love and trust to do it for you. . . . Alone, accompanied by another, or performed by two caring people, the results are the same—release from suffering and distress. . . . The only time you do not have to ask permission is when your own child, parent, or spouse is involved. The closeness of the relationship gives you the right to help them. . . .

"Find a quiet place in your home . . . a time when you . . . will be reasonably certain of quiet. . . . Relax. . . . Breathe in and out rhythmically. . . . Your favorite prayer will help. . . . Silently or vocally call the person by name. . . . Now begin your conversation. Tell the person the reason for your trying to communicate . . . [and] the circumstance of the death. Very often the dead are not aware that they have passed on, and so it is important that they be told. Be very explicit. Remain calm and don't expect answers. . . . If you have been unusually distressed, nervous, sleepless or ill since the demise, then say so, and emphasize that their presence is harming you. Reassure your loved ones that they will be looked after when they finally depart from the material world, and will benefit by the release. Last of all tell the departed to look for the guiding Light, for helpers, relatives or friends who have gone on before. Give a final word of love and blessing. . . . Repeat if necessary the entire process several times for about three days.

"Unless your symptoms both physical and emotional are from other causes, you will feel better, sometimes immediately. Sleeplessness, irritability and nervousness, unless they are old unrelated symptoms, will disappear dramatically."

Chaplin gives a case history illustrating the incredible effects of such an Act of Severance performed by a daughter-in-law for her deceased father-in-law, whom she suspected of obsessing his son, her husband.

"In spite of her knowledge and familiarity with the Act of Severance, Ruth was astonished when three hours later [her husband] returned home a different man. Restored to his normal self, he opened the door with his old but recently neglected greeting, 'Hi, honey, I'm home. How did your day go?' [Chaplin adds,] Although not everyone responds as speedily as Ruth's husband, yet . . . many experience the great release within a few days, at most a few weeks."

Ten years after Chaplin's book come out, Dr. Edith Fiore's book, *The Unquiet Dead,* was published. She was acquainted with and impressed by Chaplin's book and was doubtless influenced by Chaplin's "Act of Severance" when she wrote her own chapter on "How to do a Depossession." Condensed, her chapter says:

"It is possible for you to free yourself or another of possessing [obsessing] spirits. . . . Many of my patients have done so on their own between therapy sessions. No harm can come from a depossession. At best, the entities will leave, and the worst that can happen is that they may be somewhat upset for a while and continue to stay. . . . The possessing spirits are lost souls, literally and figuratively. Remember that they are suffering, even if they argue that they are not. . . . Rather than thinking of this procedure as 'getting rid of' the entities, think of it as a method of helping them in the greatest possible way. They go from totally hopeless and lost conditions to ones in which they can finally be at peace. . . . The main effort should be . . . to convince them of this truth. Once this is accomplished, helping them to leave becomes a simple process.

"I explain to my patients that if I would forcibly remove the possessing spirits from them without assurance that they were being guided into the higher realms, I would be creating a horrendous problem for these entities and most likely for the living people whom they would later latch onto. . . . The most important attitude to have during a depossession is a concern for the possessors. . . .

"Usually you will be unaware of the identities of the possessing agents. However, sometimes it's very clear who is with you . . . especially if they are loved ones. . . . With loved ones, it is necessary that you make a prior *firm* commitment to let go of them emotionally. Sometimes the factor that allowed the possession to occur in the first place was your own emotional dependence upon them. . . . Some people have actually begged their deceased loved ones to stay with them, [even] proudly asserted to me that they have had their parents or spouses with them for years, a constant source of comfort and support. However, because the loved ones were earthbound spirits, both were making a tremendous mistake. Occasionally, there are some minor benefits from the possession but it is *never* a healthy solution and prevents the spiritual growth of both participants. . . .

"The most effective way to do a depossession is to record it, using the transcript that follows or composing your own. Playing the tape one or more times a day if necessary educates the possessing spirits repeatedly, and calls their attention to their loved ones [on the other side]. Sometimes it takes a while for entities to really hear what is being said. . . .

"[If you are the one possessed,] [a]nother excellent way . . . is to have someone read the transcript to you. Or, if you are doing the depossession of someone else, read it to them. If you prefer, you can say it in your own words. . . .

"[In these cases,] have the possessed person relax, close his eyes and imagine himself surrounded by White Light. Then mutually ask for spiritual help and/or say a prayer. Speak directly to the entity, making the same points as described below. If you know who the spirit is, address him by name. When you know the people and the circumstances of their deaths, it is much easier to help them. You can more readily convince them of their condition by explaining how they died. Then, if they are loved ones, appeal to their love for you in order to persuade them to depart. . . . Reassure them that when people love each other they are never separated, even by death. Make it clear that they may return from the spirit world to visit. Once convinced that they are indeed hurting [the person they are obsessing] and that [they] will not be separated forever, such possessing spirits will usually leave immediately.

" . . . To help the entities overcome the most common fear—that of hell—tell them that a specialist in religious education from the spirit world is here to help them: priest, nun, minister, rabbi, etc. . . . A frequent fear of possessing entities is that they will not exist if they leave their possessees. It is imperative to convince them that that is not true. Point out that their deceased loved ones are very alive. Have them take their hands to feel how real they are. Convince them that their lives will continue! You can call on whatever spirits you need for extra help. You can ask for spirit doctors or nurses. You can ask for Saint Michael, Gabriel, or Jesus to come.

1. "Do the depossession at a time when you will not be interrupted. Allow a half hour although in most cases this much time is not necessary. Try to be as well rested and as calm as possible . . . no use of drugs, including alcohol, prior to the depossession.

2. "Begin by relaxing a few minutes. . . . Close your eyes and take three or four slow, deep breaths. . . . Recite your favorite prayers. . . . If you have faith in certain religious figures, such as Jesus Christ, Buddha, angels, etc., call upon them to aid you with this procedure. If you are metaphysically oriented, call upon spirit healers for aid.

3. ". . . to protect yourself from any possible negative forces or entities . . . form a defensive barrier. Imagine a brilliant White Light, completely surrounding you with a dazzling aura. Impress upon your mind that this aura protects you totally from any negativity or harm.

4. "Address the possessing spirit, either mentally or out loud, in a kindly and loving manner. If you know him, call him by name and explain that you are now aware that he is with you [or with your client]. Impress upon him that he is a spirit since his own body died, and remind him of the circumstances of his death. Tell him that we are all spirits and never die—that only the physical body dies. State that, without realizing it, he has been harming you [or the person he has entered] by draining your energy and confusing you, since you cannot tell his thoughts and emotions from

your own. Direct his attention to his own spirit loved ones who have come to take him home. Explain that he has a wonderful life ahead, that he will be in a perfect body, and that it is important to you and to him that he go, *now*. Tell him that hell does not exist, and that there are teachers from the spirit world to advise him about this. Bless him as he leaves, sending him off with your love.

    5. "Continue to relax. Thank your spiritual helpers and spend a few minutes in a calm state."

In her book Fiore follows this sketch with the verbatim transcript of a typical depossession that she uses in her office, varying it according to what she knows about the entity. She advises reading such a transcript slowly, with frequent pauses. And, as mentioned before, she says that you may use your own words, seeking to include the important points listed above.

In 1988, the year following Fiore's publication, Eugene Maurey published his book, *Exorcism,* describing his method. He chose to use the term "exorcism" on purpose, admitting that it might be a frightening word to some but would accurately express what he was doing. The subtitle of his book is "How to Clear at a Distance a Spirit Possessed Person."

"My experience in thousands of case studies," he writes, "indicates that more than eighty per cent of such multiple personalities are a result of spirit possession. Spirit, in this context, refers to a dead person who still has all the mental, emotional, and personality characteristics he had when alive. Possession occurs when a disembodied spirit takes control of the mind and body of a living person. This is a book about the exorcism or clearing of people who are spirit possessed. It is not about demons or the devil if such exist. This is a 'How to Do It' book. It will teach you to perform an exorcism safely in a few minutes."

Using not hypnosis but a pendulum over a chart while verbally asking questions about the remote client, he formed his own method of discovering and releasing invading entities. The one page of revised instruction for lay persons is dated 1992. As you will see, some of his instructions, like his methods, differ from those of the other therapists, but his percentage of "success" appears to be comparable. He says:

"The number of requests for an exorcism are overwhelming me. . . . The solution is for you to perform the needed exorcism. It is always done at a distance from your client. It is not difficult. My book outlines the methods used and will greatly assist you. . . . Please follow these suggestions:

1. "First of all, you must recognize the symptoms of a person who may be possessed. Look for . . . abuse of alcohol or drugs; poor or fair health; violence or criminal activity; profanity, lying or cheating; and deep depression. In general, look for characteristics that are not socially acceptable.

2. "Avoid performing an exorcism by personally contacting the invading spirit(s). They are not nice people. In the first place, if there are spirits, there must be highly evolved spirits who know a lot about the business of an exorcism. We call them spirit guides. Ask for such a guide and you will immediately have one. He or she may be your favorite saint or unknown to you. Give your guide a name, whatever name you prefer. You are now ready to perform an exorcism.

3. "Ask your guide to get hold of the intruding spirits on or around your client and introduce them to those they care for who are on the same side of the curtain of death as they are.

4. "Ask your guide to have the spirit people *think* about those persons for whom they care who are dead or may be dead. At this moment the exorcism is completed. They see their friends who take them away. Within a few days you should observe a change for the better in your client.

5. "It may be necessary for you to repeat the exorcism every time your client becomes intoxicated with alcohol or drugs. Habits are difficult to break. If you persist, eventually an exorcism will no longer be necessary. Keep what you did to yourself; if you tell the client what you did, he/she usually will not understand or believe you."

This brief instruction is what Maurey was sending to persons who requested his aid. As you perceive, some of his rules and assumptions differ from those of other therapists—for instance, that he is not dealing with "demons" or "the devil." Fiore likewise does not mention such beings in her book and even denies that she has total belief in "possessing spirits." Nevertheless, as all of us agree, it is not necessary for the therapist to "believe in" such assumptions for the results to be therapeutic. As Fiore states emphatically, "It works."

A few years after Maurey's book appeared, William Baldwin's first edition of his *Spirit Releasement Therapy* was published (1991) and the second edition came out in 1992, a very detailed study that is more than just a reference book for therapists. He calls it a technique manual.

To quote several pages (p. 317 ff):

"Rescue work has been conducted for decades, perhaps centuries. A small group of two or more like-minded people can gather with the intention of calling out to the lost spirits and directing them to the Light. The Light is invoked by a prayer or [a] meditation. . . . Questions are directed to the spirit or spokesperson for any group of spirits who respond. They are guided to look upward, to locate the Rescue Angels of Light, and to lift toward the Light. This can be very effective for people killed in earthquakes, floods, volcanoes, airplane crashes, or any other disaster. Distance is not a set-back. Time does not exist for earth-bound spirits. This Rescue work is effective for present-time events and for disasters of long ago.

"Disturbed spirits can remain in buildings or other locations on land or sea because of strong emotional ties. When such a spirit is locked into the repeating drama of the emotional and physical pain of the original event, a living human with the compassion and ability to reach out to them can help break the entrapment in the astral realm (Summer Rain, 1989)." [Here Baldwin refers to *Phantoms Afoot* by Summer Rain, 1989.]

Under "Self Protection" and "Self-clearing" Baldwin writes, (p. 384 ff):

"At the completion of a [releasement] session, the client may feel particularly vulnerable and exposed to spirit attachment [and] can make the pronouncement:

"'I take my power back from any discarnate being who wants to attach to me. This is my space and I claim dominion here and now. I refuse permission for any [negative] spirit or entity to approach me or to attach to me in any way.'"

The "sealing light meditation" is also recommended for the newly released client to visualize several times a day: to see or to imagine a light within the body, growing and spreading until it fills the entire body and then radiating outward to form a roomy protective bubble or capsule completely surrounding the person with White Light.

"After a little practice, the visualized sealing meditation becomes automatic. It is a light which is always turned on," [he says, adding,] "A new awareness of the possibility of spirit attachment can lead to a more careful approach to life. As a person learns the reasons for vulnerability there is often more care taken in terms of emotional outbursts, conscious thinking, physical risk-taking. Personal boundaries are established and maintained. A person can learn to say 'NO.'

"When a person begins to suspect that he or she is obsessed, sensing an attempted interference by a discarnate entity, she can immediately bolster the personal defenses. There is an increasing ability to sense the emotional and physical impingement caused by a discarnate being. Conversely, there is a decrease in the fear regarding the fact of spirit interference. Distaste and discomfort with the idea of parasitic attachment is replaced with righteous indignation at the violation, and [then] compassion for the plight of the lost souls caught in this intertwining mesh of consciousness. This finally extends even to the dark energy beings who, in ignorance, suffer bondage to the dark master.

"The therapist is a guide and instructor along

the way. The client can and does learn to deal with most of the entities that gain entrance in moments of vulnerability. There is improvement in the capacity to communicate with the entity. . . . The client can begin the actual process of questioning, resolution and release.

"*Clearing of others* has been accomplished by people after they have been cleared themselves and have taken time to learn the procedures. A person can learn to perform this loving service. The work must be done with unconditional love for the other person, a desire for improved communication and interaction between the two people, and a request to the High Self that the work serve the highest good of all concerned. Interference for selfish reasons or the possibility of personal gain inflicts a most undesirable karmic burden."

Skipping over other therapists (whose books are listed in the Bibliography) I come now to *my personal methods.*

In a previous book *(O Sane and Sacred Death)* I gave a sketch of the manner in which you may assist in the rescue or releasement of a deceased person. I quote it here.

"In many cases, the remedy is simple. First is the brief but very important process of centering yourself, of calming your mind and quieting your feelings before you start to help the deceased one. Souls are highly sensitive to the unspoken thoughts and emotions of the living and a false cheerfulness will not fool them. Therefore work on yourself first, talk to your own soul about the freedom you desire for your loved one (or the stranger you have in mind) until you do feel compassion and a selfless desire to help. Then ask for wisdom, guidance, protection for yourself and the other soul, discarnate or incarnate.

"Second is to call the person by name or by location or other identifying circumstance and explain to the (invisible to you) spirit of the deceased person how its body died and point out that now, although people consider the *person* dead, the *person* is still alive, listening to you. Speak tactfully and as gently as you would if you could see the person right there with you. The point is to convince the soul that although it is still aware and conscious, its body is now dead. It may not have realized this. Please be careful not to let your own emotions drop into your wording terms like 'lonely' or 'miss you' or 'need you'. Your purpose is to lift and help, not to drag down nor hold back. Your purpose is to release and to free and lighten the soul of the deceased one. It might be wise for you to write out what you wish to say to your loved one or to the stranger(s) you want to contact, in order to be sure your words will serve to help and not hinder your 'ghost'. The rule is simple: '*Accentuate the positive; eliminate the negative.*'

"You may wish to suggest that the soul sweep out old pains and weakness, old fatigue, old addictions and mean habits, etc. Be gentle as you suggest such actions, but repeat the suggestions firmly if you feel it advisable. You may feel the need to repeat your words on successive days. Do not be afraid to start.

"The third step is to direct the attention of your 'clients' toward the Light and tell them to move toward it and to watch for a welcoming person who comes as a guide to escort them home. This third step is important, for many souls have told us that when they lost their body they didn't know where to go, or that they feared to leave the earth-plane lest they go to hell. They didn't know that the Light would come visibly to receive them, so they did not look for any light and their *expectation of dim uncertainty or of darkness* provided exactly that for them—thoughts being the builders in the spirit-world. Therefore it is important to speak of the Light, its warmth, its welcome, and of the guide who will come. If you are not sure that a guide has come, then simply invite 'someone who cares about this person—a high, wise, spiritual being,' to come and escort the soul safely into the Light and home. This wording prevents any mischievous or dark entity from turning up as 'guide'.

"This third step may need to be repeated a few times, especially if the deceased one still has had feelings of unworthiness or 'badness'. The Light understands all and is more than willing to forgive all with limitless love and compassion. However, the preliminary is for the soul to be *willing* to rid itself of its old undesirable habits and addictions. This is the soul's first move, made by its own free will; then comes the Light's instantaneous response.

"When talking to the soul of a relative (or a stranger) who you may feel is lost, unhappy, or otherwise in trouble after death, you might say something like this:

"'Sally (or Sammy), I have been thinking of you and sending thoughts for your welfare and peace. You are at the beginning of a new period now, and the old time is past. I am sorry it was so rough for you, but now you can shuck off all the old feelings of anger at your helplessness, your feelings of inferiority and loneliness, and start fresh and new. You realize, don't you, that your body is gone? If you think back—without feeling any fear or pain—you will see what happened, and you will know that your body is no longer of any use to you. Neither are the old habits and addictions that bothered you. Just throw them all away and be rid of them. I think of you now as clean and clear and starting fresh. I am sorry no one realized just how desperate you were. We understand more clearly now, and we send you our thoughts and our concern. Look for the Light, Sally (Sammy), and let it shine away your unhappiness. I am thinking of you now as being surrounded and comforted by the gentle Light.'

"(If the person you have in mind has been really a dark character, you might remind your own self of what Dr. Hazel Denning said one time, 'The meaner and nastier a person is, the more he is hurting.' That thought may help you to help the mean, nasty persons more easily!)

"If it is a loved one or relative you are talking to, you might say something like this:

"'Dear Jim (or Betty), I think of you often and am so glad that we knew each other as long as we did. I put your picture where I look at it and smile every time I pass by. Sometimes I put a vase of flowers up there beside it, too. I know you have gone into the Light and are happy now. Don't worry about any of us; we'll work at our life lessons, just as you did, and make you proud of us. Sure, we miss you here, but we are glad that you are with Grandfather and Grandmother now and are free of those old problems, and we are so grateful that you were one of us this long. In my thoughts I see you strong and healthy, strolling or even running in the sunshine, or just lying in the shade of a tree and enjoying the beauty and peace all around you. Not a bad vacation after all you've been through, is it! Or are you busy doing other things? Knowing you, I bet you have found interesting things to do already! Whatever they are, dear Jim (Betty), I'm pulling for you. And I'll see you again when I come over. I love you.'"

# Resistant Entities

Resistance to being called out and sent away from the obsessed person is fairly common among the invaders we have encountered, often being a simple objection, "He needs me," or "I help her." The therapist's usual formula of persuasion is enough to enlighten most of these entities to the disadvantages of the obsessive relationship not only to the client but also to the invading entity.

Resistance may be a long-time habit of fearing change. A sad case comes to my mind of a group of souls found not obsessing a living person but wandering aimlessly in the earthbound condition, led hither and thither by their leader. When contacted, the leader proclaimed that they were "Children of the Covenant," who were "faithful unto death." It devolved that they were a group who had been slaughtered because of their religion in some long-past year. I did not know which Covenant the leader meant or which religion they followed. All were totally deaf to any voice except that of the leader, and he was totally deaf to any of my thoughts, even while answering my voice. At last, taking a chance that they were Jewish, I asked "The Master Moses" to come and speak to these Children of the Covenant. That was the word needed. Without hesitation the leader—who had rejected all my own suggestions about looking for the Light and going toward it—agreed, "We will follow Father Moses." And at long last the Children were on their way Home. Resistance had crumbled at that one name.

# Therapists' Methods
# of Dealing with Resistance

When Dr. Carl Wickland was doing the first Releasement Work in America by nonshamanic means, he would spend considerable time talking and arguing with each "ignorant spirit" (as he called the souls who did not understand that their bodies were dead), trying to convince them of their state and get them to move on into a higher level of the spirit world. Those who remained obdurate he sometimes threatened rather mildly with a term in what he called a "dungeon," a dark gloomy room. Baldwin adopted this symbolic room, suggesting that it was lined with multitudes of mirrors, a place in which the stubborn spirit would be alone with its own myriad images until it changed its attitude.

Eugene Maurey uses "picturization" to create thought-forms of neutralization of negative energies or of protection for the clients. He starts with picturing the negatives as a black cloud around the client, then pictures the cloud rising, changing color, dispersing, and going back to the person who had sent the dark thought or emotion, but in the form now of love, not of negativity.

Resistant negative entities he would visualize being put into a black box. "Some of the intruders cause so much misery that I have little sympathy for them," Maurey writes, "yet I always give them a break. If they come back after the black box treatment . . . I have them tied up, head to foot, and thrown into a box and have the lid nailed shut and tell them they will stay there forever. However, I'm not too bad a guy, and I don't really want them to be shut up forever. . . . When [a] powerful negative entity attacked me, I finally dispatched him by placing a white light around him. It worked. I believe I'll do that to a few dozen characters who are in the boxes. They are a mean lot but I have no fear of them."

Others have discovered the power of the White Light, also. When I first began Releasement Work I followed Wickland's technique of talking to and persuading the entities, and if I encountered a stubborn resistant one I offered it a choice between going into the Light or "back into the darkness, to stay there forever, and never harm any other living creature, human or nonhuman." Like Maurey, however, I feel that I'm not too bad a guy and I didn't really want them to stay in darkness forever. Therefore it seemed reasonable to offer such resistant entities a compromise, a middle choice—i.e., Wickland's gloomy room lined with mirrors, where each would be alone, unable to escape until each changed its mind and asked for the Light (sacrificing its pride, so to speak); then the Light would shine down and release the soul. This arrangement permitted each entity to control its own moment of release.

This middle option worked well. Some dark entities, both human and nonhuman, arrogantly rejecting the Light, were asked to go to the door of the "dungeon" room and look into it. Then one recoiled. "I don't want to look at myself!" it stated with a grimace. Another paused, then decided firmly, "I don't want THAT!" A few, however have chosen the "dungeon," in which case I remind each that its freedom is under its own control. As mentioned before, almost none of even the darkest entities has chosen to go back to the cold, lonely darkness, although some have escaped from our voices and no doubt are free to "walk up and down in the world."

One of my students and coworkers offered a stubborn entity as a third option not the gloomy mirror-room but a quiet garden in which it might rest and think and change its dark nature. I was impressed not only by the much more compassionate approach but also by the swift positive reaction of the stubborn entity. Since this session I, as she did, offer resistant entities this type of third choice. Rarely does an entity choose the dusky mirror room any more.

Baldwin, who used to follow Wickland's pattern of dealing with resistant dark entities by threatening to send them to a "dungeon"—although he never sent any there—has found that asking the "Rescue Spirits of Light" to surround the dark entity with "an impenetrable, impervious, inescapable capsule of light" is an excellent way to restrain their negative energies and keep them from escaping while he continues to talk to them, pointing out how they have been used as tools by dark forces that have deceived them with lies such as that light is harmful and destructive. Dr. Irene Hickman sometimes asks the helpers to send a "laser of light" right through the negative entity. She uses this technique with good results. In fact, one dark entity encountered by Hickman seemed to enjoy the laser of light and asked for "more . . . more!" until Hickman told it, "Don't be greedy." (See Hickman, Bibliography.)

## Just Ask the Obsessing Entities

Discarnate entities, human and nonhuman both, can see other entities in the person obsessed and also in persons associated with the obsessed person but at a distance. If we ask, if we inquire of it, the obsessing entity usually answers our questions, not only about the person it has invaded but about family members, friends, business associates—and the therapist! Occasionally information is volunteered by the entity, as for instance when a grandmother-soul that I was releasing from a young woman told me, "You have an entity in you, Louise." Then she described the one that she perceived in me; and a few weeks later with a coworker facilitating we contacted and released this human soul who was within me.

Other information may be something like, "There are many others in this one. She likes them; she wants to keep them. They make mockery of people. If you release them, they will come to *you*." Or, in another client's session, "There are still some small entities in her. They are harmless. They need not be sent away at this time." In such case I try to double-check with each client's Higher Mind to be sure that this is not a subterfuge to distract me from the releasement of the remaining entities.

Still other information, sometimes offered voluntarily, may relate to the type of entity being contacted (as in the case of "Legion") or even to the specific age and sex of an entity still in the client. If we are told that there is still the soul of a child in the client, we accept that and begin to offer words of gentle reassurance to the child-soul, which has been so frightened that it is trying to hide and pretend that it is not present in the client. This situation, too, has been encountered repeatedly.

After a dark being has been persuaded to "turn to the Light" it often voluntarily gives suggestions for the client as to physical or psychological means that will be helpful (as the entity within "Gina" did, telling the mother about Gina's ear infection).

If asked, the obsessing entities can often partially or wholly "fix" certain abnormal bodily conditions for which their presence has been responsible in the client (as old Cleo fixed "Annie's" hip joint but could not fix her knee because "that isn't me"; whereas Gladys, the second entity in Annie, did fix Annie's knee—which had been stiff because of Gladys' knee injury at her death when run over by the train). For this reason Baldwin asks the entities as he releases them to repair any damage in the client's body that their presence has been responsible for having caused. I usually do so, too. Even without being asked, the entities on their departure often leave the client symptom-free, although perhaps not as quickly.

Not only conditions in the living person's physical body but also the feelings, motivations, and stresses of the client are perceived by the invisible entities within, who can also perceive those of persons associated with the client (as little Casey perceived the negative motivations of "the funny lady in the mask" who was "making stars in Wayne's mind" and making his heart split in two and fall down.) No psychologist could have described more succinctly what the situation between the funny lady and Wayne was at that time.

Considering these discoveries, it is sensible for us when we talk to an entity to *ask it questions* and *listen to its answers,* always using our conscious mind to sort sensible information from fantasizing or trickery on the part of an entity. (Remember young "Johnnie," who, when asked if he ever told lies, readily admitted, "It's a possibility.") Such trickery is almost always a sign of a dark being. Human discarnate entities seem to tell the truth quite matter-of-factly, even when it is very painful truth, and their emotions usually ring true to their words. If they do not, then as mentioned above, we suspect the presence of a dark being within them, call it out and deal with it, and then return to the human soul.

## The Effects of Organ Transplants

Since the rapid increase in organ transplants, which give renewed life and health to many disabled or unwell persons, some unsuspected results have been appearing. For example, in *Science News* for September 20, 1997, an article reports a case of peanut allergy transferred to the 35-year-old male recipient by the implanted liver of a 22-year-old man who had been allergic to peanuts. There have been other reports of various syndromes transferred from the deceased donor to the living recipient along with the anatomical structures of the donated organs. It seems that the very cells of the donor are still faithful to their original owner and need to be talked to and reprogrammed just as if they were invading entities in this new (to them) body. Yes, and we can do exactly that: speak to the cells of the organ being donated, and to the organ as a whole, explain the situation, and command them to be congenial to their new environment from now on. This is quite similar to the directive words used by therapists in programming a tumor or directing the cells and functions of any bodily system.

Mentioned in the *Newsletter* of the Association for Past-life Research and Therapies for Summer 1997 is the memoir by dancer Claire Sylvia, *A Change of Heart,* telling about the changes she experienced after her heart-lung transplant which exchanged her 48-year-old organs for those of an 18-year-old boy who had been killed in a motorcycle accident.

Almost her first words to the reporter who asked her what she wanted most, after surviving the surgery, were, "Actually, I'm dying for a beer right now." The words surprised her own self, for she didn't even like beer—at least not until now. She also felt "mortified" that she "had answered this sincere question with such a flippant response."

There were other new and radical changes in her tastes and habits. While still in the Intensive Care Unit, she began to feel the presence of "something or someone else within her." New cravings appeared, new attitudes—e.g., an uncharacteristic aggressiveness and impetuosity—that she later learned "mirrors those that once belonged to her donor."

She also had strange dreams. In one, she is with "a happy young man named Tim L.," whom she kisses and inhales deeply into her. "It feels like the deepest breath I've ever taken, and I know that Tim will be with me forever." Later, as she adjusts to her new organs, which she finds healthier than her old ones (removed because of primary pulmonary hypertension), she begins to learn more facts about her donor, including his name: Tim L.

This sketch of the case would certainly indicate that Tim L.'s personality, his mind and desires and habits, had entered the recipient along with his transplanted heart and lungs and is now obsessing her, melded with her own personal likes and habits. My impression, without knowing more of the circumstances, is that Tim chose to enter Claire during or after the operation and has no idea that his presence may be obstructing or hindering her in any way. Physically the presence of his heart and lungs has definitely helped her; but she did not bargain for any transplant of his teenaged aggressiveness and impulsiveness. Those attitudes may not be positive ones in a 48-year-old lady. She now has what used to be called a "split personality"! And Tim himself needs to leave the earth-plane and go on into his new world of astral experience.

The entrance of a discarnate entity into a living person during or after an operation is not an uncommon event. The chief difference here is that the discarnate entity was not entirely discarnate, for his physical organs were being implanted into the patient. And so, also, he was not really invading, he was being *put* into her by the surgeons, as they placed the youth's organs within her body and connected them up to her own circulatory system. Tim did not need to go along with his organs. That was a matter of choice for him. But numerous souls after death of the body do feel that they must follow the body wherever it is. Tim chose to follow his heart and lungs rather than the rest of his body.

In cases of organ transplants the preliminary tests need to be as careful as those demanded by many adoption agencies before a baby is allowed to be given to a couple for their own. An organ transplant in many ways is different from an adoption. It is a melding of intimate cellular memories as well as cellular functions.

From reports like Claire's it is evident that protection of the recipient from becoming the victim of obsession by the donor's personality also needs to be included as a routine preparation just as much as determination of blood type. Such protection might be simply calling the (deceased) donor and explaining (perhaps repeating on several successive days),

> "I am speaking to you whose body was ruined in that car wreck. I do not know you, but I am sorry that your body died when you were so young. However, the organs of your body can be given to living people whose own organs are diseased or wounded, and in that way you can continue to help us; but let *your mind, your soul, rise higher and enter the Light,* free and happy. I believe that you are glad to be of such great assistance by donating your organs. And I ask the cells of your organs to adapt to their new bodies smoothly,

physiologically, and in every other way. I also ask the bodies of the recipients to accept them easily, as friendly helpful new units of their bodies."

As mentioned, two or three repetitions of this type of instruction may be necessary, and if the results are not as quick and complete as expected, the wording can be changed from, "I ask the cells . . ." to, "I command the cells . . ."—in a firm tone! As for asking or commanding the bodies of the recipients, that is an acceptable mode of therapy, for all of us are connected at the lower levels, as also at the higher levels of existence.

## Four Shelves of the Bookcase

Like any new field of knowledge or expertise, this entire field of organ transplants needs to be studied carefully in all its aspects, not merely the physical aspects of physical benefit to the recipients. The effects on the recipient's mind, emotions, personal habits need to be considered.

I am reminded of Nobel Laureate Karl Popper's metaphor of the bookcase of several shelves.

On the lowest shelf, labeled "Physical Sciences," are the books containing knowledge of all the physical realms, the fields concerning geology, astronomy, meteorology, anatomy, and so on. Nature here is considered deterministic; reality is physically measurable. These fields are called "hard science."

On the second shelf, labeled "Life Sciences," are concepts like "organism" and "growth." Here are books about physiology, hormones, enzymes, vitamins, etc., all concerned with the life sciences. These include the functions that define "life": respiration, digestion, reproduction, motion, causing the physical body to manifest livingness.

Next is the shelf that contains the books dealing with the "Psychosocial Processes" and functions of the living body and its brain: consciousness, volition, culture; emotions, ideas, thoughts; habits, feelings, desires; also frustrations, angers, fears, resentments. The cultural aspects of religion and mores also need to be here, and somewhere on this shelf we shall place the books concerned with parapsychological knowledge and knowledge of the psychic and astral talents and phenomena.

Willis Harmon (see Bibliography) suggests another shelf, which is labeled "Spiritual Sciences," on which are the books concerned with the still higher aspects of consciousness, such as motivation, purpose, planning, choice, courage; and also ethics, morality, altruism, and spirituality (as opposed to mere religiousness and "spiritism").

Maybe instead of books, the shelves contain plants, each "shelf" growing the plants of one aspect or one branch of the great Tree of Life. Then *this* book is like a plant with its main body on the shelf of psychosocial knowledge but with roots going down to the knowledges below and its blossoms higher into the spiritual knowledges.

In any case, the knowledge that I have conveyed in this book is intended not to be confined to any one shelf but to include several, and especially to extend up into the higher realm where the Law of Karma is found, with its corollaries of compensation and justice, and where also compassion, mercy, forgiveness, and love are found. These are needed by every living creature and every discarnate living soul.

The need is great; many souls are wandering or hiding, some in bewilderment, some in fear of hell, some in fear of continuing terrors of war, abuse, or betrayal. I urge you who have read this or other books with a similar message to use part of your meditation time to reach out to these souls and rescue or release some of these needy ones. It is not hard; you have only to start and you will be guided, if you ask.

## A Word to the Skeptics

Does it embarrass you even to consider *secretly* asking assistance from invisible beings to help you rescue or release other invisible beings? Friends, I know—I went through that stage myself. But think of the alternatives to your valuing your own opinions above possible facts: You who could offer help are refusing to do so in deference to your personal opinions. Yes, your opinions are permissible, they are your own, part of your nature; but please be aware that other intelligent people may hold different opinions from yours and that the universe may indeed be "too good to be true." On the other hand, the universe at times may seem too hard or too evil to be true, when the Law of Karma brings down the just reward of former ill deeds or when group karma seizes large numbers of people or other creatures. We do not yet have perfected wisdom or full knowledge of everything in the universe. That may be in the future for the race.

Meanwhile let us do whatever we can to alleviate the hardships of our fellow beings and not be hindered by our personal embarrassment nor by the overwhelming size of the problems. Mahatma Gandhi said, "Whatever you do will never be enough, but it matters enormously that you do it."

Mother Teresa said, "In this world we cannot do great things, but we can do small things with great love." So let us begin!

— PEACE TO ALL BEINGS —

# BIBLIOGRAPHY

Anonymous. *The Boy Who Saw True.* (Scott, Cyril editor) Lanham, Md.: National Book Network, 1953.

Baldwin, William J. *Spirit Releasement Therapy: A Technique Manual.* 2d ed. Terra Alta, W.Va.: Headline Books, Inc., 1992.

Boerstler, Richard. *Letting Go.* South Yarmouth, Mass.: Associates in Thanatology, 1982.

Carruth, William H. "Each Is His Own Tongue." in *101 Famous Poems,* ed. R.J. Cook (revised edition). Chicago: Book Division of The Cable Company, 1929

Chaplin, Annabel. *The Bright Light of Death.* Marina del Rey, Calif.: DeVorss and Co., 1977.

_____. *The Presence of the Light.* Marina del Rey, Calif.: DeVorss and Co., 1994.

Dass, Ram, and Paul Gorman. *How Can I Help?* New York: Alfred A. Knopf, 1987.

Denning, Hazel. *True Hauntings.* St. Paul, Minn.: Llewllyn Publishing Co., 1996.

Dowding, Lord Hugh. *Lychgate: The Entrance to the Path.* London: Rider and Co., 1945.

Eadie, Betty J. *Embraced by the Light.* Placerville, Calif.: Bantam Books, 1992.

Fiore, Edith. *The Unquiet Dead.* Garden City, N.Y.: Doubleday and Co., 1987.

Gorf, Stanislav. *Behind the Brain.* New York: State University of New York Press, 1985.

Harmon, Willis. "The Transpersonal Challenge to the Scientific Paradigm: The Need for Restructuring of Science." Paper presented at International Transpersonal Conference, Santa Rosa, Calif., October 1988.

Hickman, Irene. *Remote Depossession.* Kirksville, Mo.: Hickman Systems, 1994.

Ireland-Frey, Louise. "Clinical Depossession: Releasement of Attached Entities from Unsuspecting Hosts." *Journal of Regression Therapy,* Vol. I, No. 2, Fall, 1986: pp. 90-101.

_____. *O Sane and Sacred Death.* Unpublished, 1995.

Leadbeater, C.W. *The Astral Plane.* Wheaton, Ill.: Theosophical Publishing House, 1941. Reprinted 1996.

_____. *Invisible Helpers.* Wheaton, Ill.: Theosophical Publishing House, 1912. Reprinted 1996

Long, Max Freedom. *The Secret Science Behind Miracles.* Marina del Rey, Calif.: DeVorss and Co., 1948.

Lucas, Winafred. *Regression Therapy: A Handbook for Professionals*. Vols. I and II. Crest Park, Calif.: Deep Forest Press, 1993.

Martin, Malachi. *Hostage to the Devil*. New York: Bantam Books, 1976.

Maurey, Eugene. *Exorcism*. West Chester, Pa.: Whiteford Press, 1988.

Montgomery, Ruth. *Strangers Among Us*. Madison Hts., Mich.: Fawcett Crest Books, 1980.

Moody, Raymond A , Jr *Life After Life* Mockingbird ed. New York: Bantam Inc., 1973.

_____. *Reflections on Life After Life*. New York: Bantam Inc., 1977.

Naegeli-Osjord, Hans. *Possession and Exorcism*. (German, 1983) New Frontiers Center, English translation, 1988, Oregon, Wis.

Peck, F. Scott. *People of the Lie*. New York: Simon and Schuster, 1983.

Ritchie, George. *Return from Tomorrow*. Old Tappan, N.J.: Fleming H. Revell Co., 1978.

Wickland, Carl A. *Thirty Years Among the Dead*. Van Nuys, Calif.: Newcastle Publishing Co., Inc., 1974. (first published, 1924)

Woolger, R.J. *Other Lives, Other Selves*. New York: Doubleday, 1987.

# ABOUT THE AUTHOR

Dr. Louise Ireland-Frey began her career in hypno-therapy at age sixty-seven, a time in life when many people are planning to retire. She had already followed one career path, graduating as Phi Beta Kappa with a bachelor of arts degree from Colorado University at Boulder, a master of arts from Mount Holyoke College in Massachusetts, and her medical degree from Tulane University.

But in 1978, Dr. Frey used self-hypnosis to overcome a health problem that had plagued her for years, and her career path was changed. She and some friends had previously spent several hundred hours experimenting with "this catalyst," as she calls it. She augmented that introduction with professional training, and became a hypnotherapist in 1979.

# Hampton Roads Publishing Company

*. . . for the evolving human spirit*

Hampton Roads Publishing Company
publishes books on a variety of subjects including
metaphysics, health, complementary medicine,
visionary fiction, and other related topics.

For a copy of our latest catalog,
call toll-free, 800-766-8009,
or send your name and address to

Hampton Roads Publishing Company
134 Burgess Lane
Charlottesville, VA 22902
e-mail: hrpc@hrpub.com
www.hrpub.com